# Exploring Oklahoma With Children!

## The Essential Family Travel Guide

Sarah L. Taylor, Editor

*Thank you for your business!*
*Enjoy!*
*Sarah Taylor*

**in**print
*Publishing, Inc.*

Inprint Publishing, Inc.
306 S. Bryant, Suite C-152 • Edmond, OK  73034
(405) 340-1404 • e-mail: explore@oklahoma.net
Web site: www.exploringoklahoma.com

Inprint Publishing, Inc.
306 S. Bryant, Suite C-152
Edmond, OK 73034
(405) 340-1404
e-mail: explore@oklahoma.net
Web site: www. exploringoklahoma.com

**Editor:** Sarah L. Taylor, President, Inprint Publishing, Inc.

**Design and production:**
David, Randall & Yates Graphic+Design, Oklahoma City.

**Editorial assistance:** provided by Donald E. Hines and Pam Pittman.

**Contributing authors:**
Robbie Scott. Other writers: Susan Hollingsworth, Deborah Bouziden, Taprina Milburn, Sarah Taylor, Elaine Warner, Allison Thompson, Patty Lee, and Sarah Kobos.

**Writers of special articles:**
Lisa Marotta, Nona Leatherwood Schoenleber, Becky Tallent, Trena Thomas.

**Cover Model:** Julie Clem.

**Portrait and Staff Group photo:** Whitaker Portrait Studio.

ISBN number 0-9645685-2-7
Library of Congress Catalog Card Number: 97-071985

To order *Exploring Oklahoma with Children* and *Exploring Oklahoma Together* contact:

Inprint Publishing, Inc.
306 S. Bryant, Suite C-152
Edmond, OK 73034,
(405) 340-1404

# Dedication

This book is dedicated to my loving and wonderful family—to my husband, John, who has supported me in countless ways through the process of compiling, editing, and writing this book, and to my precious children, Kathryne, Reed, and Zane, who have been more than patient and understanding.

# Foreward

Recently, I learned the secret to one young man's success in earning a highly-prized national scholarship. His parents didn't have the financial means to provide special sports activities, music lessons, or enrichment camps. As an affordable alternative, his family spent Saturday afternoons in local museums, studying the exhibits together and taking advantage of free "edutainment." These experiences instilled in the student a sense of wonder and curiosity about the world; he became motivated to learn, thus setting the stage for his continued achievements.

It is inspiring to hear these stories, reinforcing what many of us already know: for our children to be able to develop a positive self-image and a sense of purpose and direction, we need to spend time with them, to be their role models and to listen to them. We need to introduce our children to the world and experience new places together. What better way to achieve this than to explore the diversity that is Oklahoma!

This book is designed to provide the important information that families need to make the most from travel in Oklahoma. The overwhelmingly-positive response to our first edition motivated us to expand the state's coverage in our second edition. We are proud that this up-to-date guidebook includes even more towns, museums, events, state parks, and lake areas than before.

Our sincere hope is that your family will enjoy rewarding quality time while exploring Oklahoma, and that together you will enjoy Oklahoma's pristine natural beauty, gain new knowledge and, more than anything, have FUN away from the normal routine. God Bless!

Sarah Lowrey Taylor, editor/publisher
*Exploring Oklahoma with Children* and *Exploring Oklahoma Together*
May, 1997

# Acknowledgements

This book would not have been possible without the help, support and guidance of the following special people:

**Exploring Oklahoma with Children crew and writers:**
Randy Yates, Robbie Scott, Lisa Marotta, Nona Leatherwood Schoenleber, Becky Tallent, Trena Thomas, Martha Jacobs, Susan Hollingsworth, Elaine Warner, Deborah Bouziden, Taprina Milburn, Patty Lee, Sarah Kobos, and Allison Thompson.

Our most sincere appreciation to our corporate sponsor and our many advertisers.

**Corporate Sponsor:**
**Children's Hospital of Oklahoma**
**All Advertisers (see page 259 for an index)**

**Friends and Advisors:**
Pam Pittman, Donald Hines, Melba Prior, Roy Page, Richard Bedard, Jake Lowrey, the staff of A Child's Garden, Kay Hunt, Teresa Brown, and Julie Jones from Frontier Country Marketing Association, Sandy Price, Tina Smith, Jeanette Graves, Jeanette Henderson, Carla Hill, Elise Marrs, Jenny Johnston, the staff of the Oklahoma Department of Tourism, particularly Sandy Pantlik and Barbara Palmer, and from the staff of Oklahoma Parks and Resorts, Kelly Newsom and Lisa Grant, the staff of Oklahoma Today magazine, particularly Joan Henderson and Brian Brown, Allison O'Rear, Jill Bradshaw, Ellen Mercer, Julie Clem and her parents, Tim and Debbie Clem.

A very sincere thank you to my entire family, especially my parents, Harold and Virginia Lowrey, and my mother-in-law, Mildred Taylor, for helping when I needed it!

**Invitation**
You are encouraged and invited to provide suggestions for additions and changes to subsequent editions of Exploring Oklahoma with Children. We want to hear from you!!! Please send you ideas to Inprint Publishing, 306 S. Bryant, Suite C-152, Edmond, OK 73034, (405) 340-1404, e-mail: explore@oklahoma.net.

**Disclaimer**
The information in this book has been thoroughly researched and tested to be as accurate as possible. However, the travel industry is dynamic, and the contents of this book are subject to change. Readers are advised to call ahead to verify information whenever they travel. Neither the authors nor the publisher can be held responsible for the experiences of travelers.

**Book Resources used for Exploring Oklahoma with Children:**
Footsteps through Tulsa, by Marilyn Inhofe, Kathleen Reeves, and Sandy Jones published by Inhofe, Reeves, and Jones, 1995; Oklahoma Travel Handbook by Kent Ruth, University of Oklahoma Press, 1985; Oklahoma Historical Tour Guide by Burnis Argo and Kent Ruth, Crossroads Communications, 1992; Oklahoma, A History of Five Centuries by Arrell Morgan Gibson, University of Oklahoma Press, 1981; The Oklahoma Land Rush of 1889 by Stan Hoig, Oklahoma Historical Society, 1989; Guthrie, A History of the Capital City 1889-1910 by Lloyd C. Lentz, Logan County Historical Society; The Sooner Story by Charles F. Long and Carolyn G. Hart, University of Oklahoma Press, 1980; Historical Atlas of Oklahoma by John W. Morris, Charles R. Goins, and Edwin C. McReynolds, University of Oklahoma Press, 1970; Oklahoma: Off the Beaten Path by Barbara Palmer, The Globe Pequot Press, 1996; Oklahoma Treasures and Treasure Trails by Steve Wilson, University of Oklahoma Press, 1988; various articles from Oklahoma Today magazine.

# Contents

## Northwest Oklahoma (Red Carpet Country)

## Northeast Oklahoma

## Southeast Oklahoma

# Contents

# Using this Book

This book has been designed for ease of use. Here are some helpful guidelines that will help you find your way around.

- The book is arranged geographically by section, beginning with Northwest Oklahoma, going clockwise around the state, and ending with Central Oklahoma. Within each geographic "chapter," the major towns or areas are in alphabetical order, and other, smaller towns or areas are listed "In the Vicinity" to these towns. Within each city or area, the information is arranged by Attractions (listed in alphabetical order) and Events (listed in chronological order).
- Geographic areas of Oklahoma are highlighted on an outside corner map of each page to help identify the entry's general location.
- Icons are used to help identify those places and attractions that are particularly outstanding, and those that have placed advertisements or coupons in the book. The icons and their meanings are as follows: ★ = Outstanding Attraction; ⑤ = Coupon; ⊡ = Advertisement.
- Handicapped accessibility is noted on most entries.
- A map is included in this book for general reference only. Written directions are provided for most entries. Travelers will need an official state map, available from any Tourist Information Center, most Chambers of Commerce, and the Oklahoma Department of Transportation.

# Traveler Resources

**Fishing Information** (800) ASK-FISH
**Frontier Country Marketing Association** (800) FUN-OKLA
**Governor's Office** (405) 521-2342
**Highway Patrol/Emergency** (405) 682-4343 (*55 on cellular phones)
**Hunting Information** (405) 521-2739
**Oklahoma Arts Council** (405) 521-2931
**Oklahoma Community Theater Association** (405) 236-0788
**Oklahoma Department of Transportation** (405) 521-2541
**Oklahoma Department of Wildlife Conservation** (405) 521-3851
**Oklahoma Historical Society** (405) 521-2491
**Oklahoma Museums Association** (405) 424-7757
**Oklahoma Resorts, Parks, and Cabins** (800) 654-8240
**Oklahoma Restaurant Association** (405) 942-8181
**Oklahoma Scenic Rivers Commission** (918) 456-3251
**Oklahoma Tourism Department** (800) 652-6552 (In Oklahoma City area 424-0473)
**Red Carpet Country** (800) 447-2698
**Road and Weather Conditions** (405) 425-2385

## Reference Map for Exploring Oklahoma with Children

For more detailed information, consult the official map of Oklahoma, available free through the Oklahoma Tourism Department at (800) 652-6552 and the Oklahoma Department of Transportation at (405) 521-2541.

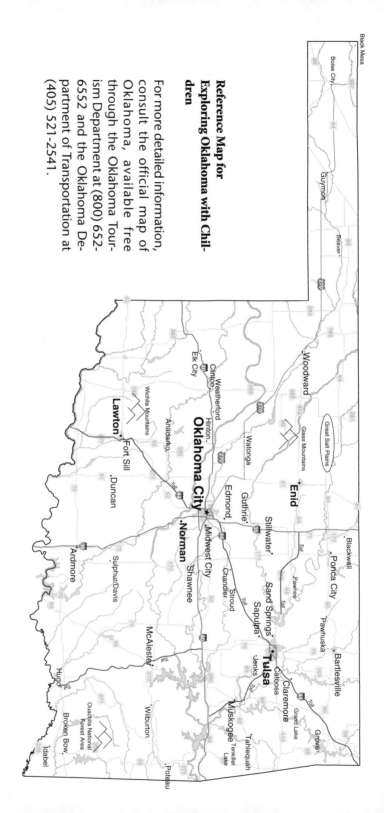

# Get the Most Mileage from Travel Time with Your Children

## by Lisa Marotta

It is rare that any of us share as much uninterrupted time with our children in a week than we spend in one afternoon on the way to a family getaway. Our busy lives can put a strain on our sense of fun and our family relationships. To be satisfying and meaningful, our relationship with our children requires extra time and attention. With young children, this time is social-skills training and an investment in the soon-to-be-challenging teen years. With our already teens (or in-betweens), extra time and attention is a buffer for the pull they feel to be separate from us.

Family time is time well spent when parents are able to recognize the value of play in making meaningful connections with children. Taking time to play with our children strengthens our family bond and helps us to understand each other more fully. However, play is most successful when certain differences between adults and children are understood and addressed.

Play is a child's number one priority; many experts agree that play is the medium by which children, particularly young children, learn best. In contrast, adults follow the motto that "play is what you do when everything else is done." This difference in our perceptions about play causes roadblocks before we even initiate playtime with our children.

From an adult point of view, there are three deterrents to making play be a valuable connection time with our children: we are often exhausted, we believe play is about performance, and we feel pressured to make playtime "perfect." In a child's world, the value of play with you is in the process of play, not the product of play. This is exciting news!!! Play with children does not require more energy of us. Instead, it's a time to reenergize by "growing-down," of becoming a child again—instead of being so grown up.

An example of this difference is when a parent sits down to "play legos" and decides to recreate the Statue of Liberty in miniature. What a nice (adult) idea. The child may go along for awhile, but nasty turns are inevitable. The parent wants the child to have a monument of their time together and quickly becomes frustrated when the child tunes him out and builds something else. However, watch the magic when the parent "grows-down" and allows

*Beaver's Bend Resort Park.*

John Taylor

the child to show him how to build a red, yellow, green, white, leaning, kind-of-looks-like the Statue of Liberty!

### How do you "grow-down" to play with your child? Here are some suggestions:

• Start with the acceptance of your child as the leader in the play arena. Teachers say that the most motivational thing for them is to have an interested student. Your child is the teacher in play; your role as parent is to be an interested student.

• Remember that play isn't about performance. Your child may choose to play something that has no rhyme or reason other than being fun. Blowing bubbles into a drink is a good example. To adults, there is no purpose to this activity, but have you ever noticed how much enjoyment children get from this simple action?

• Be ready to make mistakes and to laugh at yourself. Let your child see you laugh at your failed efforts, then "try, try again." A parent that teaches a child to avoid frustration by accepting failure with humor and attempting the task again is preparing that child for the adult world. Remember to use the motto "try, try again" for yourself frequently–perhaps even within earshot of little ears.

• Think small. Children use play to spice up their regular activities. Many families increase the volume of a kid-selected radio station to quicken the pace of cleanup time. Contrary to popular parent folklore, dancing does not interfere with vacuuming, dusting, or putting away clutter. Consider an all-out war against germs when washing the dishes, complete with sound effects and glory as everyone learns that "Grime does not pay!" Much fun can happen during regular activities if we give up the expectation that getting the job done is more important than having fun while you are working.

*Folk Festival and Craft Show, Beaver's Bend Resort Park.*

*Even dads have fun at Jasmine Moran Children's Museum, Seminole.*

• Fierce competition can ruin a playful, "connecting" moment. Even if you are an ace at checkers, playtime is not the time to prove it. Try letting your child experience some success with your helpful hints ("you might want to re-think that move, have you looked at this part of the board?") or by allowing them to make up the rules to a game. You'll soon be able to gauge when they're ready for more challenge.

Now that you are ready to play with your children, what better time to put these play skills into action than on a family trip, away from the stresses and strains of the everyday busy routine?

### Travel Tips–From Parents Who Have Been There!

• If you are very burned out before a big trip, arrange for some "un-stress-ing" time prior to the trip. Use some alone time to develop a list of the things that you love about each person in your family so that you can let them know on the journey, privately or in "strate-gically overheard" conversations.

• Dissension drains energy and zaps time. Get rid of the "grouchies" in your family by burying the grouch sock (the stinkiest one you can find) in the back-yard. In the eulogy, be sure to reflect together on how grouching and whin-ing can take away from a wonderful time. Then, when the whining begins, remind your children in a fun, gentle way that they have buried those atti-tudes. Watch out, because they will also be reminding you of the buried "grouchies"!

• Help your children be as self-sufficient as possible. Provide them with inexpen-sive lunch boxes to pack their own snacks (encourage the kinds that don't cause thirst). Let them build a "nest" around their seat made of toys and items that they enjoy in the car. Some parents even go so far as to let their children use artificial vines (purchased at a craft store) to create their own space.

• Surprise them or help them choose their own art supplies to keep handy. (Hint: colored pencils are less messy than markers or crayons that easily melt in hot cars.)

• Set up a communication system using a clothesline to pass notes back and forth.

• Inexpensive flashlights are great fun, even in the daylight hours.

• Chapter books on tape from the library are great for the entire family. Another idea is to take a familiar book and change the words to the silliest ones you can think of.

• Think of vacationing tasks that could be assigned to incorporate the interests and individual talents of each family member. Artist, writer, navigator, photographer, disc jockey, restroom critic, tour guide, problem solver, snack distributor, post card collector, quotable quoter, restaurant evaluator, mediator, humorist. . . . Brainstorm the ideas, then allow each family team member to choose one or more roles. If one role is desired by many, find a way to share the job in a friendly way. This promotes the family team spirit.

• Think of the journey as part of the process that will bond your family and help create memories, not just a means to the product (reaching your destination). Take breaks when the children are not stressed to enjoy an unusual surrounding.

• When you return, save your memories! Maybe your family started a postcard or brochure collection on the trip. Put these items with your photos in a scrapbook to tell a story about your journeys together. Refer to it often to relive the good times. (Hint: use the copy or photo store for inexpensive products and services to make your scrapbook truly special.)

Sarah Taylor

*It's so soft! Petting zoo at the Folk Festival and Craft Show, Beaver's Bend Resort Park.*

• Help the family talk about the things they liked best and least about the trip. Log this in a family journal or on slips of paper in a jar to be reviewed during the planning stage of the next outing.

• Use visualization with your children during stressful times. For example, "I got so frustrated at work that I closed my eyes and remembered how beautiful that sunset was, and I felt so much better," or "Remember when we got the flat tire and everyone pitched in to get us back on the road again?" These types of memories and visualizations help us all deal with the stresses of life.

Whether you are planning to vacation for a week or a day, or even if you are spending five minutes with your children, try to enter their world to make the connection more meaningful. It is not unusual for children to feel a little let down when their special family time is over. Do not be surprised to hear your child complain that "you never spend time with me!" on return from a wonderful family vacation. This is actually a child's way of sharing how much they enjoyed the extra time and attention. Try to respond with encouragement and acceptance: "I had so much fun, I hope we can have more time together really soon" and try, try again. "Growing down" with your children will be time well spent in building your relationships and making meaningful memories.

*Dr. Marotta is a Clinical/School Psychologist and public speaker who lives and works in Edmond, Oklahoma. She has much opportunity to "grow down" within her private practice; she works primarily with children and their families. Lisa and her husband, Sal, enjoy their playtime with their daughters, Lindsay and Katelyn.*

Sarah Taylor

*Boulder hopping at Mount Scott, Wichita Mountains near Lawton.*

# Oklahoma Archeology

## by Nona Leatherwood Schoenleber

*Oklahoma's past lies in layers of soil like the pages of a history book waiting to be read and preserved.*

Archeology is the study of past human life; through it we are able to learn about prehistoric people and how they lived. When an area reveals evidence of human life, questions such as who these people were, how they survived, with what other groups of peoples they were connected, and the effects of environmental changes on human resources, can only be answered through studying and preserving archeological sites.

In Oklahoma, state and federal agencies work together in planning and developing programs for education and for the preservation of Oklahoma's prehistoric and historic past. Read on to discover how you and your family can participate in the hands-on discovery of clues to Oklahoma's unique history.

### Ancient Hunters, Ancient Art

#### The Cooper Site

About 10,500 years ago, a band of ancient hunters painted a lightning bolt in red ochre on a bison skull and placed it in a deep canyon-like gully in what is now Northwestern Oklahoma.

The hunters skillfully drove a herd of bison down the river valley and into the gully for containment. They positioned themselves on the gully's rim and, with careful aim and deadly force, hurled spears tipped with fluted points, killing approximately twenty bison. The small ravine in Harper County was a productive site for the hunters, drawing them back for three separate hunts over a period of about ten years. Now identified as the Folsom people, they were nomadic hunter-gatherers, and Western Oklahoma was an important part of their hunting territory.

The gully eventually filled in, preserving the site until erosion began exposing the bone bed. In 1994, archeologist Lee Bement of the Oklahoma Archeological Survey in Norman, with the assistance of O.U. students and volunteers from the Oklahoma Anthropological Society, excavated the area named the Cooper site.

Discarded stone tools such as scrapers, knives, and projectile points, as well as an array of bison bones with cut marks demonstrating butchering tech-

*Oklahoma Anthropological Survey at work.*

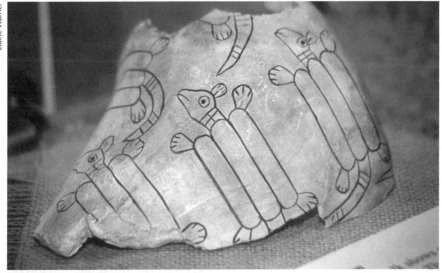

*Spiro Mounds artifact.*

niques, were found in three separate layers at the Cooper site. The painted bison skull, perhaps strategically placed in the gully by a Shaman or Holy Man to draw the herds, represents the oldest piece of art work in North America known at this time.

Artifacts from the Cooper site will eventually be displayed in the new Sam Noble Oklahoma Museum of Natural History in Norman, tentatively scheduled to open in 1999.

## Mammoth Hunters

### The Domebo Site

During the end of the last ice age more than ten thousand years ago, the climate in what is now Oklahoma was more humid. Summers were cooler, and winters were mild. Forests of pine and spruce flourished, and rich grasslands spread across the landscape like the wheat fields of today.

Members of the elephant family, mammoths roamed the river beds near the existing Oklahoma towns of Tulsa, Cheyenne and Anadarko. Giant ground sloths and camels were nearing extinction, and massive herds of long-horned bison grazed the short grasses of Western Oklahoma. Saber-toothed tigers were stalking prey in the Wichita Mountains near Lawton, and bears guarded their territory in the eastern Oklahoma woodlands. Trails across Oklahoma were being blazed by the leather-clad feet of ancient hunters cashing in on the rich stores of large game and vegetation.

One of the oldest archeological sites in Oklahoma is the Domebo Site, approximately 11,200 years old. Here, prehistoric hunters, whom we now call the Clovis people, provoked a female Imperial Mammoth (the largest mammoth species) into a narrow canyon in present-day Caddo County. Small fragments of debris from re-sharpening tools were found near the butchering site, and projectile points that were perhaps buried too deeply in the carcass to recover were left behind. The site was excavated in 1962.

The Clovis and Folsom people are typical of the period that archeologists refer to as Paleo-Indian. Dating back ten to twenty thousand years ago or more, this period is best known for its association with big game hunting and extinct animals.

Nona Leatherwood Schoenleber

### Early Villagers

As big game became extinct and deciduous forests spread, the people living during the Archaic Period (9000 B.C. to the birth of Christ) began adapting their lifestyles to include fishing, hunting game, and harvesting crops. Increasing population set the stage for Early Villagers who, beginning around 300 B.C., established semipermanent settlements. This change of lifestyle was a major link in the development of more sophisticated cultures. The use of pottery and artifacts such as stone hoes for cultivating, grinding stones, scrapers, and stone knives give evidence to the new lifestyle. Gardening became a vital part of existence, and villages began spreading across Oklahoma.

### Mound Builders

Located in Eastern Oklahoma, the Spiro Mound site represents some of the most important archeological remains in the United States. Nestled above the Arkansas River near what is now Spiro, Oklahoma, the Spiro Mounds depict a time of passage from hunter-gatherers to a more settled and structured society encouraged partially by the onset of agriculture.

By 900 A.D., Spiro was an important political and religious center. Leaders ruled from temples built on flat-topped pyramid mounds, and elaborate grave offerings were buried in mounds con-

*Lee Bement at the Cooper Site.*

structed specifically for the elite.

The Arkansas, Grand, Illinois, and Canadian Rivers (all crossing paths in eastern Oklahoma) were "highways" for easy travel, and Spiro's location on the Arkansas made it an important hub for trade routes. Farmers may have traded excess crops, such as corn, for hides brought in by prairie bison hunters or tools made by the people of the Ozarks. This phase lasted until approximately 1450 A.D.

The reasons for the population decline at Spiro, and eventually the abandonment of the site, are not entirely clear. Some evidence suggests that, as the people became more sedentary, their main diet consisted of stored crops. The prolonged storage of crops decreases the crops' nutritional value, thus explaining the malnutrition, anemia, and dental disease evidenced in this culture. The onset of a drier climate gradually reduced the production of crops, forcing people to move elsewhere. Some scholars believe that the modern Caddo and/or the Wichita tribes are the descendants of the people of Spiro.

## Visiting Oklahoma's Past

The majority of archeological sites in Oklahoma are not open to the public because the sites are on private property or are being preserved for possible further study. Spiro Mounds Archaeological Park is the only prehistoric Native American site open to the public in Oklahoma.

Other opportunities are available to learn more about Oklahoma's past. Members of the Oklahoma Anthropological Society (OAS) have been involved in archeological research since 1952. Yearly digs, field surveys, laboratory studies, publications, and seminars provide an educational experience while assisting professional archeologists with research goals.

Native Bow and Arrow Making, Rock Art, Oklahoma Battle Sites, and Flint Knapping techniques, along with the state organization reports, are a sample of programs presented by the local OAS chapters. Monthly meetings are held at each of the chapter locations, including Tulsa, Ada, Oklahoma City, Muskogee, Ponca City, McAlester, Lawton, and Weatherford. The Society invites anyone with a responsible interest in studying and preserving Oklahoma's distant and more recent past to become a member of their group. For more information, contact the Oklahoma Anthropological Society at R.R. 1, Box 62B, Cheyenne, OK 73628-9729.

The wealth of information collected on Oklahoma's archeology is primarily due to the Oklahoma Archeological Survey located on the University of Oklahoma campus in Norman. Currently, the Survey has collected information on more than fifteen thousand sites throughout Oklahoma. The Survey's staff provides educational talks to schools and civic organizations throughout the state. For more information call (405) 325-7211.

Our prehistoric ancestors did not record their history on the written page as we do. They have given us their history in bits and pieces of evidence found throughout our state. When archeological sites are destroyed or disturbed in any way, it is like tearing important and irreplaceable pages from a history book. Just as we teach our children to respect and care for books, we should also teach them to respect and care for archeological finds. If you or your family discovers evidence of prehistoric or historic life in the state, contact the Oklahoma Anthropological Society. If your family is interested in participating in organized archeological digs, contact the OAS for information about how to get involved.

*Nona Leatherwood Schoenleber, an award-winning free-lance writer and an avocational archeologist, is a long-time member of the Oklahoma Writers' Federation and the Oklahoma City Writers, Inc. She is serving a second term as Vice President of the Central Chapter of the Oklahoma Anthropological Society (OAS) and is currently working on her certification in archeology. As members of OAS, Nona and her family have participated in numerous archeological digs, surveys, and educational programs.*

# The Powwow: A Sacred Oklahoma Tradition

## by Trena Thomas

The sights and sounds of a Native American powwow are unlike any other artistic form of expression you may experience. The steady beat of the drum, the colorful movement of the dancer's regalia, and the rhythmic song as the dancers move both enchant and mesmerize. Powwows are celebrations and social gatherings, a way to connect and honor the sacred traditions to be found in the coming together of people. They may be held for many reasons: to honor an individual; as a benefit; as a special occasion; or, most commonly, as a social event.

The history of powwows is rich in Oklahoma. With many Native Americans from several tribes living in Oklahoma, any powwow may include Southern Plains style dancing, which is typically slow, and Northern Plains style, which is faster and more lively. Every powwow begins with a grand entry into the dance arena. A number of basic dances are performed at each powwow: Men's Fancy Dance and Women's Fancy Shawl Dance, Traditional Straight Dance, Grass Dance, and Jingle Dress Dance. Most dances are danced in a circle, representing the circle of unity and the cycle of life. Dancers often follow the clockwise pattern of the sun. Each dance requires specific regalia, and both the dance and the regalia may signify special events or honors in a person's life.

### Fancy Dances

This is the most athletic of the powwow dances. The men's fancy dance uses intricate gymnastic steps and requires tremendous physical stamina. The regalia is often brilliantly colored, and dancers must show coordination as they spin and turn. The women's fancy shawl dance is a spirited dance of twirling and turning, providing young women an opportunity to demonstrate individual ability and grace. This is the most modern of the ladies' dances.

### Traditional Straight Dance

This is the original dance of the Northern Plains Indians. The dance has a stately, slow-moving bounce step that dips and sways to the drum beat. The slower tempo allows for individual expression on the part of the dancer. Danc-

Elaine Warner

*The powwow tradition continues.*

ers often wear regalia that has been passed down through the generations.

## Grass Dance

This is the most ancient of the surviving tribal dances. In this dance, men hang yarn, cloth or leather from their arms and waists to represent grass; as they move through the dance, it is reminiscent of the rippling prairie grasses.

## Ladies Jingle Dress Dance

Originating from the tribes of Canada, this dance is relatively new to the Southern Plains tribes. It is a proud and dignified dance which allows a great deal of individual expression. The jingle dance regalia is not only colorful, it provides much of the musical accompaniment for the dance. Long tubular cones form a fringe-like decoration which "jingles" as the dancer moves.

Although there are ceremonial powwows held that are closed to non-tribal members, everyone is welcome at a publicized powwow. Powwows are sometimes like a reunion, and the hosts feel honored to have visitors. However, if the powwow is very religious or ceremonial, the rules would be observed even more strictly than at other powwows, and visitors should be most respectful of the proceedings.

**For newcomers to these colorful events, here are a few tips to make the experience more enjoyable:**

• Remember that the modern powwow is a link to the Native American's past; these ceremonies help Native Ameri-

Elaine Warner

*Fancy Dance competitor.*

cans maintain their rich heritage. To non-Indians, the powwow may be seen as entertainment, but the powwow is a ceremonial legacy that should be treated with respect and honor. This respect and honor should be reflected in the actions of visitors as well as the Native American participants.

• The arena is considered sacred; children should be supervised and should not run in or around the arena.

• Bring your own lawn chair. Most powwows are held outdoors and seating is not provided. If bleachers are available, bring a blanket to save your seat.

• Chairs and/or benches located around the inner circle are reserved for dancers.

• Powwow schedules are flexible. Activities will start when everything is ready.

• When the eagle staff is brought in during the grand entry, everyone stands. Hats are removed in respect.

• Always ask a dancer's permission to take their picture and avoid using flash during any dance contest. No photos are allowed during the grand entry, and videotaping is also strongly discouraged.

• Don't touch the dancer's regalia. The ornaments have special meaning, and many of the handmade outfits are cherished as heirlooms. The proper term for a powwow outfit is "regalia," not costume.

• When invited, visitors may dance during social dances and intertribal dances. Although many dances may be performed by non-Indians, some dances, such as the Southern Plains

*Indian Hill's Powwow.*

Gourd Dance, can be performed only by certain members of the tribes.
• If you are participating in shawl dance, wear a shawl.
• Alcoholic beverages or drugs are never allowed at powwows.
**The following is a list of better-known powwows and Native American dance competitions in Oklahoma.**

### Annual Tulsa Powwow

Founded in 1951 by Kenneth Anquoe, this is Tulsa's oldest powwow. Held in early June at the Tulsa Fairgrounds Pavilion. For more information see page 119 in this book or call (918) 835-8699, (918) 747-9232.

### Red Earth Festival

Held the second full weekend in June, from Thursday through Sunday at the Myriad Convention Center. For more information, see page 231 in this book or call (405) 427-5228.

### Indian Hill's Powwow

Usually held the last weekend in July at 9300 North Sooner Road, Oklahoma City. For more information, call (405) 634-5553.

### Annual Ponca Powwow

The oldest celebrated powwow, it has been held for over 121 years. Usually held the last weekend of August (Thursday through Sunday). For more information, call (405) 762-8104.

### Cherokee National Holiday

The powwow is held the Friday and Saturday of Labor Day weekend at Cherokee Heritage Center, Tahlequah. Other activities associated with the event are held from Thursday through Sunday. For more information, see page 82 in this book or call (918) 456-0671.

There are several resources for information about local powwows. Contact the Red Earth Indian Center at (405) 427-5228 for a list. You may also wish to contact each individual tribal council office or various Chambers of Commerce around the state, or you may ask the Oklahoma Department of Tourism to send the state's calendar of events and a powwow events brochure. Once you attend one powwow, you will be told of others scheduled during the summer.

*Trena Thomas is a native of Tulsa who currently resides in Jenks, Oklahoma, the Antique Capital of the World. She holds a bachelor of fine arts degree from the University of Tulsa and a masters degree in Journalism/Mass Communications from the University of Oklahoma. In addition to freelance writing and numerous volunteer activities, she is the Area Business Manager for Public Service Company of Oklahoma, an electric utility. Trena lives with her son Dylan, age seven, and dog, Beau.*

# Junior Golf

## by Trena Thomas

Interest in the sport of golf among young people has grown tremendously, due in large part to the rapid rise of amateur-turned-professional superstar Tiger Woods. Thousands of youth want to "be like Tiger," and they dedicate themselves to striving for excellence. Golf is a sport that requires patience, dedication, and concentration; the sport also provides the opportunity to see nature at its most beautiful, to make close friends, and to continue developing skills throughout a lifetime. Golf is also a wonderful family-participation sport. In fact, it's not uncommon for grandparents and grandchildren to enjoy the game together. In Oklahoma, there are many easy and low-cost ways for youth to get started in golf, due in large part to the commitment of the Professional Golf Association of America, better known as the PGA.

Established in 1916, the PGA started its rich tradition in Oklahoma during the 1920s. There are over 470 members and apprentices in the South Central Section of the PGA (which includes Oklahoma), and over 170 facilities statewide hire PGA professionals. One of the ways the PGA promotes the game of golf is to provide many opportunities for youth to be introduced to the game of golf. In large part, this goal is accomplished through the PGA's extremely popular Junior Golf program. All courses that have a PGA pro on staff offer some sort of Junior Golf program. Membership is open to boys and girls, no matter their level of playing ability. There is no minimum age, but the recommended starting age for the program is eight years.

Annual membership in the PGA Junior program is $20. Each member receives a lapel pin, bag tag and, most importantly, a tournament book listing scheduled junior tournaments throughout Oklahoma and Kansas. The average cost per player per tournament is $20. Junior members may play in as many tournaments as time and resources permit. Through tournament play, members earn points which enable them to qualify for the Junior Tour of Champions, the nation's largest youth tournament; this event is held each summer at Shangri-La Resort on the shores of Northeast Oklahoma's Grand Lake o' the Cherokees.

The majority of golf facilities offer some type of junior program designed to introduce youth to the game of golf. The cost is often $75 or less for a multi-week instructional clinic. Often, golf clubs will be provided to children to get them started, or resources will be available to purchase used clubs at a reasonable price. Most courses offer a "junior golf" green fee; however, the special fee is sometimes available only at certain times of the day. Call your local golf pro for information about local programs, or contact Walter Hopper at (918) 357-3332 for specific information regarding the Junior PGA program.

By introducing a young person to the pleasures of golf, you will have stimulated an interest in a sport that can be enjoyed for a lifetime—whatever level of play he or she might reach.

# Oklahoma Reenactments: Windows to the Past

## by Nona Leatherwood Schoenleber

Events in Oklahoma's history come to life as reenactors turn back the pages of time through real-to-life recreations of the people who affected our history. Experience the days of the cavalry and the Civil War. Visit the trappers and mountain men who display their wares and sharpshooting skills at the Gilcrease Rendezvous in Tulsa. Participate in Chisholm Trail festivals which highlight chuck wagon suppers, cowboy entertainment, encampments, and pioneer living history and displays. Enjoy the storytelling, tribal dancing, and the traditional foods at Native American powwows celebrated across the state.

Elaine Warner

*Battle of Honey Springs.*

Pictures are worth a thousand words, but participating in living history events is a learning experience not to be forgotten by children and adults alike. Most events are a celebration of culture and heritage, but some are dramatic presentations of the past. Oftentimes, in addition to watching "life as it used to be," participants are able to ask questions about particular areas of interest. For example, when enjoying a chuckwagon living history exhibit, participants are encouraged not only to enjoy the food but to ask questions about the procedure of setting up a chuck wagon meal on the cattle trail. The actors are experts, and they can help visitors understand the history in first-person voice. The following are suggested living history events for your family.

### Tombstone Tales

In a premise of "rising from the grave," reenactors resurrect the cavalrymen, Native American scouts, settlers, and World War II German prisoners of war who are buried in the Fort Reno Cemetery near El Reno, Oklahoma.

Dressed in authentic clothing, reenactors create an uncanny atmosphere as they assume the spirits of some famous and not-so-famous people such as Ben Clark, a favorite scout of General Phillip Sheridan of the U.S. Cavalry, Corporal Patrick Lynch of the Fourth Cavalry, and Chalk, an Arapaho scout for the Army. Listen as Annie Mason proclaims the perils of life for women in the 1800s. Also included in the stories are a German POW, a man from China,

*Cavalry in action at the Battle of Honey Springs reenactment.*

a preacher, and a drover; all share the communal grounds of the historic Fort Reno Cemetery, and all "come to life" during Tombstone Tales.

Tombstone Tales is a "must-experience" reenactment. An award-winning event, it is held the last week of September. For more information, contact the El Reno Chamber of Commerce at (405) 262-1188.

### Civil War Battles

The Oklahoma Historical Society captures the drama of Civil War battles fought in Oklahoma. Spectacular viewing from natural amphitheater settings and from near actual battle sites sets the stage for an unforgettable encounter with history. The air-shattering blasts of cannon fire, charging cavalrymen, and muskets fired in determined fury portray the reality of the Battle of Honey Springs, the Battles of Cabin Creek, and the Battle of Middle Boggy.

### The Battle of Honey Springs

Playing to a crowd of 10,000 spectators, more than 1,000 reenactors from eight states descend on a 360-acre site near Checotah for Oklahoma's most monumental living history event. Fought on July 17, 1863, the Battle of Honey Springs was the largest Civil War battle in Indian Territory, and it involved approximately 9,000 men. This battle, also called the "Gettysburg of the West," was the battle that gained the Union control of the upper Arkansas River, a primary artery for travel.

### The Battles of Cabin Creek

Approximately eight hundred reenactors set the stage for two Civil War battles fought in Oklahoma on July

1, 1863, and September 19, 1864. These battles were fought over Union Supply trains enroute from Fort Gibson on the historic Texas Road, a vital travel route. The 1863 battle was an unsuccessful ambush by the Confederate army to capture the Union supply train; the battle of 1864 resulted in the Confederate capture of 740 mules, 130 wagons, and more than one million dollars in equipment. This victory enabled the Confederates to continue fighting until the end of the Civil War.

### The Battle of Middle Boggy

Fought near present-day Atoka, the Battle of Middle Boggy was a key point in the federal invasions. Although the original skirmish lasted only thirty minutes, it resulted in the Union army driving the Confederates all the way to the Red River. Today, approximately six hundred reenactors recreate the intensity and dramatic effects of the battle.

These Oklahoma Historical Society (OHS) battle reenactments include Union and Confederate camps open to the public, inspection of arms, battalion drills, bayonet drills, period Civil War-era dances, and the actual battle reenactments. Held on a rotating basis every three years, the reenactment for the Battles of Cabin Creek is scheduled for 1998, the Battle of Honey Springs for 1999, and the Battle of Middle Boggy for 2000. To receive an OHS schedule of events and exhibits, call (405) 521-2491. For a listing of other living history events in the state, see the Calendar of Events in this book and/or inquire at the Oklahoma Department of Tourism.

*NOTE: Battle reenactments are important in our understanding of history, but the chaos and emotional stress of any battle engagement may be unsettling to some spectators, particularly sensitive children; parental discretion is advised.*

Elaine Warner

*Outfitters are popular at reenactments.*

*Nona Leatherwood Schoenleber, an award-winning free-lance writer and an avocational archeologist, is a long-time member of the Oklahoma Writers' Federation and the Oklahoma City Writers', Inc. She is serving a second term as Vice President of the Central Chapter of the Oklahoma Anthropological Society (OAS) and is currently working on her certification in archeology. As members of OAS, Nona and her family have participated in numerous archeological digs, surveys, and educational programs.*

# Oklahoma's Oil Industry

## by Rebecca Tallent

Oil has always been important to the people of Oklahoma. As far back as 25,000 years ago, native people used oil which bubbled up from beneath creeks as a type of medicine. Known as "rock oil," it was used to soothe sore muscles on humans and as a treatment for cuts and sores on animals. Where can someone find some of these old sites? Basically, they can be found just about anywhere in Oklahoma.

Near what is now Chelsea in Rogers County, a man named Lewis Ross, the brother of Cherokee Principal Chief John Ross, drilled a well in 1859 looking for salt; instead, he hit oil. Ross' discovery came at the same time as the well drilled in Titusville, Pennsylvania, by Col. Edwin Drake. Drake's well was the first known commercial oil well in the United States, and it helped to bring about the Industrial Revolution. If the Civil War had not happened, the rush for crude oil in Oklahoma probably would have happened much sooner than 1897.

After the Civil War, the federal Bureau of Indian Affairs wanted to protect the tribes; therefore, the government would not allow oil exploration in Indian Territory. However, in 1896, Cudahy Oil Company reached an agreement with the Cherokee Nation to lease an area along the banks of the Caney River in Bartlesville. It was one of the first oil leases allowed for Indian Territory, and the lease was made possible only because the Cherokees had passed a special law.

In January, 1897, work began on the Number 1 Nellie Johnstone. Through the cold winter, the oilmen worked until April 15th, when a crowd gathered to see the well finished. Shortly after 3 p.m., a small explosive was set off in the well, and a large column of oil, water, and debris blew out over the top of the rig. Oklahoma had its first commercial oil well. A replica of the Nellie Johnstone is in Bartlesville's Johnstone Park.

Shortly after the discovery, oil speculators began pouring into Indian Territory wanting to sign agreements with the tribes and drill for oil; however, federal laws kept many companies from leasing in Indian Territory, and Oklahoma was prevented from becoming a boom state.

Tulsa started its claim as the Oil Capital of the World on June 25, 1901, when

*Oil Rigs, a common sight in Oklahoma.*

*Tulsa—the city that oil built.*

the state's first gusher, the Number 1 Sue A. Bland, fueled a boom that forever altered Oklahoma history.

The Sue Bland made people realize that Oklahoma not only had oil, but that the oil was easy to find and a good quality. Oil speculators poured into the territory, drilling and finding dozens of small areas of oil. Everyone was still looking for the big strike, a large area of oil which could make a person a millionaire overnight.

That happened in Glenpool. In 1905, the Ida Glenn No. 1 well roared in shortly before dawn; a gusher that was the first of the famous Glenn Pool, one of the largest oil deposits ever found in the United States. The Glenn Pool was so large, averaging two million barrels of oil per month, that it made Oklahoma Territory the largest oil-producing area in the country and a major oil supplier to the world.

After Glenn Pool, oil speculators rushed into Oklahoma and found major oil deposits in Osage County, Cushing, Healdton, Ardmore, Seminole, and Oklahoma City. By World War

II, Oklahoma supplied twenty percent of all the world's oil needs.

One of the era's most famous wells was the "Wild Mary" Sudik. An early Oklahoma City field well, Wild Mary blew out uncontrolled for thirteen days in March, 1930. The well blew oil and gas so hard that oil from the well was reported blown as far south as Norman. Wild Mary caught the attention of the nation; NBC radio aired daily reports of the well's gushing, while oilmen tried to bring it under control. Before she was tamed, it is estimated that the well's owners lost between $100,000 and one million dollars. No marker is available for the Wild Mary, but the well was about two miles southeast of the field's discovery well, the Number 1 Oklahoma City, which was also a wild gusher. Today, there is a historical marker beside the Number 1 Oklahoma City on S.E. 57th street, just west of Bryant in south Oklahoma City.

In 1931, the price of oil had dropped to a nickel a barrel, and Gov. William "Alfalfa Bill" Murray decided that he had to protect the state's interest; he called out the National Guard to stand watch over the oil wells. Murray's order did not allow anyone but oil company workers within fifty feet of each of the 3,106 wells producing in twenty-seven Oklahoma oil fields. The National Guard protected Oklahoma's wells until 1933, when laws were passed to protect oil production.

During World War II, Oklahoma's oilmen created another large oilfield: the West Edmond Field. Discovered by Ace Gutowsky, Edmond was reported to have no oil or gas, but Gutowsky proved the experts wrong by drilling for more than a mile down to find high-quality oil. Some old derricks can still be seen on Edmond Road west of the city.

After World War II, there were three major petroleum discoveries in Oklahoma: The Chickasha-Watonga Trend oil field, which is located between Chickasha and Watonga; the Deep Anadarko Basin in Western Oklahoma (Beckham, Caddo, Custer, Dewey, Ellis, Roger Mills and Washita counties), which has natural gas deposits more than three miles into the earth; and the Hugoton Gas Field in the Panhandle, also a natural gas find.

Many state towns and cities were originally boom towns; they came into being because of a local oil or gas find. Some of the cities which were boom towns include Cushing, Oilton, Seminole, Oklahoma City, Tulsa, Ardmore, Ada, Enid, Ponca City, Drumright, Bristow, and Duncan. Some boom towns that didn't survive included places such as Three Sands, Big Four, Roxana, and Whiz Bang.

If you want to see an oil or gas well, you need do little more than look around you. Oklahoma produces oil and/or natural gas in seventy-one of its seventy-seven counties. Only Adair, Cherokee, Craig, Delaware, Mayes, and Ottawa counties have no reported petroleum production. However, these six counties have another form of fossil fuel: coal.

Through the years, oil has meant more to Oklahoma than just jobs and quick money. Oklahoma's pioneer oilmen and women also brought education, sports, gardens, art, architecture, and many other things into the state. For generations, oil has been the state's tax base to provide government and teacher retirements.

Some of the famous Oklahoma oil names include: J. Paul Getty, William G. Skelly, Earl W. and Harry Ford Sinclair, Dean A. McGee, Frank Phillips, E.W. Marland, Thomas Gilcrease, John and Eleanor Kirkpatrick, Lew Wentz, John Mabee, Robert S. Kerr, and F.E. Harper. Many of these names are now associated with museums, theaters, education, grant-giving organizations, art collections, highways, and buildings. Some even left their names in unusual ways: KRMG radio in Tulsa stands for Radio Kerr-McGee, part of the Kerr-McGee Oil Co.; SWGS radio at the University of Tulsa stands for William G. Skelly.

Because these famous people have gone doesn't mean that petroleum or its economic benefits have left Oklahoma. Today, there are more than 120,000 people employed in our state's oil and gas industry. Total petroleum sales are worth about four billion dollars a year, making Oklahoma the nation's third largest natural gas producing area and the fifth largest oil producer.

Why do we still need petroleum? Oil isn't used just for gasoline; it is used to make more than 3,000 products that we use every day. Some of these products include plastics, aspirin, tires, cloth-

*The Oklahoma State Capitol, circa 1935.*

ing, lipstick, toothpaste, and wax.

What does this mean for the future? The petroleum-related schools at the University of Oklahoma, Oklahoma State University, and the University of Tulsa are national leaders in developing technology and new methods of producing oil and gas. In the future, Oklahoma will continue to lead the country with improved exploration and production methods.

Currently, Oklahoma is not only leading in exploration, production and technology, its petroleum industry is also leading in something else: cleaning up the past. The petroleum industry and state royalty owners pay a voluntary assessment on all oil and gas sold, and the Oklahoma Energy Resources Board uses the money to clean up abandoned well sites and to educate people about the importance of petroleum in our state.

**Learn more about Oklahoma's petroleum heritage by reading the following books:**

*The Oklahoma Petroleum Industry* by Kenny A. Franks, Oklahoma Heritage Association, published by the University of Oklahoma Press. *Oil in Oklahoma* by Robert Gregory, printed by Leake Industries, Muskogee. *And Still the Waters Run* by Angie Debo, published by the University of Oklahoma Press.

> *Rebecca Tallent is communications director for the Oklahoma Energy Resources Board. An oil and gas journalist for twenty years, Dr. Tallent enjoys writing about Oklahoma's historic petroleum industry and taking high school students on field trips into today's oil fields. She and her husband, Roger Saunders, live in Edmond.*

# Northwest Oklahoma

## Enid

This bustling city was born with the Land Run that opened the Cherokee Outlet to white settlement on September 16, 1893. Enid was chosen as one of four government land office sites, where the approximately 100,000 land seekers had to legitimize and legalize their claim shortly after the run. Visitors can learn learn more about the Land Run and actually walk through the original land office at Enid's Museum of the Cherokee Strip and Humphrey Heritage Village. Enid is now known as the home of Vance Air Force Base and Phillips University. The town also has an attractive downtown built on a square around the Garfield County courthouse. Recently listed as one of the top one hundred cities to raise a family, Enid is an excellent place to visit. Although there are many attractions in the area, the "must do" and most highly recommended attractions in the area are Leonardo's Discovery Warehouse and Adventure Quest and crystal digging at the Great Salt Plains, located about thirty miles northwest of Enid.

*Enid is located 84 miles north and west of Oklahoma City; take I-35 north to Highway 64/412 west. From Tulsa, travel west on the Cimarron Turnpike approximately 124 miles. Enid Chamber of Commerce (405) 237-2494.*

### Attractions

### *Leonardo's Discovery Warehouse and Adventure Quest*

*2nd Street and Maple, (405) 233-2787. From the intersection of Highways 412 and 81 (Owen K. Garriott and Van Buren) go north on Van Buren to Maple. Take Maple east to 2nd Street. Adventure Quest is open (weather permitting) Tuesday-Friday noon to dark; Saturday and school holidays 10 a.m. to dark; and Sunday 2 p.m. to dark. Leonardo's Discovery Warehouse is open Tuesday-Saturday 9:30-5:30, Sunday 2-5. Both areas are closed Monday and for New Year's Day, Easter, Thanksgiving, and Christmas (open for Labor Day and Memorial Day). Adventure Quest only-$3; Leonardo's Discovery Warehouse only-$4; combined Discovery Warehouse/*

Elaine Warner

*Adventure Quest*

*Adventure Quest-$5. Group rates and yearly family memberships are available. Both the Discovery Warehouse and Adventure Quest are handicapped accessible.* ★ ☐

Dedicated to the study of arts and sciences, **Leonardo's Discovery Warehouse** operates on the premise that children and adults should share their discoveries together. . . and that learning should be fun. The space shuttle, music lab, underwater cave room, shadow wall, computer lab, puppet show area, pottery shop, general store, and life sciences room are just a few of the exhibits/play zones of the warehouse. A favorite for children is the theatrical stage. Here, they can dress up in costumes, make up a story, and watch their own performances on a video screen. The multi-cultural area and the main science topic change every month; frequent visitors will always find something new and exciting.

"The largest scientific, interactive playground in the world," **Adventure Quest** almost defies description. You have to see it to believe it. Imagine a playground inspired by the dreams and designs of children, and you might get an idea. The Adventure Quest structure is three stories tall, and is part castle, part maze, part ship, and all highly imaginative. Features include the Spanish galleon, a tot lot with a mini-city and climbing stegosaurus, a dinosaur time-line sand area, a heliostat (an instrument that allows you to safely look at the sun), a space ship, a "ball machine," mazes, catwalks, bridges, tunnels, turrets, swing sets, and more. "Waterworld" allows children to experiment with dams and dikes to see their effect on flowing water. Other features include a three-story-tall spiral tube slide, a telescope, and two separate stages for special productions and events.

Adventure Quest will fascinate children of all ages. Negotiating your way through tricky routes from one place to another is half the fun. At the same

*Future archeologist at Leonardo's Discovery Warehouse.*

time, the entire structure is wheelchair accessible, with gently sloping ramps leading to every major area of the "park."

### Helpful Hints

If you plan to have twelve or more in your group, call two weeks in advance for reservations and to save with group rates. If you are having a family reunion or group function, ask about special rooms that are available to rent.

If you or your children have questions, be sure to ask Leonardo's staff of trained volunteers; they're available to help guests have an enjoyable and educational experience. Special workshops are available with a portable planetarium and a research-quality telescope. A gift shop offers educational toys, games, fossils, shells, science kits, and other items.

## Mr. and Mrs. Dan Midgley Museum

*1001 Sequoyah Drive, (405) 234-7265. Located just south of the corner of Owen K. Garriott (Highway 412) and Van Buren (Highway 81). Open April-October: Tuesday through Friday 10-5, Saturday-Sunday 2-5. November-March: Wednesday-Saturday 1-5. Admission is free. This museum is not handicapped accessible.*

Learn the interesting history of the Midgley family by touring their home. Although they made their living by raising wheat and hay in Northwest Oklahoma, the multi-faceted couple collected exotic rocks on their many national and international trips. After World War II, they built their home by using rocks from their extensive collection. Many of the rocks on the exterior of the house are petrified wood and fossil rocks gathered near Oklahoma's Lake Texoma. Among the exhibit items of interest to children are the one hundred pound selenite crystal (the largest crystal ever removed from the nearby Salt Plains National Wildlife Refuge) and the petrified tree stump (found near Woodward, Oklahoma and weighing over 7000 pounds). Considered one of the best collections in the Southwestern United States, the home's trophy room is filled with animals hunted worldwide by the Midgleys. Visitors will also be impressed by the craftsmanship of the two beautiful rock fireplaces. Children will love the rock candy souvenirs given to them by the staff as they leave!

### Helpful Hints

Group tours take approximately one hour and must be made a week in advance. Tours are given by appointment during regularly scheduled hours and occasionally during other hours.

Located directly in front of the Midgley Museum at the corner of Garriott and Van Buren is **Champlin Park**; the park has handicapped-accessible restrooms, playground equipment, and picnic areas. Also located in the park is a tourist information center managed by volunteers.

## Museum of the Cherokee Strip and Humphrey Heritage Village

*507 South 4th Street, (405) 237-1907. Located one mile east of the intersection of Owen K. Garriott Boulevard (Highway 412) and Van Buren (Highway 81), close to the intersection of 4th Street and Garriott. Open Tuesday-Friday 9-5, Saturday-Sunday 2-5. Closed Monday and state holidays. Admission is free; donations are appreciated.*

The Cherokee Strip (also known as the Cherokee Outlet) was opened on September 16, 1893. Operated by the Oklahoma Historical Society, this museum features exhibits explaining the unique Land Run settlement. Children are mesmerized by the "grandpa" storyteller, a lifelike, robotic figure that tells stories about his younger years before, during, and after the settlement of the Strip. His story is brief enough to hold most children's attention. Be sure to view the downstairs exhibits that show pioneer life, then exit to a separate building containing antique farm machinery and cars.

The tour continues north of the museum in the **Humphrey Heritage Village**. Here you will find four buildings that represent various facets of pioneer life. These buildings, which have been moved and refurbished, include a one-room school, a small Episcopal church, a wood-frame Victorian home, and the original Land Office that was used during the 1893 Land Run. The Land Office was the place where those participating in the Land Run came to legalize their claims. By looking at the exhibits, one realizes that staking a claim was not an easy task. At times, more than one person staked the same claim, and then the adventure of proving the claim began!

### Helpful Hints

With one-week notice, the museum will give guided, one-hour school group tours. Every Tuesday, Wednesday and Thursday during the regular school year, the museum hosts a special one-room school program for fourth graders in the authentic Turkey Creek School, located on the museum grounds. It is recommended to make reservations for this popular program several months in advance.

Located just north of the museum and operated by the city, **Government Springs Park** is a good place to let the children play after spending time at the museum. For your convenience, the park has picnic shelters.

A good time to visit the museum is in mid-September during the **Cherokee Strip Days Celebration**. Living history reenactments and other special programs are offered during the festival at the museum and other locations around Enid. Also included in the festivities are a parade, an arts and crafts show, food booths, entertainment, and the Cherokee Strip PRCA Rodeo. For more information, call (800) 299-2494.

## Railroad Museum of Oklahoma

*702 North Washington, (405) 233-3051. Turn north at the intersection of Owen K. Garriott (Highway 412) and Van Buren (Highway 81). Turn east at Walnut Street. The museum is one block north at the corner of Washington and Chestnut Streets. Open Tuesday-Friday 1-4, Saturday 10-1. NOTE: The museum is undergoing complete renovation during 1997, and the hours of operation may change upon completion. Admission is free; donations are appreciated.*

Although few children have firsthand railroad experience, they have the opportunity to learn about railroads and their history at this museum. Exhibits feature railroad equipment, memorabilia, and a large model train. All visitors are given an extensive tour which usually includes railroad videos. Once outside, there are several different railroad cars available, and visitors are encouraged to climb aboard for the hands-on experience of railroading.

### Helpful Hints

Recently, the museum has added the Operation Lifesaver Program. This program features videos suited to each age group and provides solutions to safety problems that may exist, such as playing around trains, tracks and railroad crossings.

If there are more than twelve in a group, call at least a week in advance to make arrangements for a group tour. Tours last from forty-five minutes to two hours. Upon request, museum volunteers are willing to open the museum for groups during other hours.

Elaine Warner

*Telegraph demonstration at RR Museum.*

## Events

## Keeper of the Plains

*Held the third week of April at the Convention Center and in downtown Enid. The Convention Center is located at Cherokee and Independence. For more information, call (405) 234-5151. Adults $3, school-age children $1, young children are free.*

Named after a bronze sculpture by H.T. Holden which is located on the Garfield County Courthouse lawn, the Keeper of the Plains event celebrates Native American culture. It features participation by Native American tribes based in Oklahoma and by other tribes from around the United States. Activities include a three-day dance celebration, a Native American fine arts show, a trading post area, food booths (with some featuring Native American foods), tepee contests, and face painting. The Tiny Tots dance contest and the tepee-painting contest are favorites for children.

## In the Vicinity

## Great Salt Plains Area

*Located about thirty miles northwest of Enid. Take either Highway 45 or 412 a few miles west of Enid to Highway 132, north to Highway 64, then west to Jet. Travel north on Highway 38 from Jet to begin your tour. The State Park Office is open daily 8:30-5; winter hours vary. The National Wildlife Refuge office is open Monday-Friday 7:30-4.*

At the Great Salt Plains Area, families find many activities to enjoy together. From crystal digging to fishing, camping, and hiking, activities abound for every family member, regardless of age. The area provides wildlife watching opportunities virtually any time of the year. Consider a trip in late fall or early winter to observe the bald eagles and the approximately 70,000 ducks and geese that winter at the refuge.

As you wind around the lake on Highway 38, you will first come to the **Great Salt Plains State Park**. The park office staff will help you with locations for picnicking, camping and nature activities, and they will provide maps and brochures for the area. West of the dam are sandy beaches and swimming areas (no lifeguards are available). If you are interested in camping or renting one of the six cabins located in this area, contact the park office at (405) 626-4731 or the Oklahoma Parks and Resorts toll-free number (800) 654-8240. Cabins during summer weekends are booked several months (even a year) in advance. Call about one month ahead for cabins during the week and during the fall. During the off-season (about December through March), cabins are available most any time. Cabins range in price from $50-60 (off-season rates are $35-45). ⑤

While heading north on Highway 38, you will see a sign for the **Great Salt Plains National Wildlife Refuge** office (405-626-4794). The office is located down a gravel road going west. From the office, you can hike the over-one-mile **Eagle Roost Nature Trail**; interpretive signs and a brochure will help you identify the wildlife and plant species along the trail. Nearby is a children's fishing pond and the almost-three-mile **Harold F. Miller Auto Tour Route**, where visitors can observe deer and waterfowl. After the automobile tour, you can walk a short distance to the **Casey Marsh Tower** to observe many birds, including the Bald Eagle which winters in this area. For the best viewing of wildlife, be sure to bring binoculars and identification books. The Refuge recently opened a shore bird observation area. A short walk down the **Sand Piper Trail** leads to the observation tower, from which up to twenty-nine species of shore birds can be observed. Visitors will find the Sand Piper Trail on the west side of the Refuge off Highway 11.

Another highly-recommended activity for families is **Selenite Crystal Digging**. ★ This "treasure hunting" activity is fun for all children, regardless of age! The dig area is located a few miles north of the Highway 64 and Highway 8 intersection; look for the sign and travel east to the site. As an alternative, a dirt road to the site is located between Jet and the Highway 8 and Highway 64 intersection. The road leads north, then back east (look for the sign). Once at the dig site, drive only in the designated areas because of the danger of quicksand, and dig only in the designated area; other nearby areas are reserved as nesting sites for endangered shorebirds. The dig site is open daily from sunrise to sunset from April 1 to October 15. There is no charge.

Millions of years ago, sea water often flooded what is now the salt flats area. When the sea water was cut off from the sea, the water evaporated, leaving thick layers of salt deposits. Erosion from mountain ranges has covered the soil, but ground water traveling through the salty sand rises to the surface where it evaporates, leaving the crust of salt. The crystals form when the saline solution combines with gypsum.

More crystals are found when the weather has been dry. You can tell that it's been dry when the salt flats look very white with salt. A brochure explaining

# Great Salt Plains Area

## HOW TO DIG FOR CRYSTALS:

For best results, come prepared. You will need a shovel, a bucket or jug of water, and a container in which to carry the crystals, which are fragile until dry. Since crystal hunters spend most of their time on hands and knees, an old towel is handy, both for kneeling and wiping hands. Sunglasses and sunscreen are essential; bright sun combined with glare from the white salt surface can quickly result in sunburn.

Use a shovel to dig a hole about two feet deep until you reach wet sand. Allow two or three inches of water to seep in from the bottom. Use your hands or a cup to splash water gently against the sides of the hole. (Some people bring a container of water, so they have plenty of water to splash...and to drink when it gets hot!) This washes the soil away and exposes the crystals. When you find a crystal, continue splashing it with water until it is mostly exposed. Newly-exposed crystals are fragile and will break if you try to pull them from the soil. After removing the crystal, place it where the sun and wind will dry it. Egg cartons are useful for drying and carrying smaller crystals. You are permitted to remove up to ten pounds of crystals, plus one large cluster each day.

more about the crystals is available at the wildlife refuge headquarters and near the dig site.

As you observe the crystals, notice the hourglass shape formed by the sand and clay particles within the crystals. Be sure to tell your children that this hourglass shape is unique in crystal formations throughout the world!

The **Crystal Festival** is usually held the first weekend in May and includes activities in the nearby town of Cherokee as well as at the crystal dig site. Wildlife officials will be available during the festival to instruct visitors and to answer their questions. In Cherokee, festival activities include a flea market, a carnival, arts and crafts booths, food, kite flying, and more.

Another "must-do" activity in the area that will particularly interest "junior" fishermen and biologists is the **Byron State Fish Hatchery**. Operated by the Oklahoma Department of Wildlife Conservation, the hatchery's unique procedure allows visitors the opportunity to see fish hatch from eggs; the best time to see them hatch is from about mid-March to late May. Throughout the year, fish eggs are spawned, incubated, hatched, fed, sampled, counted, and harvested at the hatchery. The fish are then released in Oklahoma waters. In addition to learning about the fish hatchery, children will enjoy a visit to the harvest pond, where catfish come to the surface to feed.

Byron State Fish Hatchery is located two mile north and one mile west of the corner of Highways 38 and 11. The hatchery is open Monday through Friday 8-5. During fish hatching season (about mid-March to late May), the hatchery is also open Saturday and Sunday from 8-5. Admission is free. The hatchery is handicapped accessible. Call (405) 472-2663 at least a week in advance for group tours; tours last from thirty to ninety minutes.

## Sod House Museum

*Located about four miles north of Cleo Springs or twenty-one miles south of Cherokee on Highway 8. The museum is about twenty-two miles from* the Great Salt Plains area. (405) 463-2441. Open Tuesday-Friday 9-5, Saturday-Sunday 2-5. Closed Monday and state holidays. Admission is free. This museum is not handicapped accessible.

Imagine living in a two-room sod house, with the threat of bugs and snakes, prairie fires, and unpredictable (and sometimes dangerous) Oklahoma weather. Now imagine this same house with a family of ten living there! Sod houses were the "norm" for early-day Western Oklahoma pioneers. Made of virgin sod, dense with grass roots that held the soil together, the homes were surprisingly sturdy.

Your children will appreciate their cozy beds under a sturdy roof after they examine this sod house, the only original sod house remaining in the state of Oklahoma. It stands to remind us of the spirit and fortitude of the early settlers. The sod house is authentically furnished, and it explains much about life in a sod home. The museum also features exhibits of early pioneer life, including information regarding pioneer women's work. Be sure to pick up the brochures at the museum explaining more about sod houses in early-day Oklahoma.

# Ponca City

Much like the other land office towns in the Cherokee Outlet, Ponca City was born during one afternoon, on September 16, 1893, the day of the opening of the Cherokee Outlet. Six years later, it was incorporated as a city. The town grew slowly and steadily until one man, E.W. Marland, came to the area seeking oil. This fantastically-successful oil wildcatter changed the future of Ponca City; although his luck eventually ran out, he left three important landmarks that make Ponca City an outstanding place to visit, and his company, Marland Oil, is now known as Conoco, Ponca City's major employer.

*Located approximately ninety miles from Oklahoma Ctiy and Tulsa. From Oklahoma City, travel north on I-35, exit on Highway 60 and travel east for fifteen miles. From Tulsa, take the Cimarron Turnpike west approxaimtely seventy miles to the Ponca CIty exit (Highway 177), then travel north about twenty-two miles. Ponca City Chamber of Commerce (405) 767-8888 or (800) 475-4400.*

## Attractions

### Lou Wentz Pool

*L.A. Cann Drive, (405) 767-0436. From the intersection of 14th Street (Highway 77) and Lake Road (also known as Highland), take Lake Road east to Kygar Road (located just before the bridge). Go north 150 yards, then turn east onto L.A. Cann Drive. Follow the paved road until you reach the blue water tower. Look for the rock gate entrance. Open Memorial Day-Labor Day, Tuesday through Sunday 12-7. Closed Monday. Adults (ages twelve and older) $1.50, under twelve $1.*

Often called the most beautiful pool in Oklahoma, this pool is open to the public and overlooks Lake Ponca. Concessions and picnic tables are available.

### Marland Mansion

*901 Monument Road, (405) 767-0420. From 14th Street (Highway 77) and High-*

land, turn east. Take the circle drive around the Pioneer Woman statue to Monument Road, which leads directly to the mansion. Open Monday-Friday 10-5, and Saturday-Sunday 1-5. Closed Thanksgiving, Christmas and News Year's Day. There is no charge to visitors who tour the grounds and the museums in the guest house. Visitors pay the following admission to tour the interior of the mansion: adults $4, senior citizens $3, students $1.75. Guided tours that last approximately one hour are available during the week at 1:30, and on Saturday and Sunday at 1:30 and 2:30. If you need to schedule a tour at a different time, call a week ahead. The mansion is not handicapped accessible. The mansion also includes a hotel and conference center; call ahead for reservations. ★

E. W. Marland was one of the richest oilmen in Oklahoma's history. Although already wealthy, in 1920, Marland discovered an oil field in Burbank, about sixteen miles east of Ponca City and became an even wealthier man. A year later, he developed the successful Tonkawa oil field. Marland was founder and owner of the Marland Oil Company, which later became known as Conoco. By the beginning of the Great Depression in 1930, Marland was broke. The oilman turned to politics, serving as Oklahoma's tenth governor.

The Marland Mansion was built between 1925 and 1928 at a cost of $5.5 million; it reveals much about the wealthy man who had it built. The mansion has fifty-five air-conditioned rooms, twelve bathrooms, and a ballroom with gold leaf ceilings and Waterford Crystal chandeliers. When it was built, the mansion and estate included a polo field, an Olympic-sized swimming pool, five lakes, and many other amenities and extravagances. Children and adults visiting the mansion are often awed by the its elegance.

The former guest house now contains exhibits about petroleum, E.W. Marland, and the famous 101 Ranch located near Ponca City. These exhibits are staffed by volunteers and hours are unpredictable.

E.W. Marland helped develop the identity of Ponca City today. Besides founding the oil company, he also commissioned the statue of the Pioneer Woman which, as Marland said, is a tribute to "all women of the sunbonnet everywhere." His first mansion is now the Ponca City Cultural Center and Indian Museum. Another of his contributions is the oil well still standing today at the State Capitol in Oklahoma City; Marland encouraged the drilling of this well, the only pumping well located on any state capitol property.

## Pioneer Woman Statue and Museum

701 Monument Road, (405) 765-6108. Located at the northeast corner of Highway 77 (14th Street) and Lake Road. Admission is free; donations are appreciated. NOTE: The museum is closed until the spring of 1998 for expansion. Open Tuesday-Saturday 9-5, Sunday 1-5. Closed Monday and major holidays. Self-guided tours take about an hour. Large groups should call a week in advance for reservations.

The Pioneer Woman statue was commissioned in

1927 by oilman E.W. Marland. He sponsored a contest in which models by twelve of the country's best sculptors were taken on tour. The winning entry was determined by public vote. Bryant Baker of Brooklyn won and, in 1930, the seventeen-foot bronze statue was dedicated to the heroic spirit of pioneer women everywhere; it is now listed on the National Register of Historic Places.

Adjacent to the statue is the **Pioneer Woman Museum**. Its purpose is to educate visitors about life on the Oklahoma frontier by showcasing antiques and artifacts from the turn of the century. Visitors will see a pioneer kitchen and bedroom, and an old-fashioned beauty shop. Objects such as washboards, stoves, quilts, dishes, clothing, and more fill these rooms.

Once the expansion is completed in the spring of 1998, the museum will have 6,000 square feet of area, and it will include new exhibits about pioneering women of the twentieth century.

## Poncan Theater

*104 East Grand Avenue, (405) 765-0943. From 14th Street (Highway 77) travel north to Grand Avenue, turn west to the corner of First Street and Grand. Hours are by appointment only. Tours are $1. Tickets for performances vary in price.*

This restored 1927 theater is used throughout the year by performing arts groups in the areas of music, dance, theater, first-run movie films, and touring shows. Tours of the theater are by reservations only (call one week in advance). You may also call to receive information on shows scheduled at the theater.

## Ponca City Cultural Center and Indian Museum

*1000 East Grand Avenue, (405) 767-0427. From the intersection of 14th Street (Highway 77) and Grand Avenue, travel west to the southeast corner of 10th Street and Grand. Hours are Monday, Wednesday-Saturday 10-5 and Sunday 1-5. Closed Tuesday and some holidays. Adults (ages sixteen and older) $1, children free.*

Built in 1914, this twenty-two room home was E. W. Marland's first mansion. Exhibits here feature Native American artifacts, pre-Columbian artifacts, 101 Ranch memorabilia, an original thirteen-star United States flag, and an original sculpture by Bryant Baker, the "Pioneer Woman" artist. The self-guided tour takes about an hour.

## Standing Bear Native American Memorial Park

*Located at the intersection of U.S. 60 and U.S. 77 on the south edge of town. No fee. For more information, contact the Ponca Chamber of Commerce at (405) 767-8888.*

On the southern edge of Ponca City, sculptor Oreland C. Joe's magnificent twenty-two-foot bronze statue of Ponca Indian Standing Bear stands amid the grasses and wildflowers of native prairie. Dedicated in October, 1996, the monument honors Chief Standing Bear as an early civil rights leader. Visitors can follow the circular trail to a sixty-foot diameter plaza offering dramatic views of the statue and a panoramic view of the sixty-three acre site. Features of the plaza include the story of Chief Standing Bear, tribal seals of the six Native American tribes nearest to Ponca City, a reflecting pool, and an eternal flame. A Native American-inspired design in the plaza surface includes the names of the eight Ponca tribal clans. This sculpture is a beautiful tribute to the influence of Native Americans in the area.

## Sun 'N Fun Family Recreation

*Located near Kaw Lake, five miles east of Ponca City on Lake Road. (800) 246-5444. Go-karts, batting cages, and miniature golf open the first weekend of April and remain open through the fall. All activities, including the water park, are open the weekend prior to Memorial Day through Labor Day (hours vary so call ahead). Day rate, adults $6.50, children ages six and under $4. Adult evening rates are $5 after 5 p.m. Groups of twenty or more are $5 per person (ages seven and older).*

Water rides such as slides, the activity pool, and floating tubes are the main attraction here during the summer. The park also features sand volleyball, a tree-shaded go-kart track, an eighteen-hole miniature golf course, batting cages, arcade games, and picnic areas. Picnic shelters can be reserved at no charge by calling in advance. Food concessions and a gift shop are also available.

## Events

## Iris Festival

*Usually held the first weekend in May in downtown Ponca City. For more information, call (405) 763-8082. Admission is free.*

Celebrate the beauty of spring when you visit the Iris Festival. You may browse through a flower show, shop for arts and crafts, or splurge on a tasty treat at the Victorian Chocolate Festival.

## Christmas in July

*Held on the Fourth of July weekend at Pioneer Beach Park on Kaw Lake. For more information and directions, call (405) 269-2618. Admission is $1 per person.*

Sand castle and suntan contests are held in the afternoon of this patriotic celebration. About 9 p.m., look for the lighted-boat flotilla on the lake, then enjoy a spectacular fireworks display over the water.

## Grand National Motocross Races

*Held the first weekend in August at the Ambuc Motocross Track, 1005 West Prospect. For more information call (405) 762-5502. Open Wednesday-Saturday 8-4:30. Adults $8, children $4. The stadium is handicapped accessible.*

The Grand National Championships bring more than 1,000 of the nation's top Motocross riders (ranging from eight-year-old beginners to motorcycle professionals) to Ponca City. There are food concessions and restrooms available. Visitors may bring umbrellas and small tents. RV hookups are available.

## 101 Wild West Rodeo

*Held the third weekend in August at Ash and Prospect Street. For more information call (800) 475-4400. Wednesday-Thursday 7-9:30, Friday-Saturday 8-10:30. Adults $6-8, children $3, under age six are free.*

Polish your boots, put on your cowboy hat, and plan for fun at this PRCA-sanctioned rodeo. The 101 Wild West Rodeo follows the tradition started by the famous

Miller brothers of the 101 Ranch. More than 400 of the nation's top rodeo performers participate in steer-roping, bull-riding, and barrel racing. Children can participate in special events in the arena each night before the rodeo begins. Festivities at the rodeo also include a dance, arts and crafts, and food vendors.

## Octoberfest

*Usually held the first weekend of October on the grounds of the Marland Mansion estate. For more information, call (405) 767-0420. A small fee is charged.*

Visitors will enjoy over one hundred booths of arts, crafts and food as they celebrate fall at Octoberfest. Live entertainment, some with a German flair, includes bands, vocalists, local gymnasts, and dancers. Children's activities include face painting, sand art, and even canoe rides.

## Festival of Angels

*Held city-wide from Thanksgiving to New Years. For information call (800) 475-4400. Most events are free.*

Get into the spirit of Christmas by driving through Ponca City for this special display of lights. Be sure to see the lights at the Marland Estate, Cann Garden Center, the Ponca City Cultural Center, the Centennial Plaza, the downtown area, and residential areas. Other holiday activities include home tours, a parade, a children's play performed at the Poncan Theater, and more.

## In the Vicinity

## Blackwell

This bustling small town was planned, platted, and promoted by A.J. Blackwell before any non-Indian pioneers could settle the area. As part of the Cherokee hunting grounds, this land was not available for settlement without permission of the Cherokee tribe. However, after the Civil War, the tribe was required to provide territories for the Kaw, Ponca, Tonkawa, Pawnee, and Otoe-Missouria tribes. Excess lands were opened to other settlers through the Cherokee Outlet Land Run of 1893. Mr. Blackwell, who had been promoting the town prior to the Run, was chosen president of the town council, and he became the first mayor.
*Blackwell is located about fifteen miles west and north of Ponca City along I-35. Blackwell Chamber of Commerce (405) 363-4195.*

## Attractions

### Derailed Railroad Museum

*216 N. Main, (405) 363-2207. Open Monday-Friday 9:15-3:30, Saturday 9:15-4. Free. Call to verify hours. Handicapped accessible.*

LeRoy Jacks is a man who never outgrew his love of trains. Now a grandfather, he has, over the years, created a whole "world" in his downtown location. In the backroom is a huge model train layout

*Derailed Railroad Museum.*

which includes scenery from places the Jacks family visited, a model of the Conoco refinery where one son works, and a tiny community named after a daughter. He has close to one hundred locomotives, but most interesting is his rolling stock (the box cars) which he creatively handcrafted from cereal boxes, toothpicks, thread, pins, paper towel rolls, and all sorts of other items. Children will love to see the trains go, and they'll get a safety lesson while they are there.

## Top of Oklahoma Museum

*Top of Oklahoma Museum.*

*Electric Park Pavilion, 303 South Main, (405) 363-0209. Open Monday-Saturday 10-5, Sunday 1-5. Free; donations are appreciated.*

The history of Blackwell and its residents is displayed in the Top of Oklahoma Museum. Visitors will find exhibits depicting home and family life, local industries, Native American culture, and much more. All exhibits are housed in the Electric Park Pavilion, a remarkable building constructed in 1912-13. The building is listed on the National Register of Historic Places.

# Watonga

Children and their cartoon-loving parents will be interested to know that Watonga is the boyhood home of Clarence Nash, the voice of Walt Disney's cartoon character Donald Duck. Named after Arapaho chief Wa-Ah Dan-Ga-Ha, Watonga was once a part of the Cheyenne and Arapaho tribes' reservation. The small town has an active downtown, with many shops and attractions. Be sure to take your family to the **Old General Store and Prairie House Museum** (122 W. Main, 405-623-2444) that contains over 10,000 items showing commonly-found merchandise from 1880 to 1940. The Prairie House depicts early-day living in the plains states. With many historic attractions and the scenic wonders and activities at Roman Nose Resort Park, this area provides a wonderful family vacation destination.

*Located approximately 75 miles northwest of Oklahoma City. From Oklahoma City, take I-40 west to Highway 281. Go north approximately twenty-two miles to Watonga. Another possibility is to take Highway 3/81 to Kingfisher then take Highway 33 west approximately thirty miles to Watonga. To travel the approximately 147 miles from Tulsa, take State Highway 51 west to I-35. Go south approximately twenty miles to Guthrie, then take Highway 33 west to Watonga. Watonga Chamber of Commerce (405) 623-5452.*

## Attractions

### Roman Nose Resort Park

*Located seven miles north of Watonga on Highway 8A (turn west off State Highway 8). For Resort Lodge reservations and information, call (800) 654-8240. For infor-*

mation about camping and other park activities, call the Roman Nose Park Office at (405) 623-7281. ★ ⑤

Roman Nose Resort Park is named after Chief Henry Caruthers Roman Nose, who lived in the canyon from 1887 to 1917. The natural springs and abundant wildlife made Roman Nose Canyon a favorite refuge of the Cheyenne and Arapaho tribes, and later, a hideout for outlaws. Today, visitors to this area can enjoy golfing on a scenic nine-hole course, horseback riding, swimming, camping, hiking, and fishing. In addition, of particular interest to children is the miniature golf course, paddle boats and canoes, recreation room with an arcade and ping-pong tables, and courts for playing tennis, basketball, and volleyball. The park also includes two small lakes for fishing. The lakes are stocked with trout from October through March, and normal state fishing

*Cookout on the trail.*

licenses are required. The lodge includes a full-service restaurant.

The extensive trails which wander through the red shale canyon and gypsum hills are perfect for hiking and horseback riding. Hikers will enjoy the spectacular view, especially along the canyon rim. Interpretive **horseback rides** combine fun with learning. Dressed in period costumes, trip leaders recreate the history of the canyon by recounting stories of Native Americans, outlaws, the Cavalry, and cattlemen from the 1800s. One- and two-hour rides are offered as well as three-hour weekend dinner rides which include a complete steak dinner cooked over an open fire. Prices range from $10 an hour for one- and two-hour rides to $40 for the dinner ride. Riders need no experience, but they must be between the ages of eight and eighty, weigh less than 250 pounds, and wear shoes that cover their feet (no sandals or open-toed shoes). Reservations for rides are recommended for summer rides and weekend rides. Call the **Roman Nose Stables** at (405) 623-4354 for more information.

With its rugged terrain, Roman Nose is a great place for **mountain biking**. It is the first Oklahoma state park to host a sanctioned mountain

*Trail rides at Roman Nose.*

bike race. While on the trail, bikers should remember to yield to hikers and horseback riders. The trails are described as being steep and rough, but experienced mountain biking families will relish the challenge.

Many accommodations are available at the park, from Roman Nose Lodge with forty-seven motel-like rooms ($65-68) to tepee camping. At a cost of $15 per night, tepees come complete with electricity; they are available from May through Labor Day, and should be reserved in advance. Also available are tent camping sites ($6 per tent per night) and ten one-bedroom kitchenette cottages that each sleeps up to four ($75-78). Guests must bring their own utensils and cooking equipment for the cottages.

## T.B. Ferguson Home

*519 N. Weigle, (405) 623-5069. From Highway 33 and Highway 8 (Clarence Nash Boulevard) go north to 4th Street. Go east on 4th to Weigle Avenue, then take Weigle north one block. The home is located at the corner of E. 5th and N. Weigle. Open Wednesday-Saturday 10-4, Sunday 1-5. Closed Monday, Tuesday, and all state holidays. Admission is free. Not wheelchair accessible.*

T.B. Ferguson, the sixth Territorial Governor of Oklahoma and founder of the *Watonga Republican* newspaper, built this stately home in 1907. Filled with beautiful furnishings, period pieces, and historic photos, the Ferguson home is perhaps best known for its famous guests. Edna Ferber, a close friend of Mrs. Ferguson, stayed here while researching material for her novel *Cimarron,* a story about Oklahoma's tumultuous territorial days. Another well-known guest was President Theodore (Teddy) Roosevelt, who enjoyed hunting trips with Mr. Ferguson. Although not officially part of the tour, ask to see the museum office. This tiny room served as the Ferguson's guest bedroom. Imagine a president sleeping there now!

In addition to the house, children will enjoy seeing the first Watonga city jail and an 1870 U.S. Cavalry remount station, both relocated behind the Ferguson home.

## Watonga Cheese Factory

*314 E. Second Street, (405) 623-5915. From the intersection of Highway 33 and Burford Avenue, go north five blocks to Second Street. The Watonga Cheese Factory is on the southeast corner of Second and Burford. Monday-Friday 8:30-5, Saturday 9-1:30, closed Sunday.*

In 1941, local dairy farmers solved the problem of what to do with the skimmed milk after separating the cream: they opened this small, cheese-producing factory. Currently, the factory produces from 2,000 to 8,000 pounds of delicious cheddar cheese each day. Children and adults will enjoy watching this process through the observation window. Factory-produced cheese may be purchased at the store in two- or thirteen-pound blocks.

### Helpful Hints

To celebrate the influence of the Watonga Cheese Factory, the community hosts the annual **Watonga Cheese Festival** during the first weekend of October (Friday-Saturday). Among the many activities at this popular event are historical reenactments, a Mouse Walk and Rat Race, shows featuring arts, crafts, and antiques, cheese tasting, food contests, a flea market, and a parade. Admission is $2. For more information, contact the Watonga Chamber of Commerce at (405) 623-5452.

For authentic Watonga Cheese soup and other delicious taste treats, try the popular **Noble House Restaurant** located at 112 N. Noble in downtown Watonga.

# Woodward

Reported to be one of the friendliest towns in Oklahoma, Woodward is a wonderful place to spend the weekend and experience all that Northwest Oklahoma has to offer. From bat cave viewings to dune buggy rides to outstanding wildlife and adventure opportunities, this area provides numerous quality family activities.

Although the village of Woodward had been a railroad stop servicing nearby Fort Supply since 1887, the town dramatically increased in population on the day of the 1893 Cherokee Outlet Land Run. While traditional industries in the area have included agriculture (farming and ranching) and retailing, oil and gas companies began exploring underground resources in the mid-1950s. More recently, the area has become known as one of the few places in the world that recovers iodine from underground water.

Tragedy struck Woodward over fifty years ago in 1947 when a huge tornado flattened over one hundred city blocks and killed over one hundred residents. A drive down Woodward's Main Street tells part of the story (note that there are few historic buildings remaining); more about the 1947 tornado can be learned through photograph exhibits at the award-winning Plains Indians and Pioneers Museum. *Woodward is located 140 miles northwest of Oklahoma City on Highway 270, and 207 miles west of Tulsa on Highway 412. Woodward Chamber of Commerce (405) 256-7411 or (800) 364-5352.* ▯

## *Attractions*

### *Boiling Springs State Park*

*Located northeast of Woodward, (405) 256-7664. Take Highway 34 north about four miles to Highway 34C, go east about five miles, following the signs to the park entrance. From Alabaster Caverns, travel south on Highway 50 to Mooreland, then travel west on Highway 50B to the "backdoor" entrance of the park. For cabin reservations, call (800) 654-8240. One-bedroom cabins range from $28-43, depending on season and day of week.* ⑤

Boiling Springs is a small park developed by the Civilian Conservation Corps in the 1930s. It is named for the bubbling (not boiling) natural springs that were prevalent at the park until more recent years, when ground water depletion has caused them to stop. Known for large trees and lush forested areas, this park is a great place to take your family picnicking, swimming, fishing, and camping. It is also full of wildlife, especially deer and turkey. To see the wildlife, drive slowly, particularly in the early morning and at dusk.

Other facilities at the park include a large **swimming pool** and a small **fishing lake**. The swimming pool is open from the end of May to Labor Day, daily from noon to 7 p.m. (adults $2, children under twelve $1.50). Three nature trails are available for those who enjoy hiking, and picnic tables, shelters and playgrounds are plentiful.

Golfers in the family will enjoy the **Boiling Springs Golf Course** located near the park's entrance. The course is consistently rated as one of the top five courses in Oklahoma. Call (405) 256-1206 to reserve a tee time.

Camping facilities, including modern, semi-modern and tent sites, are available. Rustic, furnished cabins that sleep four are available by reservation. These cabins are in demand on weekends year-round, and also during the week from mid-May to October; early reservations are recommended during these busy times. Two large camps are available to rent for groups such as Boy Scouts, churches and family reunions. (Inquire about reduced group and nonprofit rates.)

During the third weekend in May, the annual **Blue Grass Festival** is held at the park. For more information, contact (405) 256-3409.

## Crystal Beach Park

*Located south of Highway 412 and north of Highway 270 on 1st Street. From the intersection of Highway 270 and Downs Avenue, turn east and travel to First Street. Turn north; the park entrance is on the east side of the road. The swimming pool is open daily during the summer from 12:30-6:30. Pool admission is adults $2, children under age twelve $1.25. The miniature train operates most summer evenings and weekend afternoons; rides cost $1 per person.*

Opened in 1932, Crystal Beach Park was built by the Works Progress Administration, and it originally featured "sparkling" beaches and a popular swimming lake. Today, families needing a travel break or spending the day or evening in Woodward can enjoy play equipment, a miniature train, a public swimming pool, tennis courts, a fishing lake (for children under sixteen and seniors over sixty-five), a nine-hole golf course, and a nearby miniature golf course. Bring bread and dried corn; children will enjoy feeding the numerous resident ducks and geese!

This park is the site of the annual **Fourth of July festivities** and the Crystal Christmas lighting display (see page 46), both hosted by the Woodward Chamber of Commerce. Call (405) 256-7411 for more information.

## Plains Indians and Pioneers Museum

*2009 Williams Avenue, (405) 256-6136. Located on Highway 270 (Williams Avenue), one mile south of the intersection of Highways 15/412 and Highways 34, 3, 183 and 270. Open Tuesday-Saturday 10-5, Sunday 1-4. Closed Mondays and major holidays. Admission is free; donations are appreciated.* ★

This award-winning and nationally-recognized museum houses history lessons about Northwest Oklahoma. Highlights include murals of scenes depicting area history by well-known artists such as Paul Laune, Pat Patterson, Fred Olds, and Jana Sol. Two remarkable exhibits outline the history of the Plains Indians and the early development of the area from just before the 1893 Land Run to the advent of the oil industry in the area. The museum's extensive photograph collection, first-person quotes, and other items are used to bring Northwest Oklahoma's history to life.

In May, the museum's prized Federal Eagle quilt is displayed. Noted as one of the best quilts in the United States, it was sewn using the intricate reverse-applique method of quilting. Made in 1820 by Anna Catherine Garnhart of Maryland, the quilt was brought to the Woodward area at the turn of the century by covered wagon. Seeing this beautiful work of art is worth the trip to the museum!

Children will enjoy being put in the city jail for being "a crook" or playing a banker in the restored Stock Exchange Bank, circa 1910. Other favorites include the exhibits featuring a saloon and historic Fort Supply. An extensive photograph collection tells many interesting stories. One well-documented story is the 1947 Woodward tornado, considered one of the most destructive storms in U.S. history. Over one hundred people died, and many others were injured as a result of this tornado. Also at the museum is an art gallery featuring work by local and world-renowned artists on a monthly basis.

Visit the agriculture building to learn about the agricultural history of the area. The exhibits start with an explanation of the Native Americans' use of the land and reliance on bison, and end with families receiving electricity and the modernization of farms after World War II. Interesting narratives, artifacts, and background murals by noted artists help to tell the story of land use and its impact on Northwest Oklahoma's economy.

### Helpful Hints

An interesting gift shop, a research area, and constantly-changing exhibits make this museum appealing, even for return guests. To arrange group tours, call two weeks in advance. Be sure to inquire about the special hands-on and audio/visual educational programs. Tours last about an hour.

## Events

## Woodward Elks Rodeo

*Usually held in mid-July at the Woodward County Fairgrounds grandstand in Crystal Beach Park. Call (405) 256-3549 or 256-7411 for general information, (405) 256-8202 for tickets. Ticket prices range from $7 to $12.*

The Woodward Elks Rodeo started as a small event in 1929; in fact, it was so small that Elks members would use their car lights to illuminate the arena each evening. Many decades later, the rodeo attracts more than 25,000 visitors each year, and it is known as one of the best outdoor rodeos in the region.

Activities held during the rodeo include a hamburger dinner on Wednesday, a "best ball" golf tournament on Friday, and a Saturday morning parade on Main Street. Each night, there are special rodeo events for children.

It is recommended to purchase box seat tickets and make motel reservations at least three weeks in advance. The most comfortable seats are on the "shady" west side of the grandstand. Ask about family night, usually held on Wednesday night; with a special pop can, children are admitted free.

## Crystal Christmas

*Held from the Friday after Thanksgiving through December 31st at Crystal Beach*

*Park. Open Sunday-Thursday 6-10 p.m., and Friday-Saturday 6-11 p.m. Admission is free; donations are appreciated. For more information, call (405) 256-7411.*

Begun in 1996, this new event features over two million twinkling lights in beautiful Christmas-theme displays. Among the most popular displays are the thirty-foot Wise Men and a Stagecoach Santa. Visitors are encouraged to walk the grounds and to enjoy the lighted bridge across Crystal Beach Lake. Family nights are held on Thursdays and feature visits with Santa, giveaway prizes, and entertainment.

## In the Vicinity

### Ft. Supply: Fort Supply Historic Site

*Located on the grounds of the William S. Key Correctional Facility in Ft. Supply. (405) 766-3767. Travel on Highway 3/270 approximately thirteen miles northwest of Woodward to the town of Ft. Supply; the entrance to the state facility is located on the north side of the highway. Follow the signs to the northeast part of the facility. Open Monday-Saturday 9-4, Sunday 1-4, closed major holidays. Admission is free, but donations are encouraged. Partially handicapped accessible.*

Explore Ft. Supply and discover a fascinating history of the Cavalry, the Plains Indians, famous and infamous military men, and early life on the plains. The few original buildings remaining on the fort's grounds tell an interesting story. Visitors can see a replica of the original cedar log stockade and visit the in-progress restoration of the Guard House and four other buildings. A kiosk area provides a map of the area and features many flyers explaining the fort's history. If at all possible, stop at the visitor center (a small white house), view the pictorial displays, and have your questions answered by the park's knowledgeable curator.

The fort was closed in 1894, but it was later reopened as Oklahoma's first mental hospital. Currently, the grounds and most of the buildings house the William S. Key Correctional Facility for nonviolent offenders. Through a joint project between the Correctional Facility and the Oklahoma Historical Society, inmates have helped restore the old fort. Plan to spend about thirty minutes to one hour at the site.

#### Helpful Hints

A good time to visit is during the annual living history event called "**Cavalry Days.**" Held the first Saturday in October, the event features reenactors and other activities. For more information, call the site's office.

Located a few miles to the south of the old fort is Fort Supply Lake and Dam. Picnicking, swimming and boating are popular family activities at this Corps of Engineers project lake.

### Freedom: Alabaster Caverns State Parks

*Located about thirty miles northeast of Woodward, just south of Freedom on Highway 50, (405) 621-3381. From Woodward, go east on Highway 412 approximately ten miles to the junction of Highway 50. Go north on Highway 50 about eighteen miles to the turnoff to Alabaster Caverns (Highway 50C). Open May 1 to September 30 from 8-5; October 1 to April 30 from 8-4. Tours begin on the hour. Cave tours for adults $5, children ages six to seventeen $2.50, children ages five* and under are free. *The swimming pool is open from Memorial Day to Labor Day, Wednesday-Sunday 1-7 and on legal holidays that fall on Monday. Swimming pool admission is adults $2, children under twelve $1.25.* ★

The Alabaster Caverns are the "star attraction" at this popular state park. Trained guides take groups of about thirty people on a fascinating trip underground to see unique rocks and minerals that began forming over 270 million years ago. The cave itself began forming 1.5 million years ago, and it continues to grow because of the stream of water that runs through the cave and the dripping water that slowly adds to its features. Highlights of the tour include viewing black alabaster (found in only three caves worldwide), observing clusters of bats (most prevalent during the winter months), and experiencing total darkness when the lights are turned out.

Inquire at the park office about information concerning the four nature trails. One of these trails has less strenuous walking than the other three. Picnic shelters are available, but the two large ones are available only by a reservation and a $30 fee. Camping facilities, including primitive and semi-modern, are available year-round. ▧ A swimming pool is open during the summer.

### Helpful Hints

Temperatures in the caves average fifty degrees; jackets are recommended year-round. The nearly one-mile tour lasts about one hour. It can be difficult for very young children because of the 340 steps in the tour. Backpacks are helpful for carrying babies and toddlers.

A **Watchable Wildlife Weekend** takes place in late April and is hosted by the park staff and the Oklahoma Wildlife Department. During the program, visitors can see and even touch some of the wild animals found in the park. They may also enjoy special talks about the animals. Five wild caves are open for "spelunkers" from March 1 through September 30. Ranging in length from 200 to 1,600 feet, these caves are available for explorers daily from 8-4:30. Even beginners can explore these caves, but they must have the proper equipment. Call ahead to get an equipment list from the park office and/or to arrange for a trained guide to help you walk—and sometimes crawl—through these caves.

Also available during a few July and August weekends to a limited number of viewers is the bat viewing at the **Selman Bat Cave**. To participate, you must preregister with the Department of Wildlife Conservation at (405) 521-4616. Call ahead to request a registration form be sent to you. Upon receiving your registration, the Wildlife Department will mail a confirmation letter that will explain the details of the bat viewing. Tickets are $4 per person. Participants first meet at Alabaster Caverns and then are taken by bus to the viewing area. The viewing is handicapped accessible.

Land containing the Selman Bat Cave was purchased in 1996 through donations to the Wildlife Diversity Program and general revenues of the Oklahoma Department of Wildlife Conservation.

During the summer, approximately one million Mexican free-tailed bats reside in the cave. Imagine seeing these bats leaving the cave en masse, almost on cue! Area landowners can attest to their nightly journeys; each night, an estimated 1.25 tons of insects are consumed by the bats.

The cave is home to mother and baby bats only. Of the approximately 500,000 migratory bats that arrive in May or June of every year, most have one "pup." The young are ready to feed themselves by early June. During the first viewing weekend, spectators may notice the babies' awkward attempts to fly. The bats leave the area in mid- to late-August.

### Helpful Hints

All ages will enjoy the bat viewing; however, it is important that everyone remains quiet and unnoticed to not bother the bats. Loud or crying children may have to remain in the parking lot. Flashlights, pets and lawn chairs are not allowed, but binoculars, video and still cameras (no flash) are encouraged. Walking from the parking area to the viewing site is not difficult. Bat viewing takes place in all weather conditions.

## Waynoka: Little Sahara State Park

*Located about forty miles east and north of Woodward, just south of Waynoka on Highway 281. (405) 824-1471. At the junction of Highways 412 and 281 in Major County, go north approximately ten miles. The entrance is on the west side of the highway. The park is open twenty-four hours a day. The six-passenger dune buggy rides are available daily from 9-4. (Other times can be arranged by calling ahead.) The cost for the dune buggy rides is $6 for adults and $4 for children ages twelve and under. Beside the cost of camping, there is a $5 per vehicle daily fee for off-road vehicles to use the dunes.* ★

Another "surprise" in Northwest Oklahoma is the Little Sahara State Park; the ever-changing sands and unique flora and fauna in this area provide a fun adventure for families.

To enjoy this park to its fullest, families should inquire at the state park office regarding a six-passenger dune buggy ride. The ride lasts about forty minutes, and it makes the trip to Little Sahara well worth the effort. The rides are scheduled on a first come/first served basis and are occasionally available into the evening. To ride the dune buggy, children must be big enough to wear a harness seat belt (this includes most three-year-olds). If you bring your own off-road vehicle, be sure to check the park rules on a sign near the entrance or pick up the safety brochure in the park office.

By following the path past the play equipment and covered picnic area near the park entrance, you can observe the dunes from a different perspective. However, for safety reasons, do not go past the fence. While enjoying the unique geography of the area, look for whitetail deer, wild turkey, coyotes, snakes, and other wildlife.

### Helpful Hints

Camping (both unimproved and RV sites) is available. The park has two comfort stations with showers available. 🅂

For a fun-filled summer trip, enjoy the Little Sahara park early in the day then visit Alabaster Caverns during the heat of the day. For a scenic trip from the Little

Sahara to the caverns, take Highway 14 north past Waynoka about ten miles until you find a sign announcing the town of Freedom. Turn west on the farm market road and enjoy the view to **Freedom**, a town brimming with western heritage.

# Northeast Oklahoma

## Bartlesville

The town of Bartlesville was named for the trader, Jacob Bartles, who moved to the area and purchased the local grist mill in 1875. This small settlement, with a history rich in Native American heritage, cowboys and outlaws, became a prosperous town when the state's first commercial oil well, the Nellie Johnstone, was drilled here in 1897. Two young, adventurous oilmen, brothers Frank and L.E. Phillips, founded the Phillips Petroleum Company, which has since grown into a powerful, international business. The community supports the arts with beautiful facilities and world-renowned, family-oriented events; several cultural and historic attractions are found nearby.

Bartlesville is the perfect weekend destination for families. Among the favorite attractions are Woolaroc, the Frank Phillips Mansion, Johnstone Park (especially its "kiddie park"), and nearby Dewey's Prairie Song. Call ahead to Woolaroc to determine the exact dates of their special summer events; the hands-on activities and many other "extras" will make the weekend even more special. *Located approximately 161 miles north and east of Oklahoma City (east on I-44 to Tulsa and north on U.S. 75 from Tulsa). From Tulsa, travel approximately forty-seven miles north on U.S. 75. Bartlesville Chamber of Commerce (918) 336-8708.* ★ ▣

### *Attractions*

### *Frank Phillips Mansion*

*1107 Cherokee Avenue, (918) 336-2491. Take U.S. 75 north to Adams Boulevard. Turn west on Adams Boulevard and follow it to Cherokee Avenue. Turn south on Cherokee Avenue. The Phillips home is located between 11th and 12th Streets on the west side of the road. Wednesday-Saturday 10-5, Sunday 1-5. Closed Monday, Tuesday and major holidays. Ring the bell at the front door for admittance. Free; donations are appreciated. There are no restrooms available, and the home is not handicapped accessible.*

Visit the mansion owned by Frank Phillips, and experience the lifestyle maintained by the founder of Phillips Petroleum Company. Built in

*Frank Phillips mansion.*

Bartlesville Chamber of Commerce

1908, the Greek Revival Style mansion has a pink brick exterior with white wooden columns. The inside of the home, which includes twenty-six rooms, reflects the style of the 1930s, when $500,000 was spent on remodeling. On the first floor, there is a video available for viewing to learn about Frank Phillips and Phillips 66.

Children will especially be interested in the "hideyholes" in the library. They will also enjoy the large bright children's bedroom upstairs along with the life-sized tiger that stands guard.

If you look closely at the bathroom fixtures in Jane Phillips' bathroom, you'll notice they're solid gold. There is a professional barber's chair in Frank's quarters where he received a shave every morning at 5:30 a.m. In 1947, an elevator was added to the interior of the home at a cost of $31,000.

The Phillips had a Japanese butler named Henry Eignaga, who lived on the third floor of the home. He came to the United States a poverty-stricken immigrant; after his death, it was discovered that he had made some very profitable investments. Frank Phillips, the millionaire, had a millionaire butler!

### Helpful Hints

If you view the video, the self-guided tour lasts approximately fifty minutes. Children over seven will benefit the most from the full tour, but younger children will enjoy seeing some of the more unusual aspects of the home. In the fall of 1997, an interpretive exhibit is scheduled to open in the massive, six-car garage. It will explain more about the personal life stories of Frank and Jane Phillips.

## Johnstone Park

*Hensley Boulevard and Highway 123 North. From U.S. 75 take Hensley (Tuxedo) west to Highway 123 (Cherokee). Turn northwest onto Highway 123 (do not go over bridge). Johnstone Park is open all year; the Kiddie Park is open summer evenings from 7-9:30. Most of the fourteen rides are thirty cents each.*

Johnstone Park pays tribute to one of Oklahoma's most important events—the drilling of the first commercial oil well. In 1897, drillers struck oil on property belonging to Nellie Johnstone. Her land had once been considered useless because a black, oily scum covered the creek nearby. The well was drilled to a depth of 1,300 feet and produced fifty to seventy-five barrels of oil a day. The land now features a replica of the Nellie Johnstone #1. The park also has a cannon that was used when oil storage tanks caught fire. The cannon was fired at the base of the tank, which released the oil and made the fire easier to extinguish.

A restored train depot has been moved to the park for public viewing. It was originally located on the Mullendore Ranch. A Santa Fe train engine is displayed nearby; it was donated to the City of Bartlesville in 1946 by the Santa Fe Railroad.

### Helpful Hints

With its playground equipment and walking trail, Johnstone Park is the perfect place to let children run off some energy and have fun. Picnic areas, both shaded and covered, are plentiful.

In the summer, the **Kiddie Park** is the main attraction at the park. Surrounded by miniature amusement rides that cost only thirty cents each, youngsters will run with excitement from ride to ride. Parents will feel comfortable letting even the little ones run free. Rides include a Ferris wheel, airplanes, a carousel, bumper cars, and many others. A passenger train large enough for adults circles the park. Also plan to visit in December, when the park hosts Fantasyland Forest, a holiday light display (see page 55).

## Keepsake Candle Factory

*West of Bartlesville, (918) 336-0351. Take U.S. 75 to Frank Phillips Boulevard (Highway 60) and turn west. Go two miles west of Highway 123 to the small blue and white Keepsake Candle sign. Turn north and follow the road until it ends; then turn east. Monday-Friday, 9-5:30, Saturday 10-5, Sunday 1-5. From Thanksgiving to Christmas, hours are extended to 6. Closed major holidays. The fifteen minute tours are conducted at 11, 1, and 3, Monday through Friday. Admission is free. The store and factory are handicapped accessible.*

Originally started as a church project in 1969, the Keepsake Candle Factory has expanded into a thriving business, selling its candles worldwide. As you approach the Keepsake Candle Factory, you will be pleasantly surprised by the scents of the season. Inside the factory, the workers keep wax heated on regular kitchen stoves as they add layer after layer to the molds. It takes about two days to make one candle, and approximately 850 candles are completed every day.

### Helpful Hints

The factory store sells candles shaped like apples, animals, antique glassware and more, in all colors. Favorite scents such as bayberry, cinnamon and cranberry can be found along with the unusual, like pumpkin pie.

Although children over seven will benefit most from the tour, younger children will still enjoy seeing the different shapes and colors of candles. The best time of day to visit is at 11 and 1, when tours are conducted and workers are available to observe.

In June, refreshments are served during the OK Mozart Festival. During the last weekend in September, the **Fall Harvest** is celebrated with special Autumn candle groupings. New Christmas candles are introduced the first weekend in November at the **Christmas Open House**.

## Woolaroc

*Located southwest of Bartlesville, (918) 336-0307. Take U.S. 75 to Frank Phillips Boulevard and turn west to Highway 123. Turn south on Highway 123 and continue approximately twelve miles to Woolaroc, which is located on the right side of the road. From June 1-September 7, open daily 10-8; from September 8-May 31, open Tuesday-Sunday 10-5. Closed Thanksgiving and Christmas. Adults $4, Seniors $3. Children under 16 are free (except for special events). Woolaroc is handicapped accessible. ★*

Located in the heart of the Osage Hills is Woolaroc, the country home of millionaire Frank Phillips, founder of Phillips Petroleum. Phillips' inspiration for his retreat's name was a combination of the natural beauty contained in the 3,500 acres of WOOds, LAkes and ROCks.

*The grand entrance to Woolaroc.*

The two-mile drive to the main buildings winds through a **wildlife preserve**. During your drive, look for four-horned sheep, yaks, ostriches, bison, and other exotic species. More than 700 animals roam these hillsides. Because the animals are unpredictable, stay in your car until you reach the museum parking lot.

The Woolaroc Museum was originally built to house the "Woolaroc" airplane. Phillips sponsored the monoplane in the 1927 Trans-Pacific Dole Flight. It won the competition, flying from California to Hawaii. The restored "Woolaroc" airplane is on display in the museum; it would be airworthy if two pistons weren't missing.

Over the years, the museum has expanded to include magnificent artwork, cultural development exhibits that focus on prehistoric man and Native Americans, and displays featuring cowboys and outlaws of the Southwest. Everything from an original Frederick Remington painting to a shrunken head is displayed in this museum.

Located on the grounds, the Lodge was built in 1926-27. It has been completely restored to the time when Frank and Jane Phillips entertained businessmen, politicians and entertainers. Children and adults will be fascinated by the large number of trophy heads that hang in the lodge, including an elephant, a giraffe, a longhorn, and a bison.

Visit the **Y-Indian Guide Center** where visitors learn about Native American culture. "Arrows Skyward" is an audiovisual presentation with showings scheduled several times a day. It is highlighted by songs presented in Indian sign language.

If you visit in early spring or late fall, you can see an authentic **1840s Traders camp** located on the five-mile North Road Tour. For those who enjoy hiking, the **Nature Trail** provides the opportunity for a close-up look at native flowers and plants. During June, July and August, a **Petting Zoo** is open for children.

Woolaroc is an excellent place for families who want to learn more about the early history of Oklahoma, to better understand the Native American culture, and to become better acquainted with Oklahoma's natural surroundings.

### Helpful Hints

If you are hungry, the Buffalo Haunt near the Y-Indian Center serves Buffalo barbecue sandwiches, Indian tacos, snacks, and soft drinks. If you bring your own lunch, you're welcome to sit on the grass and enjoy the outdoors.

Woolaroc sponsors special events each year. **Kidsfest** is held on a weekend near the end of June. This three-day celebration includes children's games, art, nature exhibits, and special entertainment. These activities help introduce children to the nature preserve and museum. **Family Day** is more crafts-oriented. It is held the first Saturday in August and includes free admission.

## Events

### Biplane Expo

*Held the first weekend in June at Frank Phillips Field. For dates and a brochure, call (918) 336-8708. Admission varies from year to year; recent prices were adults $5, children $3.*

Up to 500 vintage airplanes attend the largest annual gathering of biplanes in the world! Fans and guests from almost forty states account for about 350 of those planes, and about 150 planes range in age from the late 1920s to new, custom-built experimental models. An incredible air show, along with exhibits and educational seminars, bring guests back year after year. There is also plenty of food and good entertainment available.

### Sunfest

*Held the first weekend in June in Sooner Park. Signs along Highway 75 direct visitors to the park. To avoid parking difficulties, ride the shuttle from Eastland Center at the intersection of Highway 75 and Frank Phillips Boulevard. For dates and a brochure, call (918) 337-0999. Admission is free.*

Sunfest offers a day of fun with activities for every age. Children will enjoy free craft activities and testing their skills in games and contests. Adults can browse through arts and crafts booths or displays by juried artists. Demonstrations are presented by local clubs and organizations. Skydivers make thrilling entrances while storytellers, clowns and jugglers delight the crowd. The festival's five stages are filled with entertainment including musicians and dancers. On Saturday, visitors can board a three-car train at the old Santa Fe station for a one-hour excursion through the countryside. (There is a small fee for the train ride.)

Vendors at the fair offer Indian tacos, pork chop sandwiches, drumsticks, barbecue, corn on the cob, and a variety of other foods.

### OK MOZART International Festival

*Held for nine days in mid-June at the Community Center in downtown Bartlesville and other venues. Ticket office (918) 336-9800 and Showcase events (918) 336-9900. The Community Center is located at Adams Boulevard and Cherokee. From Highway 75, take Highway 60 west to Cherokee; the Community Center is on the right. Some Showcase events begin as early as 6:30 a.m.; others begin on an almost hourly schedule throughout the day. Concerts begin at 8 p.m. and conclude at 10 p.m. Some local establishments remain open to serve refreshments after the concerts. Ticket sales by mail begin around March 1st. This is the best way to obtain tickets to the performances of your choice. Telephone sales begin in mid-March. Admissions vary; most evening concerts are $15-25. Showcase events range from free-$20. Student and child tickets are usually available.*

OK MOZART

*Fireworks at an OK MOZART concert.*

Be prepared for an extraordinary experience as you enjoy the mixture of Old World music with New World charm. The Festival celebrates the music of Mozart and other composers, and it is recognized around the world as a major musical event. Some activities include tours, equestrian events, musical demonstrations, workshops, lectures, special events at area attractions, afternoon concerts, and evening concerts. Don't miss the opportunity to participate in this world-renowned festival!

### Helpful Hints

There is so much to see, do, and hear during the festival that patrons need to write or call the Festival office in advance for brochures. Of particular interest to families is the outdoor concert typically held on Wednesday night of the Festival. Held in a natural amphitheater on the banks of a lake, the concert concludes with a fireworks display.

## Indian Summer

*This is a three-day festival held in mid-September at the Bartlesville Community Center. For dates and a brochure, call (918) 337-2787 or (918) 336-8708. Admission is free.*

This festival includes fine arts, traditional Indian clothing, craft demonstrations, beadwork, children's art activities, and an intertribal powwow. It also features the first major organized Lacrosse Tournament in Northeast Oklahoma.

## FantasyLand of Lights Christmas Festival

*This event is held throughout the Bartlesville area, from Thanksgiving through December. For dates and a brochure, call (918) 336-8708.*

Visit the events at various locations throughout Bartlesville to get in the Christmas spirit. The FantasyLand Forest display in Johnstone Park sparkles with over a half million Christmas lights. Step back in time to Christmas in the 1800s at Prairie Song, and enjoy Christmas finery at Woolaroc.

## In the Vicinity

## Dewey

Like the nearby city of Bartlesville, Dewey was founded by Jake Bartles, the local grist mill owner who came to the area in 1875. He and his wife built a large, two-story home near the middle of town in 1899. The handsome structure was later converted to the forty-room **Dewey Hotel**. The hotel is directly across the street from the Tom Mix Museum.

*Dewey is located just a few miles north of Bartlesville on Highway 75.*

# Attractions

## Prairie Song

*Located outside of Dewey, (918) 534-2662. From U.S. 75 turn east on Durham Road. Go 5 1/2 miles east on Durham to the Moore Ranch entrance. All vehicles must stop and check in at the red brick ranch house. Public tours are given at 10 a.m. and 2 p.m. on Monday, Wednesday, and Friday; other hours are by appointment only. Children eight and under are free; all others are $7. Prairie Song is not handicapped accessible, nor is it air-conditioned.*

Visit Prairie Song to gain an understanding of life as it was in the late 1800s. As visitors enter Prairie Song, they pass the "Blue Mound" (the tall mound on the left); it was formerly a popular lookout area for outlaws scouting posses. The same outlaws visited Moore Ranch, home of Prairie Song. In operation since 1892, Moore Ranch is the oldest ranch in Northeast Oklahoma still operated by the original family.

In 1983, Marilyn Moore Tate and her husband, Kenneth Tate, began building Prairie Song as a getaway home for themselves. People became curious when word spread of a frontier town being built in the nearby countryside. Finally, the Tates opened the village to share their collection of pioneer days paraphernalia.

How can you use a hog roller? What about a train mover? Find out the answers to these questions by touring this 1880s frontier village. You'll see everything from a log church and one-room school to a train depot. There is even a working blacksmith shop where you can watch wagons being built! New to Prairie Song is Miss Rachel's Parlor, a great place for dances. Each building is authentically furnished with period furniture and artifacts.

### Helpful Hints

Be aware of the limited tour times at Prairie Song; call ahead to make special arrangements for other tour times. Ask the Tates about special events they can host, such as church retreats and family reunions. They can even provide catered meals. Picnic areas are available. Always be a polite guest; take your trash with you.

## Tom Mix Museum

*721 North Delaware, (918) 534-1555. Take U.S. 75 north to Don Tyler Boulevard in Dewey. Turn west and travel two blocks to Delaware (Highway 123). The museum is located on the southwest corner of the intersection. (There's a stop sign at the intersection.) Open Tuesday-Saturday 10-4:30, Sunday 1-4:30, closed Monday and major holidays. Closed during January and open weekends-only in February. Suggested donation: adults $1.50 and children fifty cents. This museum is handicapped accessible.*

Tom Mix was a silent movie star who made more than 330 films (only nine were talkies). He was very popular as the original "good guy in a white hat." Before he began acting, he was the Dewey town marshal, a bartender, a champion steer wrestler, and a 101 Wild West Show stunt rider. Later, he bought his own circus.

Tom Mix performed his own film stunts. He also used live ammunition, carrying he carried his own medicine chest in order to treat his own wounds. This medicine chest in on display in the museum. A replica of Tony, his stunt horse, is also on display. You'll be amazed at the picture of Tony jumping twenty-five feet across a canyon with Tom on his back!

## Helpful Hints

With advance notice, Tom Mix movies are available for viewing. They last from fifteen minutes to an hour. This small museum will take approximately thirty minutes to tour. Children over seven will benefit the most from this museum, but younger children will have fun seeing the replica of Tony and Tom's western gear.

A **Tom Mix Day** festival is held in mid-September. Activities include children's games, live music, and a Tom Mix Run.

## Osage Hills State Park

*(918) 336-4141. Located eleven miles west of Bartlesville, just south of Highway 60. Cabin reservations can be made by calling (800) 654-8240 or the park office.*

Osage Hills State Park is comprised of 1,199 acres of beautiful scenery. Visitors can enjoy traipsing along marked hiking trails or driving winding roads to enjoy the views. Other activities include tennis, swimming, boating, camping, biking, and fishing. The park includes a small, eighteen-acre lake with rowboats for rent, a creek area to explore, and a swimming pool open daily during the summer. Eight native-stone, one- and two-bedroom cabins ($53-73; winter rate $43-73) are available; call a year in advance for weekends; the cabins are almost always available on weekdays (Sunday-Thursday). Camping sites include RV sites ($12) with full hookups, and thirty-five primitive campsites ($6). Both campsites have modern bathhouse facilities. Camping at the park is only crowded during major holidays.

# Claremore

Claremore is the county seat of Rogers County. A trading post was established at the present site in 1842 and, prior to that, Osage Chief Black Dog had a settlement here. In 1874, a post office was opened, and the town was named after an Osage Indian, Chief Clermont (or Clermos), who had brought his people to the area in 1802.

A common misconception is that Claremore was the birthplace of Will Rogers; the famed entertainer and journalist was born in Oologah, but he claimed Claremore as his hometown because, as he put it, "no one but an Indian could pronounce Oologah." Claremore is the birthplace of Lynn Riggs, the playwright who wrote *Green Grow the Lilacs*. The play was later adapted and became the popular Rodgers and Hammerstein musical, *Oklahoma!*

Claremore and the nearby town of Oologah are THE places to visit to understand more about Oklahoma's native son, the remarkable humanitarian, entertainer and journalist, Will Rogers. For a wonderful memento of your visit to Claremore, take your children to the new Will Rogers statue that is located in front of the Claremore Daily Progress newspaper office at 311 West Will Rogers

Boulevard; the statue and your children make a wonderful photograph. The statue was created by Claremore-born artist Sandra Van Zandt.

While in Claremore, don't miss two other attractions that appeal to families: Swan Brothers Dairy Farm and the J.M. Davis Arms and Historical Museum. *Claremore is located approximately thirty miles northeast of Tulsa on Route 66. From Tulsa take I-44 or I-244 east to the Will Rogers Turnpike where the road joins Highway 66. Travel the historic "Mother Road" through Catoosa to Claremore. Claremore Chamber of Commerce (918) 341-2818.*

## Attractions

### J.M. Davis Arms and Historical Museum

*333 North Lynn Riggs Boulevard, (918) 341-5707. Traveling from the west on Route 66 (named N. Lynn Riggs in town) into Claremore, The museum is located on the north, just past the Will Rogers Boulevard intersection. Open Monday-Saturday 8:30-5, Sunday and holidays 1-5. Closed Thanksgiving and Christmas. Admission is free; donations are encouraged.*

The private collection of J.M. Davis now provides the basis for an interesting museum that features guns and other weapons, a near-complete collection of John Rogers' statuaries, and a variety of steins. These artifacts were originally displayed on the lobby walls of a local hotel. On the collector's 82nd birthday, this collection was presented to the state for a museum; it is presently operated by the state. Everything from ladies' small pistols to rifles and cannons are displayed here. Also featured are knives, swords, military weapons, and uniforms. Of special interest are the exhibits about outlaws.

#### Helpful Hints

Explanatory labels are found throughout the displays. If your child has an avid interest in guns, take someone with you who knows the subject. This museum is a great place for World War II veterans to take their grandchildren.

This stop will take from one to two hours. Located within the museum is a gift shop featuring reasonably-priced items. Restaurants, including fast food and a popular tea room, are nearby.

### Swan Brothers Dairy Farm, Inc.

*938 East 5th Street, (918) 341-2298. From the intersection of Lynn Riggs Boulevard (Route 66) and Patti Page Boulevard (Highway 20), go east to Maiden Lane. Turn north, and go up the hill to the dairy. Monday-Saturday 8-6. Admission is free.*

Swan's is an interesting place to take the children on your way through Claremore. Ruby and Harley Swan, Sr. started the dairy in 1923 with one cow; the business grew to include home delivery until 1946, when the route was sold. Milk was sold to processors from 1946 to 1951, at which time, the Swan's began selling directly to the public. This practice continues today. Swans does not spray chemicals on their pastures for weed control, nor do they inject their cows with hormones to increase milk production. Children will love to see the black and white Holsteins in the pasture. From behind a glass window, children can watch the afternoon milking, which begins at 3 p.m. and lasts about two hours.

### Helpful Hints

Be sure to dress for the weather; spectators stand outside. Next to the milking area is a dairy store that sells milk, cheeses, and seasonal gift baskets. A Christmas brochure is available. On Friday and Saturday afternoons, cheese samples are offered.

## Will Rogers Memorial

*1720 West Will Rogers Boulevard, (918) 341-0719. From the intersection of Route 66 (Lynn Riggs Boulevard) and Will Rogers Boulevard, turn north on Will Rogers Boulevard and follow the road up the hill and around the curve to the Will Rogers Memorial. Open daily 8-5 except for Thanksgiving and Christmas. By request of Will Rogers' family, admission is free. Donations are recommended at $5 per family, $3 per individual.* ★

Learn about Oklahoma's favorite son, Will Rogers, a simple man who became world famous. The State of Oklahoma has erected a memorial on land where Rogers planned to retire. The grounds and Memorial house the tomb, personal possessions, keepsakes, and trophies of this cowboy philosopher, performer, humanitarian, author, journalist, and Ambassador of Good Will.

*Will Rogers Memorial*

Children will love the interactive area that features activities relating to Rogers' life and times. Beginning in a turn-of-the-century classroom, children are introduced to Will Rogers through an interactive television program. They walk through a time tunnel, past representations of prehistoric Oklahoma, Indian culture, and a cowboy camp, into "old Claremore." Next, they enter "Frolic Central," where different aspects of Will Rogers' career are represented. Six interactive stations are located here: a 1930s radio studio; a vaudeville stage and costume area; an interpretive art area; a tumbling area for toddlers (complete with blocks to manipulate and saddles to ride); a video room to witness Will Rogers' rope tricks; and a library.

### Helpful Hints

Call in advance for group reservations, or to see if a large group is scheduled to visit the same day. This is particularly important if you are interested in the children's section, because each section in this interactive setting accommodates a maximum of thirty children at one time. Plan to spend at least ninety minutes at the museum. A gift shop offers books, tapes, and videos about Will Rogers, and souvenir items with a western theme.

For "unwinding" from the many activities in Claremore, try **Will Rogers Park**. Located across the highway from the Will Rogers Memorial, the park is equipped with picnic tables and playground equipment, perfect for children needing to run off some energy. If you didn't pack a lunch, a drive down Will Rogers Boulevard will reveal several eateries. Try the popular Hammett House or The Pink House, which has been restored to its original beauty. Be sure to try one of the Pink House's special desserts.

## In the Vicinity

## Catoosa

Founded in 1882, Catoosa was a Cherokee town. The town was named for the nearby Catoos Hill, which in Cherokee is "gatv gitse" and translates into "new settlement place." Today, Catoosa is the beginning of the important Arkansas River Navigation System, connecting Tulsa to the Gulf of Mexico by way of the Arkansas and Mississippi Rivers. The inland state of Oklahoma is connected to the ocean through this fascinating system! With a tour of the Port of Catoosa, children will gain a new perspective on Oklahoma's place in the world. *Located approximately fifteen miles east of downtown Tulsa. Take I-44 or I-244 east to Route 66. This historic highway runs right through town. Catoosa Chamber of Commerce (918) 266-6042.*

## Attractions

## Tulsa's Port of Catoosa

*5350 Cimarron Road, (918) 266-2291. From Tulsa, go east on I-244. Following the signs to the Port, exit at 193rd East Avenue and go north. Turn east into the entrance gate and follow the main drive to the Port Authority Building. Monday-Friday 8-4:30. Admission is free.*

With the help of Senators John McClellan of Arkansas and Robert S. Kerr of Oklahoma, the city of Tulsa is now linked with the Mississippi River and, ultimately, the Gulf of Mexico, by the once-unnavigable Arkansas River. With seventeen locks operating over the 445 mile length, economical transportation of goods is possible. Eight barges at a time can navigate the nine-foot-deep waterway; each barge can hold fifteen rail cars or sixty semitrailers. For other information about the Navigation System, check at the Port Authority Building where visitors can see the **Arkansas River Historical Society Museum** and watch a video explaining the development and dedication of the waterway. Later, drive to the 500-acre terminal area, where barges are loaded and unloaded with cargos of agricultural, industrial, and manufactured goods.

### Helpful Hints

Help make this trip more meaningful to children by taking a prior trip to the Arkansas/Verdigris River or by looking at a map and tracing the route of the River. This will help them visualize the magnitude of this engineering feat and understand the concepts of river navigation. Children will enjoy the activities at the terminal area such as loading and unloading and arrival or departures of barges. Movement of barges can be seen from any number of places along the river.

Make a stop at the Port on the way to the Will Rogers Memorial in Claremore or to any other destination going east. This is a nice morning or afternoon outing that takes about thirty minutes to an hour. Allow an extra hour if you drive to the dock area. The Port is available for group visits, but you should call in advance to schedule a tour. To avoid a crowd, check with the office prior to your visit. The building can become crowded when there are several bus-loads visiting at the same time.

Another interesting stop located just north of Catoosa along the historic Route 66 is the **Blue Whale**. Originally owned by Mr. and Mrs. Hugh Davis, the smiling whale with bright eyes greeted travelers on the Mother Road and served as a popular water park for years. Although it had fallen on hard times, the community of Catoosa has begun restoring the endearing monument. Bring a camera and a smile to the Blue Whale of Catoosa.

## Oologah

Born with the railroad in 1887, Oologah is a small ranching/farming community, best known as the birthplace of Will Rogers. The beautiful, 29,000-acre **Oologah Lake** is located approximately three miles east of town and provides many recreational opportunities, especially sailing, fishing, hiking, and swimming. *From Claremore, travel about twelve miles north and west on Highway 88. Take Highway 169 through Collinsville to Oologah. Oologah is about 142 miles from Oklahoma City and thirty miles from Tulsa. Oologah Area Chamber of Commerce (918) 443-2790.*

## Attractions

### Will Rogers Birthplace (Dog Iron Ranch)

*Located just east of Oologah, overlooking Oologah Lake. From Tulsa take Highway 169 north to Oologah. Follow the sign, turning right on County Road East-West 38 to the Birthplace Ranch. Ranch gates open at dawn and close at dusk. Free.*

Learn about Will Rogers by exploring the beautiful area that he called "home." Will grew up in the large home known as the "White House." Visitors are welcome to tour the home and to view videos about Will's life and times. A welcome addition to the ranch is the barn, built during a traditional barn raising by the Amish in 1993. The barn houses farm animals such as sheep, goats, ducks, chicks, and a pig. Longhorn cattle graze nearby. Pack a picnic lunch and spend a peaceful afternoon exploring the scenic area where Will Rogers grew up.

*Will Rogers' birthplace.*

# Grand Lake O' The Cherokees

Seventeen-year-old Henry Holderman first dreamed of harnessing the water power of the Grand (Neosho) River in 1892. However, his subsequent efforts (and those of other private investors over the next forty years), failed to accomplish much. It wasn't until 1935, when the Oklahoma Legislature created the Grand River Dam Authority, that this ambitious plan for a dam finally came to fruition. Completed in 1941, the Pensacola Dam is the longest multiple arch bridge in the world. Winding through more than sixty miles of Ozark foothills, the lake has 1,300 miles of shoreline and 59,000 surface acres of water. After a century, Henry Holderman's dreams for development have finally come true!

Grand Lake provides recreation choices for all ages, making it one of the best family destinations in Oklahoma. Families may fish, boat, water ski, camp, and much more at the lake, and they can take advantage of the entertainment offered at many shoreline villages nestled among the fingers of the lake. The lake is generally divided into three areas: the northern part of the lake, served by U.S. Highway 20; the middle section served by U.S. Highway 59; and the southern area served by Highway 28. The most developed lakeside community, Grove is found along the eastern side of the central section of the lake. Disney, another popular lakeside community, is found in the southern area. Both public and private recreation facilities abound. For a complete, continuously-updated listing, contact the Grand Lake Association (918-786-2289) for a copy of the "Guide to Grand Lake Magazine."

Of the many state parks located in the area, the four that offer the most family-oriented amenities are: **Twin Bridges State Park** (located at the northern end of the lake, six miles east of Fairland), **Bernice State Park** (located 1/2 miles east of Bernice off Highway 85A), **Honey Creek State Park** (off U.S. Highway 59 near Grove), and **Cherokee State Park** (at the southern end of the lake near Disney). ⑤ *Grand Lake is located about 190 miles northeast of Oklahoma City and about seventy miles northeast of Tulsa. Grand Lake Association (918) 786-2289.*

## In the Vicinity

## Grove

One of the oldest towns in northeast Oklahoma, Grove offers visitors a number of activities besides water recreation. A small agricultural town until the development of the lake in the 1940s, much of its prosperity now comes from tourism. A wide selection of accommodations and restaurants in the Grove area makes this a favorite vacation spot for state residents and out-of-state guests. Grove is also becoming a favorite retirement area. Locals and visitors alike relish the quaint, small-town atmosphere of the community as well as the seasonal activities offered here. *Located approximately eighty miles northeast of Tulsa. From Tulsa, take I-44 to the Will Rogers Turnpike. Exit at Afton and turn back south on Highway 59 for about ten miles. Grove is located 200 miles northeast of Oklahoma City. Grove Chamber of Commerce (918) 768-9079.*

## *Attractions*

### *The Cherokee Queen*

*Located on Highway 59 at the Sailboat Bridge in Grove, (918) 786-4272. Cruises begin in early May and continue through late September. Sightseeing cruise tickets are adult $8.50, children ages four to twelve $5, and seniors $7. Sunset Dinner Cruise tickets are adult $19.50, children $10.50. Cruise schedules and prices are subject to change. Reservations are required for dinner, dance and special cruises; call for more information. All cruises originate at Sailboat Bridge; however, some guests may be picked up at the Shangri-La marina. Cruises are handicapped accessible. ★*

The Cherokee Queen II

Families spend a pleasant afternoon of sightseeing along the shores of beautiful Grand Lake on board the Cherokee Queen II, a two-story paddleboat built to resemble the Mississippi steamboats of the mid-1800s. The ninety-minute cruises leave daily at 2 p.m. Tuesday through Sunday, with an additional cruise leaving at noon every Saturday. A snack bar on board offers hotdogs, popcorn and soft drinks.

In addition to the regular afternoon tours, families can set sail on **Sunset Dinner Cruises** every Saturday night. From 6:30 to 8:30, passengers feast on a buffet-style meal of barbecue chicken and ribs and enjoy a spectacular view of the lake at sunset. Your children won't soon forget this experience!

A special **Fireworks Cruise** is held over the Fourth of July holiday. Watch with excitement from the decks of the Cherokee Queen as the spectacular fireworks display is launched over Grand Lake.

### *Har-Ber Village*

*Located 3.5 miles west of Grove. (918) 786-6446. From the intersection of Highway 59 and Main Street in Grove, turn south at Main Street. Continue on Main to Har-Ber Road, turn west and travel for about three miles. Follow the signs to the entrance. Open daily from 9 a.m.-6 p.m. from March 1 to November 30. Closed Thanksgiving Day. Admission is free; donations are appreciated. ★*

Har-Ber Village was created in 1968 by Harvey and Bernice Jones as a gift to the traveling public. Starting with a single statue overlooking Grand Lake, Har-Ber Village has grown to over one hundred buildings housing a wide variety of collections. Built to resemble a turn-of-the century village, this unique site draws more than 400,000 visitors each year. Although there is no admission fee, posted signs remind everyone "you are welcome as long as you conduct yourselves as ladies and gentlemen."

As you enter Har-Ber Village, be sure to pick up a brochure for the self-guided tour. Simply follow the brochure as you visit each building. Stay on the sidewalk and follow the arrows for the complete tour. You may take as much time as you want to view the village.

Har-Ber Village now houses one of the largest antique collections in the United States. Buildings contain numerous collections of china, dolls, glassware, toys, household equipment, and home furnishings. There are many replicated businesses, including a dentist's office, a doctor's office, and a lawyer's office. Fishing and hunting equipment are displayed along with a collection of big-game-animal mounts. Old tractors and farm implements are plentiful, as are assorted horse-drawn wagons. Some of the very first automobiles can be found in these buildings.

Harvey and Bernice Jones have certainly fulfilled their desire to preserve "the way of life as experienced by our forefathers who carved out of the wilderness this wonderful country we know and enjoy today."

### Helpful Hints

Because the tour is long, strollers are advised for small children. The tour involves much walking, especially up and down steep hills; benches for resting are located throughout the village. Wheelchairs are offered free of charge. Cold drink machines are available, as are trash cans to dispose of any empty packages or containers. Public restrooms are easily accessible.

## Kountry Kuzins Jamboree

*The Kountry Kuzins theater is located northwest of downtown Grove on Highway 59. (918) 786-9458 or (800) 292-1974. Call ahead to confirm show dates and times. Reservations are helpful, but walk-ins are welcome. Weekend performances are scheduled on both Friday and Saturday nights in June, July and August; Saturday night shows are held in March, April, May, September, and October. Special holiday performances are conducted in November and December. Doors open at 7:15, shows begin at 8:00 p.m. Adults $10, children ages twelve and under $5.*

Expect an evening of good, wholesome family entertainment when you visit the Kountry Kuzins. For more than twelve years, the "kuzins" have entertained audiences with their old-fashioned fun as they play, sing and kick up their heels. Although homespun humor is a big part of the show, it isn't negative and it doesn't come at someone else's expense. Ranging from country/western to gospel, music is another important part of the program. Members of the Case family own and operate the Kountry Kuzins Jamboree. In addition to performing, family members may also sweep and serve popcorn.

## Lendonwood Garden

*1308 West 13th Street (Har-Ber Road), (918) 786-2938. The gardens open April 15, and they remain open through the summer. Open 8-5:30 weekdays and 8-8 Friday and Saturday. Adults $5, and children ages twelve and under are free.*

Lendonwood was created in September, 1994, as a labor of love by Dr. Leonard Miller. Covering three acres and containing more than 1,400 different plants, the gardens are part of the Oklahoma Botanical Garden System.

The gardens are divided into four different sections, with an additional area for introspection in the center. The Display Garden features ninety varieties of Chamaecyparis (false cypress) and five hundred varieties of day lillies; the Oriental Garden contains several ponds with waterfalls. Perennials, roses and flowering trees are found in the English Terrace Garden, and a pond filled with Koi fish is located in the Japanese Garden. In the center of the gardens, a fenced area marks the Zen Garden, where over one hundred Bonsai trees are displayed during the summer.

The Lendonwood Gardens bloom with beautiful colors from spring through fall. Take your child for a stroll through the garden and help identify different types of foliage (most plants are labeled), or watch the colorful Koi fish swimming in the pond. Be careful to stay on the paths and leave the gardens just as you found them.

## Events

### Grovefest

*Held the first weekend in May at the Grove Community Center in downtown Grove. Sponsored by the Grove Area Chamber of Commerce, (918) 786-9079. Admission is free.*

Bring your family and help celebrate this festival that includes music, chili and barbecue. Visitors browse through arts and craft booths and taste their way through the food fair. To sample the entries in the chili and barbecue contest on Saturday, you may purchase a tasting kit (usually $2). With over 100 entries, the Antique and Classic Car Show is popular with young and old alike. It begins at noon on Sunday, and winners are announced later in the afternoon. Entertainment begins around noon on the Community Center Lawn. Bring a blanket or lawn chair and listen as music fills the air—from toe-tapping bluegrass to sing-along gospel. Activities for children include face-painting, sand art, and a petting zoo.

### Pelican Festival

*Held in late September at Grove Community Center in downtown Grove. For more information, call the Grand Lake Association (918) 786-2289. Free.*

This festival celebrates the migration of the American White Pelican. The pelicans stop briefly (from mid-September until late October) at Grand Lake during their annual trip south. The festival features an educational area that includes materials about the bird such as films, lectures, maps, books, and photos. Guided field trips are offered for a nominal fee by the Grand Lake Association and the Grand Lake Audubon Society. Let your boat drift near the pelicans and watch them from the lake, or take binoculars to watch them from the land. Remember, these birds are an endangered species; be very careful not to get too close or to harm them.

Other festival activities include a fair, a large parade with many marching bands, arts and crafts, special children's activities, and more. Take this opportunity to learn about wildlife, especially the intriguing pelican.

# Langley/Disney

Langley, located at the west end of Pensacola Dam, and Disney, located at the east end, first began as constrtuction camps in 1938. Workers buildng the dam rested here each evening after a long day's work. Now Langley/ Disney merchants provide supplies for fishermen, campers, and sportsmen, instead of for weary laborers.

*Located on Highway 28, approximately sixty miles northeast of Tulsa. Take I-44 (Will Rogers Turnpike) to the Adair exit, Highway 28. Go east through Adair and Pensacola to the Langley/Disney area.*

## Attractions

### Picture in Scripture Amphitheater

*The amphitheater is located three and one-half miles east, and one mile north of Disney, off Highway 28. (918) 435-8207. Performances run Friday and Saturday evenings from mid-June through Labor Day. Gospel singing begins at 8 p.m. An introduction to the city of Nineveh begins at 8:45; the performance begins ten to thirty minutes later, depending on the sunset. Waterfront $10, general seats $9, children ages 4-11 $4, children three and under free if held by an adult. Meal prices vary.*

Travel back through time and experience first-hand the Biblical story of Jonah and the great fish while watching "The Man Who Ran." The realistic setting of the Assyrian city of Nineveh, along with period costumes and live animals, help this drama come to life each evening. The audience will be fascinated as the lightning flashes and thunder rolls while Jonah is thrown overboard and swallowed by the great fish.

#### Helpful Hints

Reservations for individuals and groups are required. Individuals should make reservations about one week in advance, and groups should call as early as possible. A $25 nonrefundable deposit must accompany reservations for groups of twelve or more. Specials are offered throughout the year; call the box office or check a current brochure for more information. Proceeds help support the New Lifehouse Girls Home, an outreach of Picture in Scripture Ministries, Inc.

Be sure to take a sweater; the breeze off the lake can make the evening air very cool. Also, take a can of insect repellent to protect yourself from mosquitos.

The **Christmas Caravan** is a new event for 1997. During the first two weekends of December, visitors can view a live nativity scene while walking through the city of Bethlehem. Dress for the winter weather; this activity will be outdoors. Admission $3.

## Monkey Island

Although not a town, Monkey Island is well known as being the home of Shangri-La Resort and numerous other resorts and attractions.

*From Tulsa, take I-44 to the Will Rogers Turnpike. Go northeast on the turnpike to the Afton exit. Take U.S. 59 south from Afton to Highway 125. Follow the signs leading to*

# Monkey Island

*Shangri-La which is located on Monkey Island. Contact the Grand Lake Association at (918) 786-2289 for a current listing of resorts, condominiums, and accommodations.*

## Attractions

### Monkey Island Trail & Hay Rides, Inc.

*Located on Highway 125, three-fourths mile south of Highway 85A. (918) 257-5186. Open six days a week, Wednesday-Monday. Closed Tuesday. Open 10 a.m.-dusk. Trail rides: $20/person for one hour trail ride. $15/person for one-half hour trail ride. Hay rides: $10/person for one hour hay ride. Group discounts available. Cash or travelers checks only.*

Your children will think they have traveled back in time as you explore the Grand Lake area cowboy style—on horseback! Located at Royal Horse Ranch, Monkey Island Trail and Hay Rides have horses ready for any level rider. Saddle up and ride the trails in search of deer, eagles, hawks, and (hold your nose!) skunks.

Sit tall in the saddle and take your posse for a ride. This is one way to experience Oklahoma's heritage they're sure to love.

#### Helpful Hints

All rides are guided, and riders under age ten must have a parent or guardian on the ride with them. Hay Wagon Rides are offered year-round at the ranch or your choice of location. Hay rides are available by reservation only, and a minimum of six people is required. Other activities include campfires, weinie and marshmallow roasts, horsedrawn carriage rental, and much more.

### National Rod and Custom Car Hall of Fame

*#1 Star Kustom Avenue, (918) 257-4234. From Tulsa take I-44 north. Take the Afton exit (Highway 59) then turn on Highway 85A at Monkey Island. You can't miss the Hall of Fame building once in the Monkey Island area. Wednesday-Saturday 11-5. Closed for the winter, December through February. Call to make an appointment on off days and during closed months. Adults $6, seniors (65 years and older) $5, children (ages eight to twelve) $3, under eight are free. Inquire about group rates. The Hall of Fame is handicapped accessible.*

Darryl and Donna Starbird opened the National Rod and Custom Hall of Fame in 1995 to recognize builders and designers of custom-built, exotic vehicles. At a ceremony held in August that same year, thirteen of these builders and designers were inducted into the Hall of Fame.

The lobby of the museum contains a replica of Darryl Starbird's first garage, known as the Star Kustom Shop and opened in 1954. The Shop shows work in progress on a 1947 Cadillac; this same car was Starbird's first to be shown in a national magazine.

The 12,000-square-foot, ultramodern museum houses twenty exotic vehicles. The walls are covered with memorabilia and numerous photographs related to these unique creations. A forty-five minute video presentation gives the history of the museum, as well as details about various cars on display and their makers.

A gift shop in the museum offers interesting souvenirs for car enthusiasts.

Items such as T-shirts, embroidered ball caps, car photos, and Hall of Fame License Plates are available.

## Shangri-La Resort and Conference Center

*Located in Afton, in an area commonly referred to as Monkey Island. (800) 331-4060. Shangri-La is located between Tulsa and Joplin on I-44. From I-44, take Exit 302 at Afton. Go south on Highway 69 for one mile. Turn left after Buffalo Ranch on Highway 59 South and go 5.5 miles. Turn right on Highway 125 South (look for a sign) and go 10.9 miles; the highway ends at Shangri-La. Rooms range in price from $80 to $145, with suites and the Governor's Suite costing more. The resort includes numerous activities, each priced separately. The resort is handicapped accessible.*

Shangri-La consists of 650 acres located on scenic Grand Lake O' the Cherokees. A combination of diverse guest accommodations, multiple restaurants, intriguing shops, and endless recreational activities make Shangri-La the perfect place for a family vacation. Plan to return year-after-year, as this is one resort children will gladly want to visit with their parents.

The biggest problems you'll experience at Shangri-La is deciding what activities to choose and what type of accommodations you need from the numerous options available. Accommodations at the resort include lodge rooms, one- to three-bedroom suites, estate homes, and condominiums. No matter where you choose to stay at Shangri-La, the guest accommodations are located within walking distance of resort facilities.

A total of eight restaurants, lounges and snack bars are found at Shangri-La. Whether you prefer gourmet specialties or just a regular hamburger, the resort's restaurants provide something for everyone. The main restaurant, The Greenery, is located on the second floor of the main lodge. It offers fine dining in an elegant atmosphere, where specialties include pasta dishes. Located on the first floor of the main lodge, R.D.'s Lobby Bar makes a delicious "quick stop" for those in a hurry. For a cool drink on a hot afternoon, stop by Monkeys. Located on the deck outside the main lodge, Monkeys overlooks the Shangri-La Marina, and it is a relaxing place to take a break at the end of an afternoon of fun in the sun. Snack bars can be found at the Recreation Center, on the golf courses, and at the Pool Hut.

Shangri-La provides numerous activities that appeal to a variety of ages of children. Indoor and outdoor tennis, swimming, racquetball, bowling, biking, basketball, volleyball, the Recreation Center, and golf are available. If parents need a change of pace, the Recreation Center is also home to the Pirate's Crew program for children ages four to twelve. Responsible crew leaders spend time creating crafts and participating in activities with children while parents spend time together.

Grand Lake O' the Cherokees has 1,300 miles of scenic shoreline and, during the summer, water sports are the main attraction at The Waterfront. Water sports equipment and boats of any size, including jet boats, pontoons, yachts, and cruisers, may be rented at this marina. Experience the thrills of parasailing as you glide over the lake, or take to the water on a waverunner and feel the spray of water in your face. Spend a quiet morning fishing or an exhilarating afternoon water skiing. If you want to enjoy the sun, but not the water, take advantage of the lakeside patio, the south lawn, or the beach area. Relax and work on your tan or challenge family members to a game of volleyball.

### Helpful Hints

Whether you spend the day on water or land, be sure to keep plenty of sunscreen on your children. Don't fret if you forgot to pack something; Shangri-La has several shops with everything from gifts and clothing to snacks and toiletries.

Spend the **Fourth of July** holiday at Shangri-La and take part in the "big blowout by the lake." Special activities include tennis tournaments, parasailing demos, poolside dances, and more. The whole family will love the holiday concert that Shangri-La  hosts each year for members and holiday guests. Prepare to spend the evening dancing and singing to the tunes of groups like The Coasters, featured artists for the 1997 summer concert.

## Muskogee

Historically known as the Three Forks area (the cradle of Oklahoma history), the Muskogee area has played an important role in the development of northeastern Oklahoma. The Verdigris, Grand (Neosho), and Arkansas Rivers meet here. Muskogee was named after the tribe of Indians who were forced to move to this area in 1829. The original Creek Indian Agency was located here; then later, the Agency of the Five Civilized Tribes was opened. Muskogee now has a population of 37,000 and is home to the ever-popular Azalea Festival and numerous other attractions and events that highlight the area's beauty and history.

*Located approximately 52 miles southeast of Tulsa and 138 miles east and north of Oklahoma City. From Tulsa take Highway 51 to the Muskogee Turnpike; there are five exits serving Muskogee. From Oklahoma City, travel west on I-40 to Highway 69 and go north. Muskogee Area Chamber of Commerce (918) 682-2401.*

### *Attractions*

### Ataloa Museum

*2299 Old Bacone Road, (918) 683-4581, extension 283. Take the Shawnee Bypass (U.S. Highway 62) to the Bacone College entrance; follow the road until you see the museum. Monday-Friday, 10-4 (closed from 12-1). Tours on weekends by appointment. Adults $2, children free; donations appreciated. The museum is handicapped accessible.*

At this museum, children and adults alike will delight in the unusual and interesting artifacts collected from the northern tip of Alaska to the southern tip of Argentina! As you enter the lodge, notice the rocks that make up the fireplace; they are from North and Central America. See the new collection of artifacts from Panama and Guatamala. This collection includes mola (handsewn examples of traditional San Blas Indian dress), beadwork, a miniature hut from the San Blas Indians, and woodcarvings. You will also find a petrified dinosaur egg and a juvenile Raptor footprint. See the toys Native American children played with years ago—bows and arrows, baskets, and traditional dolls. Sports enthusiasts will want to see the collection's 125-year-old hockey stick. Fifty-three colorful Navajo blankets and rugs draped throughout add to the ambiance of beauty and intrigue at this lodge.

### Helpful Hints

Families are welcome anytime during regular hours; however, groups should schedule tours two to three weeks in advance year-round. For $3.75 per person, you may eat at the Wacachee Student Dining Hall, located south of the museum.

## Five Civilized Tribes Museum

*The museum is located in Honor Heights Park. (918) 683-1701. From the intersection of Highways 62 and 69, travel south on Highway 69 to Broadway. Turn west and watch for the park's sign on the north. Monday-Saturday 10-5, Sunday 1-5; closed Thanksgiving, Christmas and New Year's Day. Adults $2, children $1, senior citizens $1.75. The museum is handicapped accessible; however, the restrooms are not.*

The first thing visitors notice when they approach the museum atop Agency Hill is its distinctive and historic building. The building was completed by the United States Government in 1875 and through the years, it has been utilized in several different ways—originally as the Union Agency building for the Five Civilized Tribes and then as an orphanage and a tea house. The museum was opened in 1966.

This museum houses an impressive collection of artifacts belonging to the Cherokees, Creeks, Choctaws, Chickasaws, and Seminoles, known collectively as the Five Civilized Tribes. Here, your family will learn about the Indian territorial days of the late-1800s and view the art work and culture of more contemporary Native Americans. Not only will children see Sequoyah's syllabary, they will learn to identify tribes by the use of color in clothing, bead work and pottery. Listen to the sound of the tortoise shell leggings which women strapped to their legs during ceremonial dances. A display of farming tools includes Will Rogers' branding iron, as well as the multipurpose gourd; gourds were used as water dippers and for storage of water, flour and grain.

The second floor of the museum houses a collection of work including paintings, pottery and sculptures by Native American master artists. The museum library holds a display of Indian Territory documents and rare historical volumes.

### Helpful Hints

Reservations are needed for groups of ten or more. There are no guided tours during the month of April; instead, the museum hosts two events for families and children during that month. The **Art Under the Oaks Exhibition and Sale** lasts throughout the month of April and includes baskets, beadwork, cabin crafts, metalwork, pottery, and textiles by contemporary artists of the Five Tribes. The **Art Under the Oaks Indian Market** is held during the second weekend of the Azalea festival in April. This event includes hands-on activities such as storytelling, stickball games, and demonstrations of dancing and flute playing. Several traditional Native American foods are offered for sale.

## Honor Heights Park

*48th Street on Agency Hill, (918) 684-6302. From the intersection of Highways 62 and 69, travel south on Highway 69 to Broadway. Turn west and watch for the park's sign on the north. Gates are closed at 8:30 p.m. in the winter and 9:30 p.m. in the summer. Admission is free.*

Laid out as a "Wreath of Honor," the park was dedicated in 1920 by the people of Muskogee as a tribute to those who served in World War I. Nationally-known for its display of flowers (particularly the azaleas in April) and its dazzling lights in December, Honor Heights Park has year-round appeal for families.

Visit the 113-acre park for picnicking, feeding the ducks, fishing in the "children-only" pond, paddle boating, tennis, or just admiring the beautiful surroundings. Besides the famous azaleas, other beautiful plants at the

*Honor Heights Park.*

park include roses, daffodils, hyacinths, redbuds, dogwoods, and creeping phlox.

### Helpful Hints

Two "don't miss" events at the park are the **Azalea Festival**, held for two weeks in early to mid-April, and the **Garden of Lights Festival** held from Thanksgiving to New Years Day. (See pages 72 and 73 for more information.)

## Muskogee War Memorial Park and U.S.S. Batfish

*Located at the Port of Muskogee, (918) 682-6294. Travel north from the intersection of the Muskogee Turnpike and the Hyde Park/Harris Road exit. Follow the signs to the U.S.S. Batfish. Open mid-March through mid-October, Monday-Saturday 9-5 (closed Tuesday), Sunday noon-5. From mid-October through November open Friday-Saturday 9-5 and Sunday noon-5 (weather permitting). Closed December through mid-March. Call to confirm times. Adults $3, senior citizens $2.50, children ages six through fifteen $1, children under six free. Adult groups of ten or more are $2.50 each; children's groups of ten or more are fifty cents each. Picnic tables are available at the park.*

Named for a ferocious West Indies fish, the U.S.S. Batfish was commissioned in 1943 and served in the South Pacific during World War II. The U.S.S. Batfish sank three submarines and eleven other vessels in less than four days; this feat earned it nine Battle Stars. The crew received one Navy Cross, four Silver Stars, and ten Bronze stars. Children will want to experience the crew's tiny quarters, and to see and touch the equipment inside.

Adjacent to the submarine, visitors will see fifty-two monuments dedicated to the memory of submarines and their crews lost during battle. Children enjoy climbing on the red caboose and Army trucks that are also located on the museum grounds.

## Thomas-Foreman Home

*1419 West Okmulgee Avenue, (918) 682-6938. From the intersection of Highway 62 (Okmulgee Avenue) and Highway 69, travel east on Highway 62 about 1.5 miles. Open Saturday and Sunday 1-4, and on weekdays by special arrangement. Admission is free. Park along the west side of the home. The home is not handicapped accessible. Group visits require reservations.*

Federal Judge John Thomas built this home in 1898, and eventually it passed to his daughter Carolyn, and her husband, Grant Foreman. The Foremans were experts in Oklahoma history and the Five Civilized Tribes. Together, they wrote twenty-seven books and numerous magazine and newspaper articles about these subjects. In addition to writing, the couple traveled the world and could be called the "Indiana Joneses" of the early-twentieth century. Pictures and souvenirs are displayed throughout the home, capturing the excitement of their travels. The photos show the couple riding elephants, camels and donkeys, as well as "shooting the rapids" in Africa; others show the couple with princes and other royalty. Memorabilia from their travels includes an applique from an Egyptian tomb. When Carolyn died in 1967 at the age of ninety-four, she had visited every country in the world except for three Scandinavian countries and Russia.

### Helpful Hints

Children six years old and up will enjoy this home and its furnishings, including the collection of bells the Foremans accumulated from all over the world. Remind your children that this home is "hands off."

## Events

## Azalea Festival

*Held for two weeks during the first part of April at Honor Heights Park. Honor Heights Park is located at 48th Street on Agency Hill. For a brochure, contact the Muskogee Parks and Recreation Department, (918) 684-6302. Admission is free.*

Approximately 500,000 people attend the Azalea Festival each year. In addition to the beauty of millions of azalea blossoms, several activities are held in conjunction with the festival, including a chili and barbecue cook-off, Art Under the Oaks and Indian Market at the Five Civilized Tribes Museum, a photography contest, parades, and craft shows. The parade and cook-off are held the second weekend of the festival. Activities take place throughout the town of Muskogee; call for locations and directions. Don't miss the spectacular beauty and fun of this festival!

## Renaissance Faire

*Usually held the first and second weekends in May at The Castle of Muskogee, 3400 Fern Mountain Road, (918) 687-3625. From the Muskogee Turnpike, take the Highway 69 exit and go south to Fern Mountain Road. Turn right and follow the signs to the castle. Adult three-day pass $13, student/senior citizen three-day pass $11, child three-day pass $7; adult per day ticket $7, student/senior citizen per day ticket $6, child per day ticket $4. Children five and under free.*

For those fascinated by history, the Renaissance Faire offers a unique opportunity to revisit the distant past. For three magical days, the hills of Oklahoma become the enchanted forests of the Old World. Villagers in medieval garb and knights astride thundering horses provide entertainment and excitement for all.

Visitors can shop the booths of artisans and merchants, dine on medieval fare, and interact with scores of dashing nobles. Jousting tournaments are held, medieval weddings are presented, and a "living chessboard" illustrates the classic game. Children have fun in their own "realm" where storytellers, puppeteers and ventriloquists entertain them. What a surprise—finding Camelot in Oklahoma!

### Helpful Hints

Several activities relating to the Renaissance Faire and with a medieval theme are held throughout the year, including the Boars Heade Feast, the Haunted Castle, and the Renaissance Christmas Festival. Contact the Castle of Muskogee for information about the Renaissance Faire and other seasonal events.

## Muskogee Air Show

*Usually held on a Saturday and Sunday in October at Davis Field Airport. Located on Highway 64 and Davis Field Road. Call the Muskogee Area United Way at (918) 682-1364 for information and current ticket prices. Tickets can be purchased four to six weeks in advance through all area Git N' Go stores and other locations. The show usually begins in the early afternoon and lasts for about three hours.*

The Muskogee Air Show features civilian, experimental, and military airplanes on display. Climb aboard and be fascinated by the unique instruments or look to the sky and be dazzled as the planes fly over. Other than the air show, visitors can enjoy the Bedouin Shrine Temple Classsic Car Show or check out the souvenir and food booths.

### Helpful Hints

Seating is on the airport tarmac; visitors are advised to bring their own lawn chairs. Sunglasses and plenty of sunscreen are always a good idea. Proceeds benefit the Muskogee Area United Way and the Bacone College Student Scholarship Fund.

## Garden of Lights Festival

*Held from Thanksgiving to New Year's Day at Honors Heights Park located at 48th Street on Agency Hill. For more information, call Muskogee Parks and Recreation Department. (918) 684-6302. Sunday-Thursday, open until 10 p.m. Friday and Saturday, open until 11 p.m. Admission is free.*

Enjoy more than 500,000 twinkling lights in displays such as swans, deer, doves, and ducks. You may ride in your car, walk, or take a hayride through the park.

## In the Vicinity

## Fort Gibson

Located near the place where the Verdigris, Grand (Neosho) and Arkansas Rivers meet, this area was easily accessible by water. Trappers and traders entered this area, then known as Three Forks, shortly after the Louisiana Purchase was finalized in 1804. The Osage Indian tribes had already settled here and had claimed much of the land drained by the Arkansas River. Conflict ensued when the Cherokees, who had settled in western Arkansas, began to move into this area. It was the duty of the military troops stationed at Fort Smith, Arkansas to control these confrontations, but by 1824, it was clear another post was needed; Fort Gibson was established for this purpose. Visitors today can explore the fascinating history through the Fort Gibson Historic Site and the nearby national cemetery.

*Fort Gibson is about seven miles east of Muskogee on Highway 62. Fort Gibson Chamber of Commerce (918) 478-4780.*

## Attractions

### Fort Gibson Historic Site

*110 East Ash, (918) 478-3355. Located approximately eight miles east of Muskogee. Take Highway 62 east to the Highway 80 turnoff; drive north through the town of Ft. Gibson to the end of Lee Street. Open daily from 9-5. The site is closed New Year's Day, Thanksgiving Day, and Christmas Day. Admission is free, but there are fees for special events. Most of the site is handicapped accessible.*

Named in honor of Col. George M. Gibson, the Commissary General of the United States Army, Fort Gibson was instrumental in promoting relations with western Indian tribes, and it was a base of operations for many expeditions. The fort was abandoned in 1857, but was reactivated during the Civil War and used as a base for postwar Reconstruction activities. The site was permanently abandoned by the Army in 1890.

Begin your tour at the Visitor Center, housed in the 1840s Army Commissary building at 907 North Garrison Avenue. Visit the original buildings on the site, then walk the trail or drive to the reconstructed log garrison.

#### Helpful Hints

No matter when you visit, dress for the weather; the tours are held outside. The best time to visit the fort is during one of the many special events, most of which have living history reenactments. Usually held the last Saturday in March, **Public Bake Day** gives visitors a chance to bake bread in the Fort's wood-burning Army oven. During the fort's existence, an average of two hundred loaves a day were baked by Army cooks, fifty loaves at a time. On Bake Day, the public can bring their own dough to bake; those without dough may purchase baked goods. Each year in mid-May, the Fort hosts an **Armed Forces Day Military Timeline** which depicts soldiers of every war, from 1812 through Desert Storm of the 1980s. Another special event is the **Candlelight Tour** of the Fort. Typically scheduled during the second weekend in December, this event allows visitors to experience firsthand an 1848 Christmas at the Fort. Guests are led by candlelight through the log fort as they observe scenes from Christmas past. Watch as reenactors present history as it happened at a frontier fort; the soldiers celebrate Christmas, the officers talk politics, and the wives tend to their household duties—all without the recognition of an audience! The tour ends with music from the nineteenth century and hot cider served with freshly-baked cookies served around a roaring fire. Tours take about fifty minutes; they start at ten-minute intervals beginning at 6 p.m. This visit is sure to create magical holiday memories for your children.

## Fort Gibson National Cemetery

*From the Muskogee Turnpike, take Highway 62 east approximately eight miles. Turn north at Wiley Road and travel one mile. At Cemetery Road, turn right. (918) 478-2334. The gates to the cemetery are always open; office hours are 8-4:30. Admission is free.*

This cemetery was created in 1868, during President Lincoln's administration. Many of the 3000 soldiers buried here have been relocated from other forts and of these, over 2200 are graves of unknown soldiers. A visit to this reverent place reminds all of the sacrifice of wars. The oldest graves are those of two veterans of the War of 1812. Some of the more well-known historic figures buried here include John Reese, the only Medal of Honor recipient in the cemetery; Talahina Rogers, Sam Houston's Cherokee wife; Vivia Thomas, rumored to have disguised herself as a man to join the service; and John Nix, the first postmaster to serve Fort Gibson and the second to serve in the state of Oklahoma. Children in the fifth grade and up will be especially interested in this cemetery.

## Greenleaf State Park

*Three miles south of Braggs on SH-10A, (918) 487-5196. From Muskogee, travel approximately seventeen miles east and south on Highway 10. For cabin reservations, contact (800) 654-8240. There is a disabled accessible cabin.* ⑧

Greenleaf State Park is one of Oklahoma's most beautiful state parks. Central to the park is its 930-acre sparkling blue lake! For a relaxing weekend retreat, stay in one of the fifteen cozy stone cabins; some have fireplaces, making them particularly nice for off-season trips. There are also five camping areas with 178 campsites, including modern, semi-modern, and primitive campsites.

Families visiting Greenleaf have an abundance of activities from which to choose. For those who enjoy swimming, there is a swimming pool with a double drop slide and a log roll. There is also a swimming beach by the lake. For the more adventurous, mountain bikes may be rented for $3 an hour or $10 a day. Other activities include playing softball, volleyball or horseshoes.

To fully appreciate the beauty of the park, take the eighteen-mile primitive hiking trail which passes over a swinging bridge. The return loop passes through the **Cherokee Wildlife Game Management Area**. The trail begins and ends in the park and is designed for overnight backpacking as well as day hiking.

Find the marina and you'll find many more activity choices. For your day on the lake, you may rent paddle boats, kayaks, canoes, fishing boats, and house boats. Greenleaf Lake is a wonderful place for fishing; dedicated fishermen will especially appreciate the  enclosed and heated fishing dock that is open 24 hours a day. If you should find yourself at the lake during mealtime, stop by the floating grill for hamburgers, french fries, funnel cakes, and other fast food.

Be sure to visit the park's **Nature Center**, open daily. Groups tours are available by appointment. Housed in a recently-remodeled 1930s bathhouse constructed by the Civilian Conservation Corps, the Nature Center features artifacts found at the park as well as live and hands-on wildlife exhibits. Other activities include storytelling of Indian legends, hayrides, astronomy programs, nature walks, campfire programs, canoe races, sack races, and games on the beach. The Nature Center provides much fun for the family!

Before you leave Greenleaf State Park, stop by the gift shop for some souvenir T-shirts and caps. They'll help you remember the great time you had at Greenleaf!

# Pawhuska

Visit this small but sophisticated town and relive the history of the early twentieth century. As the county seat of the largest county in Oklahoma (Osage County), Pawhuska reflects the influence of the Osage Indians, one of the wealthiest tribes in North America. A drive through downtown Pawhuska will reveal historic buildings and quaint shops. Especially notable on Main Street is the **Constantine Center**, the recently-renovated and incredibly elaborate theater. In 1911, Charles Constantine bought the local hotel and transformed it into a spectacular theater, complete with handpainted curtains, oversized seats, mosaics in the lobby, and much more. Although later the theater fell into disrepair, concerned citizens have revived the theater; now a variety of performances are held each year on its stage, and tour groups visit to see the lovely details of the building.

Be sure to also drive by the **Immaculate Conception Catholic Church**, located nine blocks north of Main Street (Highway 60) on Lynn Avenue. Completed in 1915, this is one of the most elaborate Catholic churches in the state; it features huge panels of gorgeous stained glass windows.

Explore the land of the Osage through the two museums and the Tallgrass Prairie Preserve, one of the few remaining tallgrass areas in North America.

*Pawhuska is located approximately 160 miles north and east of Oklahoma City and about 57 miles north and west of Tulsa. From Oklahoma City, take I-35 north to U.S. Highway 60. Follow this highway east to Pawhuska. From Tulsa, take Highway 75 north to U.S. Highway 60 and travel west into town. A more scenic route can be taken by traveling from Skiatook west on Highway 20 to Highway 99. Pawhuska Chamber of Commerce (918) 287-1208.*

## Attractions

### Osage County Historical Museum

*700 North Lynn Avenue, (918) 287-9924. From Highway 60, turn north at the light and travel one block to the museum. Open Monday-Saturday 9-5, Sunday 12-5. Closed Christmas and Thanksgiving. Admission is free; donations are appreciated. The restroom is not handicapped accessible.*

Housed in an old train depot, this small museum is filled with history. The museum has five main areas: the Boy Scouts area and its artifacts (find out about the first Boy Scout Troop in America that began in 1909 at Pawhuska); the Western Life section (branding irons, barbed wire displays, and a chuck wagon); the Pioneer Life area (old photographs, clothing, furniture, and quilts); early-day oil history including boom-time oil recovery operations in Osage County and the Native American section (especially emphasizes the local Osage tribe). Located on the museum grounds are an 1890 gazebo, two Santa Fe railroad cars, and an authentic one-room schoolhouse. Ask for the keys to explore the schoolhouse.

### Helpful Hints

Younger children will enjoy the railroad cars, but children over eight will benefit most from this museum.

## Osage Indian Tribal Complex and Tribal Museum

*819 Grandview, (918) 287-4622. From U.S. 60 go north on Grandview. The museum is on top of the hill and at the end of the tribal complex on your left. Monday-Friday 10-5, occasional Saturdays 1-5. Closed Sunday and holidays. Call to confirm. Admission is free; donation are appreciated. Call two weeks in advance to request a personal tour. Tours last approximately twenty minutes, and they are recommended for children over eight. The building is handicapped accessible, but the restrooms are not.*

All Osage business is conducted at this complex, and tribal decisions are made in the council chambers. Visitors are invited to walk through the **tribal museum** for a better appreciation of Osage culture. Opened in 1938, the museum is the oldest continuous tribal museum in the country. Displays include articles such as treaties and Native American apparel and beadwork. To revive and preserve the Osage culture, classes in moccasin making, finger weaving, ribbonwork, and the Osage language are held here periodically.

Petroleum deposits located in Osage County and Osage tribal lands are responsible for making the Osage tribe one of the wealthiest tribes in North America. Ask at the museum about how to locate the "Million Dollar Elm." In 1924, an auctioneer is said to have auctioned nearly $11 million worth of oil and gas leases for the Osage tribe. These leases were purchased by some of the biggest names in the oil business such as Skelly, Phillips and Marland.

## Tallgrass Prairie Preserve

*(918) 287-4803. The Pawhuska office is at 100 West Main. To get to the preserve, take U.S. 60 to Osage Avenue (the corner with the triangle-shaped building). Turn north on Osage Avenue, and follow the Tallgrass Prairie Preserve directional signs to the headquarters. Hours are dawn to dusk. Admission is free; donations are appreciated. The headquarters is handicapped accessible.*

Step back in time to view the prairie as it appeared long before the white man came to own it. Owned by the Nature Conservancy, the purpose of the 38,000-acre preserve is to protect the quickly-vanishing native American Tallgrass Prairie ecosystem. The grass can stand as tall as eight feet, and it shelters numerous birds, mammals, insects, and reptiles.

The prairie lands once belonged to the 100,000-acre Chapman-Barnard Ranch. The preserve headquarters is the restored 1920 Chapman-Barnard

Ranch bunkhouse. The drive through the preserve is approximately fifty miles and, including stops along the way, it can take more than two hours at a recommended maximum speed of 35 mph. A drive that long and that slow is typically too difficult for children to enjoy. But there is good news: you don't have to drive the entire trail to learn from the preserve; the seventeen-mile trip from Pawhuska to the headquarters will give your family a typical view of the preserve, including a bison pasture.

About five hundred bison graze in an area to the west of the headquarters. They survive entirely on the nutritious prairie grasses, just as they did for hundreds of years before settlement. This herd will be allowed to grow until it reaches two thousand.

The preserve has over six hundred species of plants. Wildflowers peak in color from mid-May to mid-June, then again in August and September. The tallgrasses reach their maximum height in August and September; they die back in the winter.

Nature trails are located near the preserve headquarters (watch for "Trail Parking" signs). The short trail is one mile, and the longer trail is two miles. While on the nature trails or while driving through the preserve, take the opportunity for a close-up look at the prairie. You might want to suggest an activity for your family, such as trying to guess where certain animals make their homes. When hiking, dress appropriately, including wearing long pants and proper footwear; the native grasses can hide dangers such as snakes, ticks and holes. As a preventive measure, stay on the established trails.

### Helpful Hints

As you continue your drive, remember to always stay in your car—these are wild, unpredictable animals! Don't try to feed the animals or honk your horn.

While on the preserve, follow these important rules. Always stay on the main public county road. Don't go onto private roadways. Avoid causing wildfires; do not smoke outside of your car and don't throw cigarettes out the car window. A common land management tool is controlled burning; in order to avoid possible hazards in the road ahead, don't drive through smoke. Leave the prairie lands as you found them. Do not litter. Do not remove any of the natural features or artifacts. Teach your children an environmental lesson by leaving the area just as you found it.

Keep in mind that this is a tallgrass prairie preserve. You will see mostly native grasses. On a good day, you will see much of the wildlife that inhabits this preserve.

The last ten miles of the trip from downtown Pawhuska is a rural, gravel road. Be sure to buy gasoline before leaving town; there are no gasoline stations in the preserve. Restrooms are available only at the preserve headquarters. Picnic tables for lunches or snacks are available near the preserve headquarters, but bring your own trash bag.

# Pawnee

This small town was officially organized in 1893 with the opening of the Cherokee Outlet. Prior to the Run, the area was the location of the agency servicing the Pawnee Indians who were moved here to a reservation from Nebraska. The influence of the Pawnee tribe on the area is still evident today. The town hosts a long-standing powwow, one of the oldest in the state. First held in 1946 as a means of honoring returning World War II veterans, the **Pawnee Indian Homecoming** is now held on a weekend near July 4th, and it involves the entire community in the celebration.

Pawnee is the hometown of two famous celebrities, Chester Gould, creator of the "Dick Tracy" cartoon, and Gordon W. Lillie ("Pawnee Bill"). The life and times of Pawnee Bill can be fully explored by families through the Pawnee Bill Museum and Ranch and the recreation of his "Wild West Shows" during the summer. Pawnee provides a "don't miss" small-town adventure for families!

*Located approximately 55 miles west of Tulsa and 91 miles north and east of Oklahoma City. From Tulsa, take Highway 64/51 west to the Cimarron Turnpike (Highway 412). From Oklahoma City, travel north on I-35 to Highway 51. Go east to Highway 18 then north to Pawnee. Pawnee Chamber of Commerce (918) 762-2108.* ★

## *Attractions*

### *Pawnee Bill Museum and Ranch*

*Located on Highway 64, a mile west of Pawnee. (918) 762-2513. Tuesday-Saturday 10-5, Sunday-Monday 1-4. Admission is free; donations are encouraged.*

Owned and operated by the Oklahoma Historical Society, the Pawnee Bill Museum sits on a hilltop known as Blue Hawk Peak. It pays tribute to Oklahoma's first "king of the cowboys," Pawnee Bill, whose real name was Gordon W. Lillie. Lillie came to Oklahoma in 1877 and, by the time he died in 1942, he had experienced the opening of the West and had witnessed its closing. He saw the last Pawnee Indian buffalo hunt; in his later life, he worked to restore the bison to the plains. In 1883, Lillie went on the road with his Wild West Show. Traveling around the world, the Wild West Show featured authentic cowboys and full-blood Indians displaying the skills that were once required in the untamed West. In 1908, his show and the competing Buffalo Bill's Wild West Show were merged, and the combined show was continued through 1913.

After the first combined-show season in 1908, "Pawnee Bill" returned to the ranch and began building a large brick show home with the money he had made. Completed in 1910, the fourteen-room house was used to display the artwork and keepsakes he had gathered while touring the world.

Visitors can tour the house and museum, visit the blacksmith shop and the large barn, and walk the nature trails. Children will especially want to see a stagecoach, a miniature scene of the Wild West Show, period clothing, and a small hands-on exhibit of animal skins and buffalo horns and teeth. For a view of buffalo, longhorn cattle, horses, and elk, take time to drive through the ranch.

### Helpful Hints

The best time to visit is when the Pawnee community recreates the Wild West Shows on the Pawnee Bill Ranch grounds (see below for more information). A picnic area is available at the ranch. Classes in primitive art such as arrowhead making and buckskin tanning are offered throughout the year; for information, call the Oklahoma Historical Society at (918) 762-3614.

## Events

### The Oklahoma Steam and Gas Engine Show

*Held the first weekend of May at the new Steam Engine Park on the Pawnee Fairgrounds north of town. For brochures and date, call (918) 762-2108. Adults $5; there is a nominal admission fee for children. A senior citizen discount is available on Friday. Parking is free.*

Steam traction engines were popular in the late 1800s. Proving more efficient than horses, the engines allowed farmers to raise crops on larger sections of land. Gasoline and diesel-powered engines replaced steam engines in the 1930s, making the steam engine obsolete. Only a few remain operable today, and most are owned by those fascinated by the engine's properties.

Visitors to this popular show can see antique tractors, cars and trucks or browse arts and crafts booths. Working exhibits include corn grinding, lathe turning, clothes washing, water pumping, spinning, weaving, cream separating, and toy making. A parade and entertainment make this annual event fun for everyone.

### Pawnee Bill's Wild West Show

*Held on Saturday evenings from late June to early August at the Pawnee Bill Museum and Ranch. For information and reservations, call (918) 762-2108. Barbecue dinners are served at 5 p.m. and cost $6 for adults and $3 for children. The Wild West Show begins at 7 p.m. and costs $8 for adults, $2 for children ages seven to twelve (free for children six and younger). Local merchants sell tickets in advance for $7 per adult; group rates are $6 each for groups of thirty or more.* ★

Watch with excitement as a recreation of the Pawnee Bill Wild West Show is performed. Over 1,000 spectators attend each week to see trick riding, buffalo hunters, sharpshooters, daring cowgirls, singing cowboys, and more. A downtown celebration is held each Saturday with a parade (usually starts at 3 p.m.) and other activities. This is small-town Oklahoma at its best!

### Helpful Hints

Although bleachers are provided, visitors are encouraged to bring their own blankets or lawn chairs.

# Tahlequah

In 1839, the Cherokees settled in Tahlequah, after being forced to leave their homes in Georgia and Florida and enduring the journey now known as "The Trail of Tears." An organized and educated tribe, the Cherokees brought their language, government and customs with them. Government buildings were built, newspapers (printed in both English and Cherokee) were circulated, and academically-challenging schools were built for young men and women.

Visitors to Tahlequah will experience the rich history of the Cherokee people through attractions such as the outstanding Cherokee Heritage Center. Families could stay in the area a number of days and still not experience all of Tahlequah's history, scenic wonders, and outdoor adventures at nearby places such as Fort Gibson Lake, Tenkiller Lake, and the Illinois River.

*From the Oklahoma City metro area, travel approximately 116 miles east on I-40, then north on Highway 82 another thirty-three miles to Tahlequah. From Tulsa, travel seventy miles (south on the Muskogee Turnpike, then east on Highway 51). Tahlequah Area Chamber of Commerce (918) 456-3742. ★*

## Attractions

### Cherokee Heritage Center

*Located three miles south of Tahlequah off Highway 62; watch for the sign. (918) 456-6007. Open April-December: Tuesday-Saturday 10-5 (last tour of the villages is at 3:30); the Cherokee National Museum is additionally open Sunday 1-5. Hours during the summer may be extended; call ahead to confirm. Admission to the Cherokee Heritage Center, Ancient and Rural Villages for adults is $5, children (ages six to twelve) are $3; children ages five and under are admitted free. Trail of Tears drama show tickets are adults $9, children $4.50, with slightly higher prices for Saturday night tickets. Dinners are adults $8, children (under age twelve) $5. The museum*

*Tsa-La-Gi Ancient Village.*

*and grounds are handicapped accessible.*

Plan to spend the day at this extensive center, experiencing the culture and heritage of the Cherokee Indians. The Center includes the Tsa-La-Gi Ancient Village, the Cherokee National Museum, the Adams Corner Rural Village, and the Trail of Tears Drama.

**Tsa-La-Gi Ancient Village.** (Tsa-La-Gi is the native word for Cherokee.) This village depicts authentic Cherokee culture prior to contact with European settlers. Tribal members in native apparel guide visitors through a sixteenth-century mud-walled village. Re-enactors demonstrate the skills of basketry, pottery, cooking, and flint-knapping, as Cherokee children play their favorite game—stickball.

**Adam's Corner Rural Village.** This rural village is a replica of an Indian Territory Cherokee community from 1875-1890. The village consists of a settler's cabin, a one-room school house, a log cabin church, a smokehouse, and other dwellings.

**Cherokee National Museum.** This museum reveals the Cherokee people's story, from their arrival in North America to the present. Exhibits include prehistoric Indian artifacts and Native American art.

The plight of the Cherokee Tribe is reenacted in a 1,500-seat amphitheater through the **Trail of Tears Drama**, held seasonally through the summer, typically from late June to mid-August. Starting with the forced removal of more than 16,000 Cherokee from their original homeland in Southeastern United States in 1838, and continuing through Oklahoma's statehood in 1907, this drama reveals the hardships and agony they endured along the trail and the new life they created in present-day Oklahoma. The road they traveled became known as "The Trail Where They Cried," (later named The Trail of Tears) because more than four thousand people died along the way. First opened in 1969, the play has recently been revitalized and restaged, and a traditional Cherokee dinner has been added to the evening activities.

### Helpful Hints

This is a "must do" experience for families to understand more about the Cherokee Tribe's heritage. Call for reservations for the drama and dinner about one week in advance. Be aware that the Trail of Tears Drama is two hours long; young children may become restless.

A curriculum for educators has been developed by the Cherokee Heritage Center. You may make a written request for material to prepare for a field trip by using school letterhead and writing to: Cherokee Heritage Center Education Department, P.O. Box 515, Tahlequah, OK 74465. The Center is open year-round for school groups (group rates available), but for two days in April, they host special education field trip days and a student art show for grades 2-12. Groups should call two weeks in advance to participate in this event.

Another opportunity to experience Cherokee culture is during the annual **Cherokee National Holiday,** held on Labor Day weekend at various locations around Tahlequah. About 50,000 visitors from around the world attend this festival to enjoy a parade, a powwow, a dance competition, demonstrations of

Cherokee games, and much more. For more information, call (918) 456-0671, extension 2542 or (800) 850-0348.

## Murrell Home

*Located three miles south of Tahlequah on Highway 82, not far from the Cherokee Heritage Center. (918) 456-2751. Open Wednesday-Saturday 10-5 and Sunday 1-5. Closed Monday, Tuesday, and state holidays. Admission is free; donations are appreciated. The first floor of the home is handicapped accessible; a ramp is located on the west side of the house.*

Located in the town of Park Hill amidst other homes of prominent Cherokee tribal members, this home belonged to George M. Murrell and his wife, Minerva Ross, the niece of Cherokee Chief John Ross. The area became a religious and social center for the Cherokee Nation. Fort Gibson officers, women from the Cherokee National Female Seminary, and others were entertained at the homes in this prestigious area.

Although looted, the Murrell Home is the only antebellum home in eastern Oklahoma left intact after the Civil War; others in the Rose Hill community and in other locations were destroyed. Many original pieces of furniture, as well as exhibits featuring the Murrell family keepsakes, are found in this two-story, Southern plantation-style home built in the mid-1800s. After a tour of this historic home, take advantage of the walking trail and a lovely picnic area.

## River City Players

*The Northeastern Oklahoma State University Playhouse is located on the corner of Muskogee Avenue and Downing Street. (918) 458-2072 or (918) 456-5511, extension 2789. Performances are held from the first week of June to the first week of August, Tuesday-Saturday at 8 p.m. Ticket prices are adults $10, children under age twelve $4.50.*

Treat your family to a musical extravaganza featuring the talented students from Northeastern Oklahoma State University and the surrounding areas. This high-energy, fast-paced musical presentation includes music ranging from "oldies" to current chart busters and is appealing to children of all ages. Staged in a reproduced nineteenth-century opera house near the campus of NOSU, the show draws sellout crowds throughout the summer.

### Helpful Hints

Take a walking tour of the small but beautiful campus of Northeastern Oklahoma State University located just north on Muskogee Avenue; make a game of locating the "castle-like" university building. Muskogee Avenue, the main street of Tahlequah, also has an assortment of shops and university student-related shops that will appeal to children.

## Events

## Illinois River Balloon Festival

*This event is held on a weekend in mid-August at various locations around Tahlequah. For more information and admission prices, call (918) 456-3742*

Watch as approximately forty colorful hot-air balloons participate in a "Balloon Glow" in the evenings and lift in mass ascension on Saturday morning. Although other activities associated with the festival vary each year, they may include square dancing, a kiddie carnival, an antique car show, food, and music.

## In the Vicinity

### Illinois River

*Located east of Tahlequah. From Tahlequah, turn left onto Muskogee Avenue (the main thoroughfare) and go north to Downing Street. Turn right on Downing (U.S. 62/Highway 51) and go east three miles to Highway 10. Designated as a scenic route, Highway 10 winds around hills between the Illinois River and overhanging bluffs. Public access to the river is provided at four areas. Several resorts along the highway offer float trips and camping facilities. Refer to the following list or for a Floater's Guide, contact the Oklahoma Scenic Rivers Commission at (800) 299-3251. Call ahead in early spring to see when the suppliers will open. Both the beginning and the end of the float season depend on the weather and the water level of the river. Most outfitters are open daily between Memorial Day and Labor Day, and on weekends in May and September, with a few offering services year-round. Reservations are strongly recommended. Rates range from $7 per person for a two to three hour float to $30 per person for a three-day trip; rates are higher for those renting rafts and kayaks. Some suppliers offer family rates or reduced rates for children.*

For a day or weekend of outstanding family fun and togetherness, consider a float trip down the scenic Illinois River. Situated in the Oklahoma Ozark Hills, the river offers a wonderful view of wildlife and nature. With more than 60,000 visitors each year, the Illinois River is one of Oklahoma's most popular outdoor attractions!

A short float is five to seven miles long and takes approximately two to four hours to complete. A longer float is twelve miles and can take six to seven hours to complete. If you plan to float longer than twelve miles, you must break your trip into two days and camp out.

### Helpful Hints

The Oklahoma Scenic Rivers Commission recommends that children be six or older to float the river. Families will want to ask about the newer kayaks and/ or rafts that may be safer for children. Canoes, especially if manned by untrained paddlers, tend to tip over. To many, this is part of the fun. Although difficult to tip, rafts are also difficult to paddle. Kayaks are new to the river and are considered more stable and maneuverable than canoes.

Life jackets are provided when you rent canoes, but bring your child's own preserver for a guaranteed fit. Also bring lots of waterproof sunscreen and water shoes or other footwear; the rocky bottom of the river is tough on tender feet.

The river conditions are usually safer in mid-June through August because of less rainfall. Expect crowds Memorial Day weekend through Labor Day; you can avoid crowds by floating the river during the week.

Bring along picnic supplies, but glass or styrofoam containers are prohibited. Store food and extra clothing in watertight containers. Many outfitters offer picnic lunches, or you can stop at one of the locally-owned cafes along the river.

## Illinois River Outfitters

**Arrowhead Camp**, (918) 456-1140 or (800) 749-1140. Canoes, cabins, camping, playground, and store. **Diamondhead Resort**, (918) 456-4545 or (800) 722-2411. Canoes, rafts, kayaks, motel, bunkhouse, camping, play area, game room, and store. **Eagle Bluff Resorts**, (800) OK-RIVER. Canoes, rafts, lodge, campground, play area, snack shop. **Falcon Floats**, (800) OK-FLOATS. Canoes, rafts, bunkhouse, play area, and camping. **Hanging Rock Camp**, (918) 456-3088 or (800) 375-3088. Canoes, rafts, motel, camping, and cafe. **Peyton's Place**, (918) 456-3847. Canoes, lodge, cottages, kitchenettes, camping, picnic supplies, and deli. **Riverside Camp**, (918) 456-4787 or (800) 749-CAMP. Canoes, rafts, kayaks, lodge, cabins, camping, play area, and store. **Sparrow Hawk Camp**, (918) 456-8371, FAX (918) 458-0124. Canoes, rafts, paddle boats, innertubes, bunkhouse, camping, play area, playground, and trampolines. **Thunderbird Resort**, (918) 456-4747 or (800) 749-4700. Canoes, rafts, lodge, and camping. **War Eagle**, (918) 456-6272 or (800) 722-3834. Canoes, rafts, kayaks, motel, bunkhouse, camping, play area, game room, swimming pool for lodgers, and water slide.

## Tenkiller Lake

*This lake is located between the towns of Tahlequah at the northern end and Gore at the southern end, approximately seventy miles southeast of Tulsa and 148 miles northeast of Oklahoma City. For a current vacation guide, call the Lake Tenkiller Association at (918) 457-4403. Information includes camping and resort information and a directory of local goods and services.*

Known for the pristine beauty of its crystal clear lake, its tree-covered banks, and high rocky bluffs, Tenkiller Lake is one of Oklahoma's most magnificent reservoirs. The lake winds for thirty-four miles through the Ozark-like Cookson Hills, and it has over 130 miles of shoreline. The recreation opportunities of the beautiful lake will keep your family more than happy! Boating, swimming, biking, hiking, fishing, wildlife watching, scuba diving. . . .there's much to do for everyone!

There are many places to stay around the lake ranging from private resorts to state parks and Corps of Engineers camping areas. Two popular resort parks for families are Tenkiller State Park and the Fin and Feather Resort, a privately-operated facility.

**Tenkiller State Park** offers thirty-nine one- and two-bedroom cabins ($50-76) and a three-bedroom cabin ($125-150). These cabins are fully equipped; call ahead for reservations, particularly for weekends during the busy summer season. In addition, there are 240 campsites in ten camping areas available on a first-come, first-served basis for $6-14.

The park offers a swimming pool, volleyball court, basketball hoops, a horseshoe area, bike rental, and a Nature Center, with daily activities conducted by the park's naturalist.

*# 918. 487. 5148*

Since 1960, the **Fin and Feather Resort** has provided outstanding facilities and services to its guests. Perched high atop a hill, the resort overlooks the south end of Lake Tenkiller. The resort has eighty-two rental units and a large dining room that seats 250 and serves delicious buffets. From one-bedroom cabins to five-bedroom houses, guests have many choices of accommodations. Rates range from $56 to $285 for a house that sleeps twenty.

Guest facilities at the Fin and Feather include an indoor pool and whirlpool spa, tennis and basketball courts, a small movie theater, a fully-equipped game room, a playground, and a grocery store. This resort is ideal for families and family reunions!

## Western Hills Guest Ranch/Sequoyah State Park

*Located on State Highway 51, about seventeen miles west of Tahlequah. Western Hills Guest Ranch (918) 772-2545; Sequoyah State Park office (918) 772-2046; for reservations or other information try (800) 654-8240.* 🅂 ★

Nestled in the foothills of the Ozarks is Fort Gibson Lake. Created in the 1940s with the completion of Ft. Gibson dam, this popular 19,900-acre lake offers an incredible variety of recreational opportunities for families, particularly during the summer months. Situated on a peninsula, Sequoyah State Park has campsites, a lodge, and cabins for those who wish to stay overnight. There are six camping areas with 339 total campsites and a large group camp. Western Hills Guest Ranch has 101 hotel-style rooms and suites (some open to the swimming pool), and 54 cottages (sleep two to six; some have kitchenettes). Lodge rooms rent for $62-70 ($45 in the winter); cabins rent for $70-105 ($60-75 in the winter).

Western Hills Guest Ranch provides numerous activities for children during the summer (Memorial Day weekend to Labor Day weekend). With a full and active recreation staff to serve as guides, the park hosts several activities daily that appeal to a wide variety of ages, especially children ages six and older. Among the offerings are swimming lessons, frisbee golf tournaments, badminton, archery lessons, horseback riding, hay rides, arts and crafts projects, tennis instruction, nature hikes, miniature golf and mini-golf tournaments, shuffleboard, ping pong, scavenger hunts, Western dance instruction . . . the list goes on! To keep guests informed, listings of daily and weekly activities are posted throughout the lodge and the activity center. Located within walking distance of the Recreation Center is a Nature Center with exhibits about Oklahoma wildlife; nature-related activities at the Nature Center continue year-round. Families can also rent pontoon boats, wave runners, and other boats through the nearby marina or enjoy the eighteen-hole golf course at the park.

### Helpful Hints

Activities are available to all park guests, whether camping or staying at the lodge. Reservations for this popular park and lodge are recommended at least two months in advance for the busy summer months. Drop-off activities through the Recreation Center are available for children ages seven and up; inquire at the center about which activities are child-only and which ones are for parents and children.

Because this park is not far from the Illinois River, many people spend one of their vacation days floating the river.

## Tulsa

Tulsa is a cosmopolitan city with the friendliness of a small town. It is a great place to spend a day, a week, or even a lifetime! Created out of the determination of its early settlers and enhanced by the fortunes of its famous oilmen, Tulsa is a city with many fine attractions. From down-home ranches to uptown theater, Tulsa offers a wide variety of activities.

Around the 1830s, permanent settlers began to arrive when Indians from the eastern seaboard straggled in from the Trail of Tears. Forced to move to the Indian Territory by the Indian Removal Act of 1830, these resilient Native Americans turned "wilderness" into home. Council grounds were established, local governments created, and social structures and customs reinstated. Some Indians became businessmen; others became farmers and ranchers. The Indians were so successful at creating "something from nothing" that, after the Civil War, the railroads came. Residents were able to ship cattle and prairie chickens east on the rails, and Tulsa went from a small Creek settlement to a rowdy cowtown, complete with cowboys and cattle drives.

In 1905, the famous Glenn Pool oil discovery took place and Tulsa became known as the Oil Capital of the World. More oil companies and oil-related industries located here than in other city on the globe. Tulsa led the oil industry for almost half

*Tulsa's Philbrook.*

a century. At this time, the town changed from a rowdy tent city of oil field workers to the sophisticated metropolis it is today.

Tulsa prides itself on being a clean city, dedicated to family values and economic diversity. Its history is evident in the area attractions and events. Here, you can go to an ethnic festival, or listen to bluegrass, country or jazz. You can attend your first opera or enjoy the ballet. Whatever you're looking for, you'll find it—in Tulsa!

*Tulsa is located in the center of the beautiful, green hills of Northeast Oklahoma. From Oklahoma City travel approximately 115 miles northeast on the Turner Turnpike (I-44), or take the more scenic "backroads" and relive history on old Route 66. Tulsa Conventions and Visitors Bureau (918) 585-1201.* ▣

## *Attractions*

### *Allen Ranch*

*19600 South Memorial, Bixby, (918) 366-3010. From Memorial go south past 191st Street to the Allen Ranch entrance gate. Follow the road to the cluster of* *western-style buildings. Daily, one-hour trail rides: $10 per person. Chuckwagon Supper and Cowboy Music Show (price subject to change): adults $12.50, children under age twelve $10. Other activities are priced on an individual basis.*

Cowboys will never die—as long as there are little boys who dream of becoming one! The image of the weather-beaten cowboy persists today. To see real cowboys, visit the Allen Ranch, a working ranch. You can take trail rides or hayrides, escorted by real cowboys. There are also daily trail rides, weekly moonlight rides, monthly breakfast rides, and horseback overnight camp outs. Hayrides for groups can be arranged throughout the year. Individuals may experience the **Trail of Fear** hayride the last two weeks in October or the **Holiday Hayride** weekend nights in December. Every year, April through November, on Friday and Saturday nights at 7 p.m., Allen Ranch hosts a **Chuckwagon Supper and Cowboy Music Show**. Let "Ole Cookie" prepare a special country meal for you just like the ones cowboys ate when they were out on the trail. Afterwards, enjoy the cowboy music show; listen to the same tunes that cowhands used to sing under the stars.

### Helpful Hints

The Allen family is very accommodating, and they offer a variety of activities on any given day, both for individuals and groups. This is a wonderful place for a group to visit! The Allens will help you arrange almost any type of outing you want. Along with the hayrides, you can schedule a private bonfire for a wiener roast, a walk through their miniature "zoo," a trial by their "kangaroo court," or a reenacted gunfight. Pony parties and birthday parties can be arranged in advance. If you have a need for any of these activities at another location (a company party or church event, for example) the Allens can provide them.

Call ahead to make sure that you can participate in the activity of your choice, and be sure to inform them of a cancellation should your plans change. Guests should wear jeans and boots; long pants and tennis shoes are acceptable for city slickers wishing to take a trail ride. Casual attire also is best for any of the other activities, including the dinner and music show.

To inquire about the wide variety of activities offered and to make your reservations, call one day in advance for individual activities and several weeks in advance for group functions. If you are going for an afternoon or evening, eat before you go, take a picnic basket, or make arrangements for a meal with the Allens.

## Amish Dinner

*Located in rural Oklahoma, between Chouteau and Wagoner along Highway 412 and Highway 69. Serving hours vary, depending on the family contacted, the size of the group, and the day the meal is scheduled. Most families prefer that evening meals be scheduled no later than 7 p.m. Saturday lunches are often served, as well as an occasional breakfast. No meals are served on Sunday. Prices range from $12-15 for adults; children's meal prices vary from one home to another. Verify childrens' ages and prices when writing for reservations.*

Return to times past when you have dinner with an Amish family. Most of all, savor the delicious meal that is not only home-cooked, but also home-grown. Meals include a pre-arranged entree, mashed potatoes, gravy, green beans, coleslaw, noodles, hot rolls, and pie for dessert. After dinner, stroll outside or purchase baked goods and cookbooks to take home. You'll leave full and refreshed, knowing that the simple joys of life can still be found.

Most of these family cooks require a minimum of twenty people. Choose several dates and write (the Amish have no telephones) to one of the families asking if they have one of the dates open. Plan to visit in the winter, spring or fall; the families do not typically serve in the heat of summer since they have no electricity. There are four main families who do most of the serving, although others join in from time to time. Names and addresses are as follows: Mrs. Norman C. Miller, Route 1, Box 326, Chouteau, Oklahoma 74337; Mrs. Fanny Yoder, Route 1, Box 318, Chouteau, Oklahoma 74337; Christie and Edna Miller, Route 1, Box 76, Chouteau, Oklahoma 74337; Eli and Ina Detweiler, Route 1, Box 244, Inola 74337.

### Helpful Hints

Be sure to ask for directions to the host's home. These two families live within a six-mile area, and there are few places to stop and ask for directions.

Go hungry; there's lots to eat. But please don't be wasteful. Left-overs are put to good use, sometimes going to the local school for lunch. Gratuities are not included in the price of the meal. Remind your children that this meal is being served in someone's home, not a fast-food restaurant; appropriate manners are appreciated.

## Bell's Amusement Park

*3901 East 21st Street, (918) 744-1991. Located halfway between Harvard and Yale on 21st. Turn north at the appropriate sign for parking and park entrance. Open April, May and September, weekends only (call for specific days and times); June, July and August, Monday-Thursday 6-10, Friday 6-11, Saturday 1-11, Sunday 1-9. Park entrance $1. Ride coupons $1 each (rides require 1-3 tickets). All-you-can-ride wristbands: $14.25 plus tax for adults, $9.25 plus tax for children under forty-eight inches. Wristbands do not include miniature golf. Senior adults sixty-five and older ride free with gate admission. Checks are not accepted, but major credit cards are.*

Family-owned and operated since 1951, Bell's offers entertainment for all members of the family at this old-fashioned amusement park. Younger visitors are thrilled by the traditional rides such as motorized cars, low-flying airplanes, and the merry-go-round. Older visitors prefer the Ferris wheel, Tilt-a-Whirl, Scrambler, and other rides. On those hot summer days, cool off by riding the bumper boats, the White Lightnin' log ride, or the Chilly Pepper Plunge, a combination water slide/roller coaster. After dark, check out Phantasmagoria, the haunted house.

Adventurous visitors will want to ride Zingo, a wooden roller coaster with plenty of plunges. If you want to take a break from the rides, play a game of miniature golf or have a drink and snack at one of the concession stands.

### Helpful Hints

Before visiting Bell's, check the local newspaper or coupon books for special admission rates. Monday through Wednesday evening, the park offers a Family Four Pack; a family of four can ride all rides, as many times as they like, for $22. If no coupons are available, the best value is the all-you-can-ride wristband. With prior arrangements, group rates are available.

## Big Splash

*21st Street and Yale Avenue, (918) 749-7385. From the intersection of 21st Street and Yale Avenue, turn west onto 21st Street. The park's entrance is visible from here. Open weekends before school is out in May and after it resumes in August; call the office for specific times. From Memorial Day-Labor Day, Big Splash is open Monday and Wednesday 10-6, Tuesday and Thursday 10-10, Friday and Saturday 10-8, and Sunday 12-8. Adults and children $12, children ages three and under and seniors ages sixty and older are free. Night Splash (4pm-close) $6. Family nights are held Tuesday and Thursday from 6-10 p.m.; admission is $25 for five people. All prices include sales tax. Prices and times subject to change without notice; for the latest information, call ahead. For group rates and booking information, call the office.* ⑤ ★

"Fun in the sun for everyone" is what you'll find at Big Splash! From the Giant Pepsi Wave Pool to the seven-story speed slides, from the Master Blaster Water Roller Coaster to the three flume slides, from the Log Roll at the Activity Pool to the Kiddie Pool, you're sure to find your favorite here.

Be prepared to spend a full day at Big Splash. With more than ten different water rides, children will want to stay as long as possible. For the younger swimmers, Little Splash offers just the right water depth for toddlers. Paradise Cove, the activity pool, is everything its name implies for children and their parents; youngsters will be busy playing with the many water toys and activities while parents watch and relax. "Motion Ocean" is the wave pool where teenagers spend their time body surfing. Everyone loves the three water flumes: T-Town Twister, Gully Washer, and the Sooner Flumer. For adventurous thrill-seekers, two speed slides are available; guests may hit speeds up to sixty-five miles per hour before reaching the bottom of the seven-story slide.

### Helpful Hints

Many chairs are available for those wanting to work on their tan, and a few shaded areas are available for those wishing to protect children in strollers from being sunburned.

Certain rides have height restrictions; others require an innertube. Tube rental ranges from $3 for a single to $5 for a double. Toddlers may bring their own tubes, provided the tubes meet park requirements. Locker rental is $3 per day.

Family nights are every Tuesday and Thursday night. From 6 to 10 p.m., five people are admitted for a total of $25. To make family nights even more special, free music acts or other events are usually scheduled during this time. Aside from these package deals, discount admission coupons (see the coupon in this book) or certain kinds of pop cans can be redeemed for discounted admission prices. Season passes are also offered. Only those with season passes are allowed to leave the park then reenter without paying more admission. Call the office for prices on season passes.

For small children, bring their own life jackets or rent one for $1. If you forget to bring sunscreen or sunglasses, you can buy them at the park. You may want to take an extra adult or teenage helper if you are bringing children of varying ages with you.

No outside food or drink is allowed at Big Splash. However, there are plenty of places to eat or just have a snack. Everything from pizza, tacos and hamburgers to frozen drinks and ice cream are available inside the park.

During the summer, children may take Red Cross-certified swimming lessons. Cabanas may be reserved for groups or birthday parties. Any child would love to have his/her birthday party at Big Splash. Cost is $10 per person (ten-person minimum), with each person receiving park entry, pizza, drinks, and a popsicle. The birthday child and one parent are admitted free for a total of twelve people for the price of ten.

## Casa Bonita

*2120 S. Sheridan, (918) 836-6464. From I-44, exit at the Sheridan/41st Street exit and travel two m iles north on Sheridan. The restaurant is in the Alameda Shopping Center on the west side of the road. Meals for children twelve and under are $2.99; meals for adults range from $5.49-8.29. This restaurant is handicapped accessible.* 🖆

Casa Bonita is a wonderful place to take your family for an evening of dining and entertainment. Parents will love the Mexican food, and children will appreciate the opportunity to eat their favorites AND to play in the large game room. Dine in the festive atmosphere of a Mexican village, complete with a twenty-foot waterfall, dancing fireflies, and strolling mariachis who serenade guests with their Mexican ballads. Dinner consists of complimentary chips and salsa and heaping portions of your favorite Mexican dishes.

As soon as the meal is over, children will want to make a dash for the game room, a large area filled with party lights and music. An ornate carousel featuring different animals beckons the small ones for a ride. Older children will enjoy skee ball and bank-shot basketball (tickets may be redeemed for prizes). Plenty of arcade games are available, including a fortune telling machine similar to the one in the Tom Hanks movie, *Big*. On weekends, a puppet show is performed in the puppet theater; check the calendar for performance times. Casa Bonita also has a gift shop featuring pinatas, jewelry, and more.

## Celebration Station

*4518 East Skelly Drive, (918) 493-3331. When traveling east on I-44, take the Yale exit; Celebration Station is on the service road, almost directly aligned with this exit. Turn right onto the entrance road and follow it south to the front of the complex. When traveling west on I-44, take the Yale exit and turn south, under the expressway. Continue south through the intersection, and turn right at the Celebration Station sign, immediately behind the gas station. Follow this entrance* road past Don Pablo's restaurant, turning left to enter the parking lot. Access is also possible from 51st Street. Hours vary according to season; call to verify. A variety of admission promotion packages is available. Call for information. All-You-Can-Ride Wristbands can be purchased for $10.78 (including tax) for all ages. (Prices subject to change.)

Both young and old alike will enjoy playing games at Celebration Station. Built to resemble a child's dream of Wonderland, Celebration Station is a fantasyland of fountains, rivers and hot air balloons.

For more entertainment, step inside and find a multitude of arcade and video games. Try your skill (or luck) playing everything from sophisticated media games to simple toss-and-score amusements. Stop at the snack bar and enjoy hot dogs, pizza and other favorites. If you have trouble finding a place to sit, eat in the theater and watch the Dixie Diggers, a life-size animated band. Step outdoors for activities such as miniature golf, go-carts, bumper boats, batting cages, and even a playland area featuring rides for little tykes.

### Helpful Hints

With advance notice, birthday parties, group outings and fund-raisers can be arranged. Birthday parties must have a minimum of six participants, and party rooms are reserved for two hours. Take along extra money; even though promotional packages include game tokens, almost every child will want more.

Special rates are available for groups with a minimum of fifteen guests; group reservations are required.

## Chainsaw Sculptures of Clayton Coss

*The sculptures are scattered throughout the city. A listing of several easily-accessible sculptures follows. A local guide, "In the Trees of Tulsa," can be purchased in area bookstores for $18.95. If you're unfamiliar with Tulsa, look in the Tulsa telephone directory or pick up a Tulsa street map at a local bookstore or car rental agency. Remember that streets running East-West are numbered, streets running North-South are in alphabetical order. North-South streets east of Main are named after cities east of the Mississippi River; streets west of Main are named after cities west of the Mississippi. Carvings owned by individuals are on private property, and they should be regarded as privately-owned works of art. Please do not enter the yards for a closer look or to take photographs without the owners' permission.*

As you travel through Tulsa, be sure to keep your eyes open for the chainsaw creations of Clayton Coss, one of Tulsa's better-known artists. Using his chainsaw, Coss has created bears, eagles, cardinals, macaws, raccoons, pelicans and dolphins. He's carved boys with baseball bats, men with fishing poles, and children with their favorite pets. He's sculpted Mother Teresa, St. Francis of Assisi, and a victorious Vietnam veteran. Coss strives for realism. As the artist states, "The more realistic the piece, the more unbelievable it is that it was done with a chainsaw." Each piece is special, with a unique story to match.

**Sculptures in public places:** Christ the King Church, 16th and Quincy; Utica Square, 21st and Utica; River Parks, 41st and Riverside; Veteran's Park, 18th and Boulder; Expo Square (inside the Expo Building), 21st and New Haven; Letter Carrier's Union meeting hall, 1st and Denver; Gilcrease Museum, 1400 Gilcrease Museum Road; Tulsa Zoo, Mohawk Park.

**Sculptures on private property**, to be viewed from the street: 36th and Atlanta; 36th and Florence; 36th and Delaware: 38th and Toledo; 42nd and Jamestown; 31st and Woodward; 44th Place and Columbia; 39th Place and Delaware; 31st and Woodward; 31st and Peoria; 37th Place and New Haven.

**Sculptures located out of town:** Sapulpa City Hall; Sapulpa High School; Jenks East Elementary; Will Rogers Memorial, Claremore; Honor Heights Park, Muskogee.

## Discovery Zone Fun Center

*9919 East 71st Street, (918) 459-5437. Located at approximately 71st Street and Mingo in the Union Plaza Shopping Center. From Highway 169 take the 71st Street exit and turn west. Discovery Zone is on the right, approximately 1/3 mile from the exit. Monday-Thursday 10-8, Friday 10-9, Saturday 9-9, and Sunday 11-7. Weekday admission is $3.99 plus tax for one- and two-year-olds, $5.99 plus tax for ages three-twelve. Weekend admission is $5.99 for all children. Children twelve months and under and adults are free. Weekday-only annual passes are $49.99 plus tax per child. Look for special price promotions throughout the year. For groups of ten or more, special rates are available by reservation.*

Children love to go to Discovery Zone, where they can climb, crawl and swing! For toddlers, there's a Starter Zone;  and, for young ones under forty inches tall, there is a Mini Zone. These two areas are separate, and bigger children are not allowed. The Mega Zone is for larger kids—even parents. At the back of the building, there is a section of video games and motorized rides. Your children will want to spend hours at DZ!

### Helpful Hints

To make supervision easy, Discovery Zone is arranged so that parents can see the entire play area. Snacks, soft drinks and fruit juices are available at the concession area. For twenty-five cents, lockers are available; knee pads for grown-ups are free. To avoid crowds, visit on weekday mornings. Birthday parties are available for groups of seven or more during the week and ten or more on weekends. Group rentals are available after hours. Reservations are required for parties and groups.

## Discoveryland's "OKLAHOMA!"

*(918) 245-6552. Located ten miles west of Tulsa on West 41st Street. Take I-244 or I-44 to 51st Street exit and go north to 41st Street. Turn west and continue approximately ten miles, passing through a part of Sand Springs locally known as Prattville. Turn right at the big "Discoveryland!" sign. The show runs from Monday-Saturday*

each week from mid-June to mid-August. The park opens at 5:30; dinner is served from 5:30 to 7:30. A performance by Native American dancers begins at 7 p.m.; the Western Musical Review begins at 7:30 p.m.; "OKLAHOMA!" starts at 8 p.m. Adult tickets $14.95; senior citizens $13.95; children under twelve are free. Barbecue Dinners: Adults $7.95, Senior Citizens $7.50, children $4.95. For groups of twenty or more, show tickets are $3 per ticket less, and dinners are $1 less. Group reservations are required. ★ 🅂

Bring your family to Discoveryland for a wonderful evening of entertainment! Start the evening with a delicious ranch-style dinner. After the dinner, take time to visit Aunt Eller's Gift Shop, filled with western crafts and souvenirs, and the Indian Trading Post to purchase Native American art, beadwork and jewelry. Everyone will delight in the pre-show entertainment consisting of Native American dancers, singers performing favorite western songs, cloggers, and square dancers.

At 8 p.m., Discoveryland's talented cast of fifty will perform "OKLAHOMA!", the musical masterpiece by Rodgers and Hammerstein. Originally created for Broadway, the show is even more dramatic in this outdoor setting with live horses, real wagons, and a surrey with "fringe on the top."

### Helpful Hints

Every Saturday night, Discoveryland hosts the Wild West Family Festival. Children enjoy special entertainment and activities such as the Haystack Treasure Hunt.

Tickets are easily accessible during the first month of the show, but most shows are sold out by late July and August. Reservations are required for both the musical and the barbecue dinner before the show.

Even in July, be sure to bring a sweater; the night air can feel cool. Insect repellant will also make the evening more comfortable. If rain is in the forecast, you may bring an umbrella, but the theater's overhang usually keeps most of the audience dry. Seldom does it rain enough to cancel the show.

During intermission, old-fashioned snacks and desserts are available. The cast gathers for pictures and autographs after the production; a photo taken with Curly, Laurie, Ado Annie, Will, or other cast members makes a wonderful memento of the evening. The show ends around 11 p.m.

## Downtown Tulsa Mystery

*Located in downtown Tulsa, on the Boston Avenue pedestrian bridge that links Archer and First Street.*

Expect the unexpected. This is not a tourist site or a public event. Instead, it is simply a little mystery that's fun to explore if you happen to be in the area. As you walk across the pedestrian bridge that passes over the railroad tracks, notice the brick circle in the center of the walk. In the very middle of this brick circle is a worn concrete center that seems to possess unusual qualities. When you are standing in the very center of the circle and talking to someone nearby, listen for unusual voice distortions, similar to an echo. Observers don't hear anything unusual. When you step outside the circle, your voice returns to normal.

Architects speculate that the design of the bridge and the proximity of nearby planters create the effect. Others aren't sure what the causal factors are. It's a fun phenomena to explore if you get the chance. Be sure to take your camera, too. The nearby sculpture "Artificial Cloud" by Robert Haozous, makes an interesting picture with the Williams Center Tower as a backdrop.

## The Fenster Museum of Jewish Art

*1223 East 17th Place (17th Place and Peoria in the B'nai Emunah Synagogue), (918) 582-3732. From I-44, take the Peoria exit and go north to 17th Place. Parking is located on the west side of the building. Open Sunday-Thursday 10-4. Closed Friday, Saturday and all Jewish holidays. Admission is free.* ★

The largest collection of ceremonial and aesthetic Judaica in the Southwest is on display at the Fenster Museum of Jewish Art. Interpretive, well-explained exhibits are rotated regularly. Some exhibits show artifacts that are considered sacred (those that signify the ceremonial events in a person's life), and other displays show items that are simple expressions of faith (represented by everyday objects). The Torah Scrolls are the most sacred items in the museum. Treasurers in this museum span 4,000 years of Jewish Heritage. The most moving exhibit recalls the Holocaust.

The purpose of the museum is to "encourage understanding between people of all religions through an appreciation of their common history and values." This museum is both educational and inspirational.

### Helpful Hints

Be sure to ask the knowledgeable and helpful museum staff members if you or your children do not understand parts of the exhibits. They are happy to answer questions and provide information regarding Jewish culture and heritage. With advance notice, docents are available to present "hands-on" explanations for young children. For younger children, this stop will take only about forty-five minutes; older children and anyone with an interest in history may want to stay longer.

For group reservations, call ahead two weeks. To avoid crowds, call ahead to see if other groups are scheduled.

## Frankoma Pottery

*2400 Frankoma Road, Sapulpa. Take I-44 west to Route 66 and continue to Sapulpa. Turn north (right) at the first light onto Frankoma Road. Follow this road to the factory and showroom, located on the eastside. The gift shop is open Monday-Saturday 9-5; tours are held at 9:30, 10:30, 11:00, 11:30, 1:00, 1:30, and 2:00. There is no admission.*

In 1927, John Frank, the creator of Frankoma Pottery, moved from Chicago to Oklahoma. Initially, Mr. Frank taught art and pottery at the University of Oklahoma. Utilizing knowledge gained from the Southest Indians and using a special clay found on Sugar Loaf Mountains in Sapulpa, Frank developed a unique product—pottery that keeps food and beverages warmer than similar items and is easy to maintain. This distinctive pottery has been sold in Oklahoma and around the world for over forty years!

## Helpful Hints

A tour of the factory is a "must do" activity for families visiting the Tulsa area. Tours are twenty minutes and can accommodate twenty people at a time. Watch as local artisans mold, trim and glaze pieces of pottery. After the tour, spend time looking for bargains and special pieces in the gift shop. For group reservations, call several weeks prior to your visit.

If you are visiting Frankoma Pottery in the morning, plan a stop at **Norma's Cafe**. Located just past the stoplight on the main road into town, Norma's serves the best cinnamon toast around!

## Gilcrease Museum

*1400 Gilcrease Museum Road, (918) 596-2700. From Highway 51 West take the Gilcrease Museum Road exit and go north to Newton (or from I-244 or Highway 75 go north on the Osage Expressway to Pine). Go west on Pine to Gilcrease Museum Road and turn left. The museum is located just south of the intersections of Pine and Gilcrease Museum Road (formerly 25th West Avenue). Tuesday-Saturday 9-5. Sunday and federal holidays 11-5. Also open Mondays from Memorial Day to Labor Day 9-5. Closed Christmas Day. Admission is by donation; recommended adult donation is $3, family donation $5. Memberships are available.*

Visit Gilcrease Museum to see an extensive, world-renowned collection of western art and artifacts. After traveling in Europe, founder and oilman Thomas Gilcrease realized that not enough of American's Western history and culture had been preserved so he began his own private collection. The Gilcrease collection records the development of man on the North American continent. Life in the American West is well documented in displays including everything from pre-Columbian artifacts and a certified copy of the Declaration of Independence to the rugged sculptures of Frederick Remington and the often-humorous art of Charlie Russell.

In the summer of 1995, the museum opened a permanent exhibition featuring the museum's Mexican artifacts. The gallery has several interactive displays that appeal to children. Exhibits feature both audio and video stations, activity stations, stone work reproductions, and "Please Touch!" objects. Children use flip books to clarify the use of various articles, and they rub icons to help trace their progress through the exhibit. In an effort to reveal the many cultural aspects of Mexico, children are allowed to touch, hold, match, and replicate items normally contained under glass.

All galleries are interesting, but those focusing on Native Americans, early-American history, and cowboys generally attract the most attendtion from young visitors. Children especially enjoy the visible storage area downstairs with Native American pottery, baskets, headdresses, and more. They also like the recreated artist's studio. When you need to rest, visit the Vista Room and take a moment to view the lovely hills and surrounding countryside.

## Helpful Hints

Several gardens are located outside the museum. Covering twenty-three of the museum's 460 acres, they represent significant gardening developments in North America. Founder Thomas Gilcrease enjoyed maintaining the grounds himself, and he was once mistaken as the hired groundskeeper. At the front desk, you may request a brochure describing the gardens.

In the springtime, the museum hosts the **Gilcrease Rendezvous**. Dating back to the 1800s, rendezvous gatherings were held by groups of mountain men in order to trade, socialize, and hold friendly competitions. This camp-like atmosphere is recreated during this event on the grounds of Gilcrease Museum. At the event, mountainmen show off their shooting accuracy, and Native Americans pitch tepees with great speed; storytellers fascinate crowds with their tall tales, and traders gladly display their merchandise. Visitors are encouraged to participate in all activities. This is a great opportunity for children to "relive history."

Throughout the year, Gilcrease Museum hosts special traveling exhibits. From February 8 through May 10, 1998, the museum will host a major retrospective exhibition of the American landscape painter, Thomas Moran. For more information about this exhibit and others, call the museum.

The museum also has a beautiful gift shop offering a variety of items such as art work, jewelry and publications. Many items, both unusual and reasonably-priced, may be purchased as souvenirs or gifts.

At 2 p.m. daily, the museum offers free public tours given by museum docents. To arrange a group tour, call (918) 596-2705 two weeks before you visit. If it is not possible for you to take the tour, be sure to pick up the gallery guide.

Gilcrease

*Hands-on art at Gilcrease.*

The **Rendezvous Restaurant** is located on site. Lunch is served Tuesday through Saturday 11-2, and brunch is served on Sunday beginning at 11. Menu selection is varied, and all items are reasonably priced. If you'd rather enjoy the great outdoors, bring your own picnic lunch to enjoy the Gilcrease gardens; benches are scattered throughout the grounds.

Special art classes for children are held during the summer and during winter and spring break. Call in advance for a brochure; registration is required and class size is limited. Gilcrease provides speakers to various civic and school groups. For information about the Speakers Bureau, call (918) 596-2705.

## Hands-On !! Children's Museum

*Currently being relocated, the museum should reopen in 1997, during late summer or early fall. Call (918) 712-2228 for information regarding hours, admissions, and food service availability.*

Tulsa children love Hands-On!!, an interactive, educational museum designed for children ages two through nine. Young people can explore different countries and cultures, view a Native American village, visit a fire station and a doctor's office, and play in a mock grocery store and restaurant. Children also enjoy the face-painting station, the giant bubble-maker, and much more. Arrangements can also be made for groups and birthday parties. Hands-On!! is a fun way to spend a day!

## Harmon Science Center

*5707 E. 41st Street, (918) 622-5000. Located on the corner of 41st Street and Hudson Avenue. From I-44 take the 41st Street exit and go west to Hudson. Turn north on Hudson then immediately turn right into the parking lot.* Admission is $5 for everyone over age three (cash only). Call the Science Center's main number to verify hours, group rates, and to acquire a listing of upcoming events. ★*

At this exciting science and math museum, children turn, twist, and manipulate the levers and dials on countless mechanical exhibits. Run a timed race with a cougar or a rabbit and crawl through the simulated tunnels of downtown Tulsa. Watch a demonstration of a heat pump, or create and tape your own weather forecast. Experience the sensation of travel as you sit inside the Simulated Ride Vehicle, or view the visiting and rotating exhibits that come to the museum on a regular basis. But shhhhh. . . don't tell your children that they're learning math and science!

Each weekend, the science center hosts Science Sunday. Beginning at 2 p.m. Sunday afternoon, special programs with guest presenters are available to the public. Topics are announced by voice mail (918-622-5000) or in the local paper. Harmon Science Center is open during the week for school field trips and home school outings. Special arrangements

*Harmon Science Center.*

can be made for birthday parties, scouting merit badges, and group overnights.

## Hockey Coliseum

*65th and Mingo, (918) 459-8203. From Highway 169 take the 61st Street exit and travel west. At Mingo, turn south. The rink is located approximately 1/2 mile ahead, on the east side of the street. Call to verify admission and hours (public skate times vary), and call for class offerings and schedules.*

Several years ago, Connie Baldwin's son wanted to be the goalie on his youth hockey team. Noticing a lack of equipment suppliers in the Tulsa area, she opened her own store. Three years later, she opened her own rink. The new rink and future home of the Tulsa Youth Hockey Association meets the size requirements of the National Hockey League. Locker rooms, a video room, concession stand, and pro shop are additional features of this new facility. The upstairs deck provides bleacher seating for observers. Two of the Tulsa Oiler players are affiliated with the Coliseum. In addition to skating lessons and hockey camps, clinics and schools for all ages are offered. Men's leagues and all-girl teams play here as well.

## The Ida Dennis Willis Museum of Miniatures, Dolls and Toys

*628 North Country Club Drive. From Highway 51 West, take the Gilcrease Museum Road exit and turn north, continuing to Edison. Go east on Edison past the golf course at Tulsa Country Club, and turn left onto Country Club Drive. The museum is in a renovated mansion on the left. Wednesday-Saturday 10:30-4:30. Closed Sunday, Monday, Tuesday, and holidays. Adults $3, children ages seventeen and younger $2. Memberships are available. ★*

You and your children will be amazed by this collection of dolls and doll houses. Featuring every kind of doll from handmade folk dolls to dainty porcelain figurines, this museum celebrates dolls and the special relationship that girls have with them. Pop-up storybooks sit open beside character dolls who look as if they've stepped from the pages. Baby dolls lay in bassinets and strollers, awaiting the loving hands of a "mother" to take care of them. Especially fun are the promotional dolls from the past that were marketed to promote a particular product; Coke and Green Giant vegetables are both represented. Doll houses abound; from the inexpensively mass-produced to the painstakingly handmade, all of them are works of art.

### Helpful Hints

Plan to spend about an hour at this museum. Reservations are required for groups. Mrs. Willis runs the museum. Children can often tour the museum with her, listening to her stories and enjoying her elementary-school teacher-style of explanation. With advance notice, Mrs. Willis will prepare a presentation featuring dolls and information on a particular subject. Mrs. Willis has a wonderful way of imparting knowledge of antique dolls and toys and her love for collecting.

## Laser Quest Tulsa

*2909 South Sheridan Road (Boman Acres Shopping Center), (918) 663-5551. Monday, Wednesday and Thursday, 6-10, Tuesday, members only 6-10, Friday, 4-midnight, Saturday, noon to midnight, and Sunday, 1-10. Cost is $6/game. Membership $20/year, $10 to renew; members pay $5/game. Group rates and birthday party packages are available. Free parking.*

Laser Quest's slogan is "You don't just play the game . . . you're in it!" Recommended for ages seven to seventy-seven, laser tag is a live-action game that combines tag with hide and seek. Choose a code name, such as Darth Vadar, strap on your harness, then enter the arena and prepare for twenty minutes of intense fun. A dark maze filled with fog and music sets the stage for heart-pounding excitement. Each participant receives a laser weapon with unlimited ammunition (laser bullets). The object is to make more hits on others while you are getting hit as few times as possible. At the end of each game, scores are posted for each code name.

Birthday party packages are available. For $10 a person, the packages include two laser quest missions per person, a "2-for-1" pass per person for future use, a Laser Quest gift for the birthday person, and the use of a private party room. Parties must be booked in advance, and a 50% deposit is required.

Other activities at Laser Quest include video games, bank-shot basketball, air hockey, billiards, and a picture booth.

## LaFortune Park

*5501 South Yale, (918) 596-8627. LaFortune Park is located between 51st and 61st Streets, Yale and Hudson Avenues. From Yale, parking is available in the lots at 52nd, 55th and 58th Streets. Smaller lots provide limited parking off Hudson Avenue. Open daily 7 a.m.-11 p.m. Admission is free.*

Take your family to LaFortune Park and enjoy this gift of gratitude donated to the city of Tulsa from one of its early citizens. About 1918, R.A. LaFortune arrived in Tulsa. He worked briefly as a newspaperman, but his success came as an oilman. In 1958, Mr. LaFortune purchased a 270-acre tract of land at a cost of $250,000, and donated the land to the city to be used as a park. Today, visitors can play golf, tennis and baseball, or swim, jog and picnic at this wonderful park.

Tennis and golf are popular at the park. Two golf courses are located at this park, the par 72 Championship Golf Course and the only eighteen-hole, lighted Par 3 course in the region. Call the Pro Shop at (918) 596-8627 for tee times and more information. A tennis complex is located along Hudson Avenue.

Beat the Oklahoma heat by diving into the Olympic-size swimming pool. The pool's shallow end is approximately four feet deep and two diving boards are located in the deep end. Near the larger pool is a kiddie pool. An enclosed snack area offers treats for hungry swimmers. Admission is adults $2, children ages six through eleven $1.50. Children under six are free.

Baseball players can practice their skills at the ball field complex on 58th Street. Fields are usually scheduled for league play, but they are available for practice on a first-come, first-served basis. For those future baseball greats, batting cages are located nearby. Hours are Monday-Friday 9-3, Saturday 10-9 and Sunday 12-9. Call (918) 481-6688 for price information.

Small children enjoy feeding the ducks and geese at the "big pond," located next to the Community Center. Families will enjoy the many sensory ways to enjoy nature by visiting The Gardens. This special area contains a flowering arbor and sensory garden that features aromatic plants with unusual textures. Braille identification plates have been placed for the visually impaired. An exercise course for those confined to wheelchairs is nearby. Also located in The Gardens is a croquet and lawn bowling green. Call the Community Center at (918) 596-8620 for more information or to reserve this area for a group.

Children enjoy the picnic shelters and playgrounds found in the park's center section and at the southwest corner of the park. Children can climb, crawl, swing, and slide on this equipment or spend time exploring the nearby rocks and creek. Family gatherings, church outings and high school reunions are held at the park on a regular basis. Shelter reservations are taken for weekends and holidays as far as a year in advance. A nonrefundable payment is due two weeks in advance. Reserve shelters by calling (918) 596-5990.

The Community Center offers classes ranging from cooking to karate. Pick up a schedule of classes which comes out every quarter in a regularly-published newsletter. Day camps, home school activities, and special events for children are also offered. The Community Center can also be rented for private events during special hours. Call (918) 596-8620 for more information.

## Mac's Antique Car Museum

*1319 East Fourth (4th Street and Peoria), (918) 583-7400. From Highway 51 (Broken Arrow Expressway) take the Peoria exit and go north to 4th Street. Mac's antique cars are housed in the white brick building with bright red letters on the east side of the street. Open Saturday and Sunday, 12-5. Group tours are available weekdays by appointment. Adults $3.75, children ages six to twelve $2.*

Mac McGlumphy has always treasured cars, especially those built before World War II. Now the successful owner of Mac's Electric Supply Company, he's been collecting vintage automobiles for several years and, in the early 1990s, he opened his collection to the public. The museum covers 2,000 square feet and houses forty-five classic automobiles. Mac's oldest car is a 1912 Model T Depot Hack, and his favorite cars are his six Packards, one of which is worth more than $400,000. These classic cars feature sleek exterior paint jobs and hand-worked interiors.

Mac's Antique Car Museum is a great place for grandparents to go with their grandchildren. Take time to visit with Mac; he has some great stories to share!

## McLean's Historic Home

*Located in Jenks, which is ten miles south of downtown Tulsa on U.S. Highway 75 (take the Jenks Road exit and drive east into Jenks). The home is located at 123 E. "A" Street, (918) 446-2745 or (918) 299-8634. From Main Street in Jenks, turn north on 1st and go one block to "A" Street. The McLean home is on the corner. Tours of the home are on Saturday afternoon from 1-5 and on other days by appointment. Adults $2, children $1. Adults who tour the home, then return later with a guest, are admitted free. Melinda Bennett, Dr. McLean's great niece, is the curator.*

Look back in history as you visit Dr. McLean's home, located at 123 E. "A" Street. Dr. McLean's father-in-law and brother-in-law built the home in 1913. It was used as a home and a doctor's office. The house has been restored to reflect the furnishings and accessories of the 1930s. Equally fascinating is the display of medical equipment used by the doctor.

### Helpful Hints

The Jenks area is known as the "Antique Capital of the World." Families with older children will enjoy the numerous quaint shops in downtown Jenks. Maps of the downtown area listing stores, malls, and eating establishments are available in most shops or at the Jenks Chamber of Commerce (918) 299-5005. Most stores are open Tuesday through Saturday 10-5. A few shops are open on Sunday and Monday. Some stores are open by appointment. Most stores accommodate strollers, but toddlers should be closely supervised. Picnic areas are available at the city park located at Main Street and North Elm.

Before you visit Jenks, check the community calendar for special events such as the **Jenks Country Fair** in June, and the **Teddy Bear Convention** and the **Holiday Open House**, both held in November.

## Mohawk Park

*36th Street North and Sheridan. For more information, call Tulsa Parks and Recreation Department at (918) 596-7877 or 596-PARK. From I-244 or Highway 11 take the Sheridan Road exit and go north to 36th Street North. Turn right onto 36th Street North and then immediately left into the park entrance. Open daily, 5 a.m.-9 p.m. $1 seasonal parking fee.*

With more than 2,800 acres, Mohawk Park has more to see and do in one day than is possible for families with small children; it may take several trips to take in all the activities here! The Oxley Nature Center (see page 103), the Tulsa Zoo (see page 113), two golf courses, and a polo field are included in the park. Also, there are horseback riding trails, a hiking trail, playgrounds, and picnic shelters. It's no wonder that this park has become a favorite spot for family picnics and church outings!

A variety of **special events** (from powwows to rock concerts) are staged here each year. In the spring, children compete in the **Zebco Fishing Derby**. On warm, breezy days, children bring their kites to the park.

If you are planning a group outing, call ahead to reserve a shelter. Depending on which shelter is reserved, up to forty-five people can be accommodated. There is no charge for reservations.

Two golf courses are located in the park. For more information about the golf courses or to arrange tee times, call (918) 425-6871.

## Oral Roberts University

*7777 South Lewis, (918) 495-6807. From I-44 go south on Lewis to the university entrance, the Avenue of Flags. Follow the drive to the right and park in the parking lot. Monday-Saturday 10:30-4:30, Sunday 1-5. Admission is free. The university is handicapped accessible.*

An accredited institution, Oral Roberts University offers its 4,000 students almost seventy undergraduate degrees and four graduate and professional schools. ORU started in 1963 with only three small buildings; it is currently considered one of the most architecturally-unique campuses in the world.

Various departments at the school offer performances open to the public;

many are held in the beautiful Mabee Center. For an events calendar, call (918) 495-6400, or call the Student Activities Office or the School of Arts and Sciences for information about upcoming events.

The University sponsors varsity sports at the NCAA Division I level. Basketball, baseball, tennis, golf, soccer, track, and women's volleyball are offered and games are open to the public. Ticket prices range from $1-10, depending on the sport and the age of the spectator. Tickets to all sporting events can be purchased at the athletic ticket office or at the gate.

## Oxley Nature Center

*Located within Mohawk Park at 36th Street North and Sheridan Road. From I-244 or Highway 11 take the Sheridan Road exit and go north to 36th Street North. Turn right onto 36th Street North, and then immediately left into the park. Drive the main road through the park, past the zoo to the Oxley Nature Center entrance. Turn right and pass through the gate to the parking area outside the center. The nature trails are open daily 8-5; the nature center is open Monday-Saturday 10-4:30 and Sunday 12-4:30. Admission is free.*

Located in northeast Tulsa, this 800-acre wildlife refuge allows guests to observe wildlife in its natural habitat. Start your tour in the **Nature Center**, where visitors can view interesting and educational exhibits that serve as an introduction to the world outdoors. Next, venture outside for a hike along one of the Center's seven nature trails, each named for elements that can be found on each hike. The Red Fox and Blue Heron Trails are more developed and have printed trail guides. They are handicapped accessible. The remaining trails, Green Dragon Trail (a wildflower), Blackbird Marsh Trail, Beaver Lodge Trail, Coal Creek Trail, and Lake Trail, are more primitive. There are also trails to the Wildlife Study Area and the North Woods.

### Helpful Hints

For your best chance to observe wildlife, visit this unique retreat early on a spring morning or at dusk on an autumn day.

Call to ask about special tours and events, or to be included on the Center's mailing list. The best way to enjoy the trails is by a group tour, led by a naturalist from the center. Tours are held on a regularly-scheduled basis; you may also form your own group of six or more and call for reservations. Special classes are offered periodically and require advance registration. Some may even charge a small fee.

## Paint'n Place

*8179 S. Harvard Avenue, (918) 491-6900. Located at the southeast corner of 81st and Harvard, one mile east of Oral Roberts University. Winter hours: Monday-Wednesday, and Friday-Saturday 10-6, Thursday 10-8, and Sunday 1-5. Summer hours: Monday-Saturday 10-8 and Sunday 1-5. The studio is handicapped accessible.*

Children will love to be creative at the Paint'n Place. Bright colors of red, yellow, green, purple, and blue are splattered on the walls, creating a festive atmosphere and stimulating young artists' imaginations. The colorful surroundings, along with the helpful teachers, provide the perfect environment for future artists.

The Paint'n Place carries an extensive line of ceramic figurines and other items that may be painted, preserved, then taken home to be admired and/ or used for years. Children are welcome to paint at the studio on a regular basis. Selections of figurines range from small animals ($3) to large gargoyles ($60). Prices are reasonable because all pieces are created from start to finish at the studio.

Instructors from the Paint'n Place regularly attend scout meetings, day care centers and school classes. They bring paints, brushes, smocks, and numerous ceramic figurines. Children are closely supervised as they select their ceramics, choose their colors, and create their masterpieces. Once completed, the pieces are sprayed with a gloss ceramic sealer, making them safe to take home.

This activity is fun for the entire family. Although the studio originally opened as a place for children, parents soon became interested in painting ceramic pieces of their own. Unique creations such as custom-painted plates, mugs, canisters, and vases are just some of the favorite items adults that like to fashion for their own homes or as gifts for friends.

### Helpful Hints

The Paint'n Place is a popular spot for birthday parties. For $6 per child, children are allowed to select and paint their own figurine. Tables are provided for the party but you must bring your own birthday cake and ice cream. Call for more details.

## Perryman Wrangler Ranch

*11524 South Elwood Avenue, Jenks, (918) 299-2997. From Tulsa, go south on Highway 75 to 111th Street South. Turn left (east) onto 111th and continue to Elwood. Turn south onto Elwood and travel to the ranch entrance. Hours are by appointment. Call ahead to make reservations for company outings, group dinners, hayrides, and birthday parties. $4 per person, or priced by event.*

Go back in history as you visit the Perryman Wrangler Ranch. Only 280 acres remain as a working ranch of the once-extensive holdings of the Perryman family. Currently owned by the heirs of the Perrymans, the home and land are operated as a dude ranch by Wes Dickinson. A wide range of activities is available for groups and a variety of entertainment is offered for large gatherings. After visiting here, you'll understand the special appeal of a "home on the range."

Call Wes for information and prices. Because a large number of activities are offered here, each activity must be individually negotiated. Call several weeks in advance for birthday parties and several months in advance for group bookings. A deposit is required. Be sure to verify terms and conditions for refunds.

## Philbrook Museum of Art

*2727 South Rockford Road, (918) 749-7941 or (800) 324-7941. Located approximately one block east of Peoria on 27th Place. From Peoria, turn east onto 27th Place and continue one block to the parking lot. Free parking in the museum lot.*

Open Tuesday-Saturday 10-5 (open Thursday evenings until 8), Sunday 1-5. Docent tours are available to the public at 2 p.m. each Sunday. Closed Mondays and major holidays. General adult admission is $4 plus tax; free to members and children ages twelve and under. Admission for students with I.D. and seniors age sixty-two and over is $2 plus tax. Group tours can be arranged by calling (918) 748-5309 at least two weeks in advance. A wide variety of art classes for both young and old is offered through the Floyd Museum School. Call (918) 748-5374 for specific class information. No admission is charged to those who visit only the museum shop, restaurant or grounds. Memberships, with a host of benefits, are available. This museum is handicapped accessible. ★ 🚹

Elaine Warner

*The gardens at Philbrook.*

Villa Philbrook, the home of oil man Waite Phillips and his wife Genevieve, was designed as an Italian Renaissance home overlooking twenty-three acres of gardens. After living in the home for eleven years, the Phillips' donated the elaborate home to the citizens of Tulsa to be used as an art museum.

This beautifully-appointed home-turned-museum showcases Philbrook's permanent collections of European, Ancient, Asian, twentieth-century American, African, and Native American art and artifacts. Special exhibitions are held in the new 150,000-square-foot Kravis Wing, built in 1990. Exhibitions include not only art but information about the culture represented by the art and the artist. Children will enjoy both the lovely home and the art work, but they must be closely supervised if they and other patrons are to have an enjoyable experience. Young people enjoy art, especially when it is presented on their level. Before you go, think of games to play such as imitating the people in the painting and picking out your favorites. These kinds of activities will help involve the children in what they're seeing, making the visit more interactive and exciting.

Art class at Philbrook.

After viewing the art, enjoy the manicured and incredibly-beautiful gardens surrounding the museum. The landscaped gardens include a terraced garden, a rock garden, and a reflecting pool. The gardens provide an excellent opportunity for children to relax after being on their "best behavior." Information to share with your children about the gardens and its plantings are found on plaques throughout the grounds. Audio tapes for self-guided tours are also available for rent.

This museum is one of only three in America with the unique combination of historic home, collections, gardens, and the interpretations of different cultures. Philbrook is "your window on the world."

### Helpful Hints

Call the Education Office at (918) 748-5309 to ask about the **art classes** offered for families and children. You may also ask about special exhibits or events that may be scheduled.

The **Museum Shop** offers beautiful gifts and souvenirs, along with a guide to the collections, villa and gardens. For "fancy" family dining, try the museum's

**la Villa Restaurant**. The beautiful restaurant overlooks the sculpture garden and offers lunch and Sunday brunch.

A picnic lunch can be eaten on the south lawn. Please remember to bring a sack to carry out your trash. Fast food restaurants are located only a short distance away on Peoria Avenue.

## Playhouse for Kidz

*825 West Houston, Broken Arrow, (918) 258-7006. Located on the southwest corner of the intersection at 161st Street East and 81st Street South, this play place is easy to reach. From Highway 51 (Broken Arrow Expressway) take the 161st Street exit. (In Broken Arrow this street is called Elm Place.) Go south to 81st Street and turn right into the shopping center. Open Saturday 10-7, Sunday 1-6; call for available hours Monday-Friday. Admission is $5.95 for the first child, $4.95 for the second child, and $3.95 for each additional child. Group discounts for groups of ten to twenty are $4 per person, and groups of twenty or more are $3 per person.*

Children love to spend the afternoon at the Playhouse for Kidz. The Playhouse has one of the biggest indoor play toys around. They can climb cargo nets from one level to another or crawl through tunnels to reach steep slides. The newest attraction is the Bungee Run. A harness is placed around the child's waist, then the child runs down a padded area until the bungee pulls him/her back. The more adventurous may choose to take a spin in the Space Ball. This ride is similar to a piece of equipment used to train entry-level astronauts at NASA.

Two separate play areas are available. One area is limited to young children from ages two to five; the other area is for children ages six to twelve. Seating for parents is conveniently located between the two areas. Staff attendants not only help supervise the play activity, but often join in as well. Kids may want to take a break from climbing and crawling to play arcade games or air hockey. There is also a concession area and a TV lounge.

### Helpful Hints

Socks and comfortable clothing are suggested for climbing and crawling. Parents are encouraged to take part in the fun. Check the Tulsa phone book or one of the local fund-raising coupon books for discount admission. Call ahead to find out about weekly daytime specials. To avoid crowds, check the group schedule or visit on a weekday. The Playhouse for Kidz is a wonderful place for birthday parties. Call in advance to reserve one of two party areas.

## Redbud Valley Nature Preserve

*Approximately 161st Street East and Pine, (918) 669-6460 or 669-6644. From I-244 go west to 161st East Avenue. Turn left under the expressway and left again at the stop sign. Go west around the truck stop and then north on 161st East Avenue for three to four miles. Watch for the signs. Maintained by Tulsa Parks and Recreation Department. The nature preserve is open Wednesday-Sunday 8-5; the Visitor's Center is open from 11-3. Closed Monday, Tuesday and holidays. Admission is free.*

Three geographical land forms converge in this near-urban setting covering

220 acres. The preserve consists of fertile bottom land, limestone bluffs, and western prairie. All three areas can be observed from the primary one-mile hiking trail. Cottonwoods, maples, elms, and oaks grow in the fertile bottom-land. In the valley, redbuds create a colorful sight in spring. Mysterious caves can be found in the bluffs. From the bluffs, find an opening among the trees. Look over the prairie and view the change from fertile woodland to open prairie. What a beautiful sight!

### Helpful Hints

Since the trails are primitive, hiking is rugged and, in places, difficult. The trails are recommended only for adults and children ages five and up. Hiking boots or sturdy tennis shoes are suggested. Take a cooler full of juice and water to quench your thirst after the hike.

Rules at the preserve are strictly enforced. No pets or fires are allowed. Picnicking is allowed only near the Visitors Center. Nature lovers should bring a wildflower guide, but they should be sure not to pick any samples. Remember to keep children on the trail. The beauty of the preserve depends on the pristine quality of the area. Restrooms are located next to the Visitors Center.

## River Parks

*Located along both banks of the Arkansas River and maintained by the River Parks Authority. The east side of the park runs from 11th Street on the north to 81st Street south, with playgrounds at 19th Street and 41st Street. The west side begins at 11th Street on the north and runs south to 31st Street with an Old West Playground located in between. Admission is free. A curfew is enforced from 11p.m.-5a.m.*

Beginning in Leadville, Colorado, the crystal-clear Arkansas River runs eastward down the mountains. Making its way through the plains, the river slows as it spreads across the land and becomes the wide (although sometimes shallow) waterway of Tulsa.

Because of its saltiness, the river was used for only a short time as a source of water for the city; however, the river provides many recreational opportunities for Tulsans. On any given day, you may watch joggers, bicyclists and roller bladers as they take advantage of the trail that runs along the east side of the river.

The historic center of the park is located at 31st Street and Riverside. Here, the Midland Valley Railroad built a bridge across the Arkansas River. When it was no longer needed, the railroad donated the bridge to the City of Tulsa. Now known as the Pedestrian Bridge, it links the east and west banks of the river. Below the bridge, Zink Dam has been constructed to create a small lake upstream where rowing, canoeing and sculling is permitted. With its jets of water shooting sky high, Blair Fountain is the scenic focal point of this area.

The Old West Playground is located on the West Bank halfway between 11th and 31st Street. It features a child-size version of a western town and fun and unusual playground equipment. Also located on the West Bank is the Reynolds Amphitheatre, the park's floating stage with seating for 3,000 spectators. Crowds gather to hear popular entertainers at concert prices, or spend an evening un-

River Parks

*The River Parks floating stage.*

der the stars, free of charge, listening to Tulsa's own Starlight Band, a community band which plays music ranging from popular to patriotic.

Throughout the year, River Parks offers numerous special events, including the annual **Easter Egg Hunt** and the **Sand Castle Building Contest** in July. For more information, call the River Parks Authority or check the local newspaper.

Picnic tables and benches are scattered throughout the park. The Rivers Edge Bistro and Cafe, located at 19th Street, is the only restaurant on the river. Open daily year round, the cafe serves salads and sandwiches for lunch and dinner. Restrooms are available at 19th, 31st, 41st, and 56th Streets.

## The Spotlight Theater, "The Drunkard"

*1381 Riverside Drive, (918) 587-5030. Located on the edge of downtown, the theater is on the corner of Riverside Drive and Houston. Parking is available on adjacent streets. Performances are held on Saturdays only, with group singing at 8; curtain at 8:15. The theater is available for private performances. $8.50 per person, groups of six to nine $8.25 per person, groups larger than ten $7.75 per person. Group tickets must be purchased at one time, at least twenty-four hours in advance.*

Families will love the audience participation at this melodrama production, Tulsa's longest-running continuous program. Prior to the start of the show, a sing-along is held featuring some of America's favorite songs; words are printed in the program, and audience members are encouraged to join in. When the show begins, the audience quickly becomes involved in the story. Boo the villain or scold the drunkard; have compassion for the heroine and applaud the hero. Learn about the evils of drinking through the story. Participation by the audience makes this production a night to remember.

## Helpful Hints

Tulsa's Spotlight Theater was formerly the home and musical studio of an early Tulsa piano teacher. The building was designed by Bruce Goff and is well-known for its Art Deco architecture. Windows and black insets can be found outside of the building above the double staircases. Notice that their placement resembles keys on a piano.

Young people ten and older will enjoy this production. Free coffee and sandwiches are served before the variety show, which features unusual local entertainment. Pretzels are served during the performance. Soft drinks, beer, malt coolers, and sparkling water may be purchased. Be sure to make reservations several days in advance. Tickets may be available the day before the show. However, be aware that the theater is small, and it is often filled with groups, especially during the holidays. Plan to be at the theater until late. If you stay for the Olio (Tulsa's version of Vaudeville), you may not get home until midnight.

## Tulsa Ballet Theater

*Performances are held at Tulsa's downtown Performing Arts Center (call for directions); TBT's office is located at 4512 South Peoria, (918) 749-6030. From I-44 take the Peoria exit and go south on Peoria to 45th Street. Continue south, just through the light and turn west into the parking lot. This is the home of Tulsa Ballet Theater. Located here are the ballet company's studios, wardrobe rooms, scenery storage areas, administrative offices, and the guild gift shop. Offices are open Monday-Friday 9-5. Ticket prices for performances range from $11 to $57. Discounted tickets are available for children under age twelve, students, senior citizens, and groups of ten or more. ★*

Watch with amazement as the magic and beauty of ballet comes alive! In 1956, the Tulsa Ballet Theater was founded by Roman Jasinski and Moscelyne Larkin, both principal dancers with the Ballet Russe de Monte Carlo. Although the school and civic ballet started slowly, it now includes thirty professional dancers and a full-time staff of support personnel. Full-length classic ballets as well as entertaining variations and contemporary performance pieces are included in the company's repertoire. The regular season of the Tulsa Ballet Theater includes two fall productions, two spring shows, and a series of *Nutcracker* performances during the Christmas holidays.

### Helpful Hints

Make reservations several weeks in advance in order to obtain the best seats. The Chapman Music Hall at the Performing Arts Center seats 2,300 patrons on three levels, but most audience members prefer to watch the performance from the orchestra or front mezzanine seats. Ten public school performances are held each year. During these presentations, students learn what to look for in a dance performance, and they view an actual ballet.

Children who are fascinated by ballet and theater will enjoy a tour of TBT's facility; call the office in advance to schedule.

## Tulsa Ice Arena

*6910 South 101 East Avenue, (918) 254-7272. From Highway 169 South take the*

*71st Street exit and go west to the first traffic light. Although not visible from the street, Tulsa Ice Arena is located at the end of this small service road. Turn right up the road and, at the end, turn left into the Arena's parking lot. Call for the current schedule. Admission for everyone is $5.50. Skate rental is $1.50. Nonprofit youth organizations and home-school associations receive group rates.*

Glide along the ice with the ease of a professional as you skate in this large arena. The seating area above the ice provides a magnificent view of the skaters and holds approximately four hundred observers. Hockey equipment and skating apparel are available for purchase at the on-site pro shop. Snacks and drinks are for sale in the concession area. Figure skating and hockey lessons are offered on a continuing basis.

The Arena is always busy; call in advance for information regarding skating classes, hockey lessons, puck sessions, public skating, and birthday parties. Call ahead to find out what hours public skating sessions are held; they change from season to season.

You will want to wear warm, comfortable clothing and heavy socks when you go skating. You may bring your own skates or rent a pair at the Arena.

## Tulsa Drillers Baseball

*Games are held in Driller Stadium, 4802 East 15th Street, (918) 744-5901. From 15th Street and Yale, turn west onto 15th Street and go approximately one block to the park entrance. Turn left into the stadium parking lot. The season runs from April to August. Games begin at 7:05 or 7:35, depending on the time of year. Sunday games begin at 2:05 or 6:05. Ticket prices range from $4 to $7. Occasional $1 discounts are given to children ages fourteen and under and seniors. Children ages*

Tulsa CVB

*The Drillers in action.*

*three and under are admitted free if they do not occupy an individual seat. Tickets may be purchased in person at the ticket office, by phone, or by mail. Drillers tickets are also available in advance at any of the four Tulsa Dillard's locations. Call the Driller office for a schedule and details about the games.*

Take part in America's favorite pastime while attending a Tulsa Drillers baseball game. The Drillers are a Class AA farm team of the American League's Texas Rangers. Tulsa's baseball history is closely tied to the oil business. Starting in 1905, after oil was struck in the Glenn Pool, Tulsa was occupied by many oil and oil-related businesses. Tulsa quickly became known as the "Oil Capital of the World" and the city held that title until the 1960s. Professional baseball teams located in Tulsa have carried on the baseball legacy. The Drillers baseball caps display a large capital "T" with a silver derrick gushing oil superimposed over the letter.

Besides the game, there are many activities at the ball park. Gates to the ballpark are opened approximately ninety minutes before the game. From the time the gates open until twenty minutes before the game starts, players and coaches are available for autographs. Concession stands are conveniently located around the stadium, offering everything from hot dogs to nachos and hamburgers to fajitas. For fans interested in showing off their own baseball skills, a speed pitch machine is located along the third base concourse. One dollar buys three pitches, and a correct guess of ball speed on the third pitch wins the participant a batting helmet from his favorite major league team. Just inside the gate, a souvenir stand offers Drillers merchandise along with major league souvenirs.

### Helpful Hints

For groups of twenty-five or more, group rates are offered. Several packages are available for groups, including a picnic buffet prior to the game for groups of fifty or more. For smaller groups (up to twelve people), VIP suites are available. To have birthdays shown on the scoreboard during the seventh inning, write down all necessary information and hand it to an usher before the third inning begins. These requests will be taken on a first-come, first-served basis. Contact the Drillers Group Sales Department if you wish to schedule a birthday party (minimum of fifteen children). For those wishing to avoid beer-drinking fans, a "no alcohol" section is available. Don't bother bringing portable stadium seats; each seat in the stadium now has a back.

Call ahead for a game schedule and promotional offers. Several promotional giveaways occur throughout the season. The first fans in the park may receive anything from hats, bats and gloves, to notebooks, backpacks, and pennants. Other attractions to be enjoyed during the season include fireworks, laser light shows, 25-cent hot dogs, and the Famous Chicken mascot entertainer.

## Tulsa Oilers Hockey

*Tulsa Convention Center (100 Civic Center), (918) 663-5888. To reach downtown, take either I-244 or Highway 51 (the Broken Bow Expressway). If you are approaching Tulsa from the east on I-244, follow the signs for the Downtown-7th Street exit. If you take Highway 51 west into town, follow the signs for Bartlesville, then immediately* take the 7th Street exit which curves up and around into downtown. Go west on 7th Street to Denver. Turn north onto Denver and continue to 6th Street. Turn left onto 6th Street; the Convention Center is on the right in the middle of the block. Paid event parking is available in lots north of the Convention Center. Some fee-based parking is available in lots adjacent to the arena. A skyway connects the Convention Center with parking and the Doubletree Hotel across the street. The schedule runs from October to March. Play begins weeknights at 7, Friday and Saturday at 7:30 and Sunday at 2:30. Adults $8 and $11, children ages twelve and under $6 and $9, children ages two and under are free if they don't occupy a seat. Group discount nights are available. Season tickets are available ($10 discount if paid in full by July 1). Tickets prices subject to change. Call (800) 654-9545 for phone reservations. There is a convenience and shipping charge applied to phone orders.

Hockey has quickly become one of the most popular sports of the decade. Watch in amazement as the Oilers take to the ice for a night of nonstop action. At times, audience participation can be as entertaining as the hockey game itself. As part of the Central Hockey League, the Oilers play teams such as arch-rival Oklahoma City Blazers. For a night of fun and excitement, make the trip to the Tulsa Convention Center to support the Tulsa Oilers.

### Helpful Hints

Concessions and souvenirs are available in the arena concourse. Several promotions are held during the season. To determine if anything will be given away the night of your visit, call the Oilers' business office a week before you go. Should you desire to dine before or after the game, several restaurants are located in the downtown area. A schedule for the Oilers' home games can be obtained by calling the Tulsa Oilers' business office. You may purchase tickets at the office or at any Dillard's Department store in Tulsa. Tickets can also be purchased at the Brady Theater, 10 Southwest Brady Street.

## Tulsa Zoo

5701 East 36th Street North, inside Mohawk Park, 36th Street North and Sheridan Road. From I-244 or Highway 11 take the Sheridan Road exit and go north to 36th Street North. Turn right onto 36th Street North and then immediately left into the park. There is a $1 seasonal parking fee. Once inside follow the main road through the park. The Zoo is visible on the left, with parking and the entrance well-marked. Open daily 10-5. Closed Christmas Day and the third Friday in June. Adults (ages 12-61) $5, senior citizens (ages 62 and over) $4, children ages 5-11 $2, children four and under free. Reduced admission is offered on several holidays and during Polar Bear Days, declared in January and February when the temperature drops to thirty-two degrees or below. Tulsa Zoo Friends, a support and promotional organization of the zoo, offers yearly memberships which include free admission to the zoo, quarterly newsletters, and preview nights for special events. For more information regarding membership, call (918) 669-6603.

Every child loves the zoo and so do the adults who accompany them! For a day of fun and excitement, spend a day at the Tulsa Zoo. Enter the zoo through the new entrance gate, then turn left to the new gift shop, or turn right to the train station and the sidewalk leading to the exhibit buildings. Directly ahead is a small, paved plaza, with engraved bricks. Take time to read the inscriptions— some are humorous, some touching, but they all helped provide funds for the zoo's extensive renovation. Also located here is an events board detailing special presentations, animal feedings, and training sessions. At the plaza, rent a stroller or a wagon to carry your lunch, jackets or camera. The zoo covers seventy acres, and it takes at least two hours to visit; it's an easier task if you're not carrying too much. Strollers rent for $2 and wagons for $3. Feel free to pack a picnic lunch (a shelter and tables are located on the grounds) or have lunch at the Safari Grille. Other concessions are available on a seasonal basis.

As you tour, be sure to read the exhibit labels as you walk through the zoo. They contain information concerning each animal's natural habitat and its current status in the world. Start the tour to the right and visit the **Chimpanzee Connection.** Patrons can see the chimps "up-close and personal," separated only by thick panes of glass. The chimps have access to two playgrounds and freely roam inside and outside. Take a trip across the continent as you enter the **Robert J. LaFortune North American Living Museum.** Four different buildings each represent different regions of our country: Artic tundra, Southwest desert, Eastern forest, and Southern lowlands. Inside the buildings are exhibits about the land, the native culture, and the indigenous wildlife. Next stop along the trail is the **Children's Zoo,** where children can watch playful groundhogs or view educational presentations in the amphitheater. Tired adults can take a break while the youngsters take advantage of the "just-for-kids" playground. This is a good time for a break because restroom facilities are located nearby.

*A beautiful tiger at the Tulsa Zoo.*

The **Main Zoo Building** houses aquariums, birds and reptiles. Children especially enjoy the reptile incubator and nursery found here. Eggs of various species are prominently displayed; often, newborn reptile babies can be seen. The sea lions are located directly in front of this building. Daily feeding and training sessions are at 2 p.m. As you stroll along, watch the "big animals." The lions, tigers and bears are located in cliff-type enclosures set in a large circle. A playground located between the rhinos and lions is a recent addition to the zoo. Children will enjoy climbing, running, hanging, and sliding on this equipment. Nearby is the station marking the halfway point for the train; weary sightseers can board the train here (one-way tickets $1, round trips tickets $1.50) for a quick and effortless return to the main gate. For those not boarding the train, the return trip to the entrance begins with the **African Savannah**, where giraffes, zebra, wildebeests, and other African animals live. Next, children will enjoy the recently-completed **Elephant Encounter**. After watching these huge animals up close, youngsters can go inside to participate in the interactive exhibits that explain, among other things, how elephants use their ears to stay cool. Children can even try to maneuver a mechanical elephant trunk!

The Zoo sponsors a variety of special events. **ZooFari**, an event especially for children, is held each April, and it includes children activities, entertainment, and food stations. May brings the Tulsa Philharmonic to the Zoo for the enjoyment of patrons and animals alike. In June, summer workshops for children begin, as well as the Photo Safari Contest. In July, **Sunset Safaris** begin. On Tuesday and Friday evenings, the zoo offers reduced admission from 5-8 while providing various forms of entertainment. **HallowZOOeen** is held the five days prior to Halloween. Little Goblins can spook down the Trick-or-Treat Trail to collect treats or play games at the booths. End the year with a trip to **ZooLIGHTful**, a "wild light safari." During the month of December, the zoo is open evenings and decorated with thousands of tiny lights.

## University of Tulsa

*600 South College. Located between Delaware and Harvard, 4th Place and 11th Street, the college is easily accessible. As on most university campuses, parking is at a premium at T.U. In each lot, some spaces are reserved for visitors. Other parking is available on adjacent streets. Dates and hours of activities vary from school to school and season to season. For specific information, contact the appropriate department. The university is handicapped accessible.*

Now considered one of the region's major universities, the University of Tulsa had its humble beginnings as a church school for Indian girls. Originally located in Muskogee and named Henry Kendall College, the school moved to Tulsa in 1907; it was renamed the University of Tulsa in 1921.

In addition to touring the campus, visitors may enjoy the arts and sports events at T.U. Three to four performances are staged each year by the Theater Department. Tickets are $7 for adults and $5 for students and senior citizens. Tickets may be reserved by calling the box office at (918) 631-2567 or 631-3857. Throughout the year, free concerts and recitals are offered by the School of Music. For information on music events, call 631-2262.

Guests will also want to stop by Phillips Hall. It now houses the School of Fine Arts and the **Alexander Hogue Gallery**. Alexander Hogue, an artist himself, was director of the university's School of Art from 1945 until 1963. The gallery exhibits are rotated monthly and include works by faculty, graduates and undergraduates. The Gallery (918-631-2202) is open weekdays 8-5, Saturday 1-4, closed Sunday and university holidays.

The University of Tulsa offers a wide variety of sports: basketball, football, golf, soccer, softball, tennis, and volleyball. Football and soccer games are held in Skelly Stadium, the forty-thousand-seat arena partially funded by W.G. Skelly. Seasons and admission vary from sport to sport. For more information, call the Ticket Office at 631-4688.

## Ursula's Bavarian Inn

*4932 East 92nd Street, (918) 496-8282. Located at about 91st Street, one-half block east of Yale. From I-44 go south on Yale to 91st Street. From the Creek Turnpike exit at Yale and turn left. Go north to 91st Street and turn right. Ursula's is on the right. Tuesday-Thursday 5-9, Friday and Saturday 5-10. Closed Sunday and Monday. There is no admission or cover charge. Reservations are suggested.*

Ursula's Bavarian Inn is known for its excellent German food and gracious service. Although dining here any evening is a treat, Thursday evenings have become the most popular. On this night, Carl and Shirley Stoops wear traditional German clothing and play the accordion and sousaphone. Other instruments are provided for would-be musicians (restaurant patrons) to play, including bells, tambourines and little German whistles. Audience members volunteer or are called upon to provide accompaniment while the Stoops sing German folk songs. The highlight of the evening takes place when everyone joins in the "Chicken Dance."

### Helpful Hints

When you are making reservations, ask for a table close to where the Stoops will be playing. The children will be able to see all the activities and won't be so bashful if called upon to participate. Since this is not typical American food, a snack before leaving home may be appropriate for those finicky eaters. Otherwise, enjoy this great taste of German culture!

## Woodward Park

*21st Street at Peoria Avenue. From Peoria, go south of 21st Street approximately one block and turn east to drive-through or park. Open daily, 6 a.m.-9 p.m. Free.*

Take a stroll through beautiful Woodward Park. At one time, this land was accessible only by wagon, and it was considered too far out in the country for a city park. Tulsans were outraged when the city paid $100 per acre for the land. Now considered the pride of the city, the park is landscaped with more than 15,000 azaleas along the sloping creek bank. Take a leisurely walk along the trails that wind through the blooming azaleas or pause for a moment on a park bench. Rock ledges and edgestone help frame the perfect family photos. How about a picnic under the trees? This is a perfect place to spread a blanket and read a book.

Several small gardens invite visitors to stroll down their rock-hewn paths. East of the azaleas is a rock garden with beautiful seasonal plantings. Water trickles down a fountain through the garden. Children love to climb over the boulders and around the small pools that form in the crevices of the rocks. A visit here on Easter morning is like an Easter parade, with families posing for pictures amid the flowers. South of the rock garden is a circular herb garden, where visitors can pinch and smell the herbs.

Guests delight in visiting the Municipal Rose Garden from May through October. The garden contains approximately 9,000 plants of over 250 varieties, and it was built in 1935 in Italian Renaissance style. The beautiful colors of roses in bloom are reflected in the fountains and pools. Watch for squirrels darting across the path and listen as the birds sing overhead; the rose garden offers a relaxing break from busy and often-chaotic lives.

The Tulsa Garden Center is adjacent to the rose garden. Once a private residence for a local merchant, the building now houses the headquarters

*A peaceful afternoon in Woodward Park.*

for the Tulsa Garden Club. Located inside are restrooms and an excellent gift shop offering garden-related treasures. The club sponsors various types of activities, and the home is available for special events. Behind the Garden Center is the Conservatory and Arboretum. The city showcases seasonal displays in the Conservatory. Trees and shrubs that will grow in this climate with perpetual care are found in the Arboretum.

## Events

### Eagle Watch

*Held on a mid-January weekend on the North bank of the Arkansas River. Call the Tulsa City-County Library (918) 596-7977 for the president's name and phone* number. *Situated on the north bank of the Arkansas River, below the dam and east of the project office. Take Highway 51 west to Keystone Dam and enter the parking lot below the dam.* Volunteers will assist with parking, and Audubon Society members will accompany observers to viewing sites. Admission is free. Parking and viewing are handicapped accessible.

View the majestic eagle at one of its winter feeding sites. Each year, the bald eagle migrates south in search of a milder climate. The birds find the mild winters and numerous lakes in Oklahoma a suitable habitat. Many of the birds choose to roost along the Arkansas River, below Lake Keystone Dam, where they can often be seen feeding along the banks of the river. For the watch, Audubon Society members provide several high-powered telescopes to help participants watch as the eagles nest and feed. Society members are available to answer any questions you may have. Be sure to dress for the weather; it can be very cold in January. Near the water, there can be a twenty degree difference in temperature. In the event of light rain or drizzle, the event will proceed as scheduled; it is cancelled only when ice is on the ground. Remember to bring your binoculars.

Held in conjunction with the Eagle Watch, an overnight adventure is offered for avid bird watchers. Lodging and seminars are available for those wanting a more in-depth study of the bald eagles. For more information or reservations, call (918) 865-4991.

## Indian Powwows

*The following highly-recommended powwows are held at the Tulsa County Fairgrounds, 21st Street and Yale. From Highway 51, take the Yale exit and go north on Yale to 21st Street. Turn left on 21st Street and travel to the first stoplight. Turn right into the Fairgrounds and proceed to the appropriate building (listed below).*

Witness the beauty and pageantry of an Indian Powwow. Audience members are fascinated as they watch dances ranging from the simple gourd dance to the inspiring fancy dance. Powwows are an integral part of Native American culture; they provide a means to pass on tribal culture and traditions; they often serve as social events, bringing together longtime friends and family acquaintances. For more information about attending a powwow, the traditions of powwows, and the etiquette required at the events, read the article on page 18 of this book.

## Tulsa Indian Art Festival

*Held in February in the Expo building at the Tulsa Fairgrounds. Call (918) 583-2253 or 744-1113 for more information.*

This powwow features a major art show along with special dance performances, historical exhibits, workshops, and artist demonstrations. A celebration of art, education and dance, this three-day event begins with demonstrations for children on Friday. Singers, dancers and storytellers showcase their talents on Saturday and Sunday.

## Annual Tulsa Powwow

*Held in early June in the Fairgrounds Pavilion. Call (918) 835-8699 for details.*

This is Tulsa's oldest powwow. Born near Anadarko, founder Kenneth Anquoe moved to Tulsa in 1941. After winning the state Golden Gloves championship that year, he entered the Marines and fought in World War II. After his return to Oklahoma, he organized the first Tulsa Powwow in 1951. The first powwow to be held in an urban setting, it was so successful that it became an annual event. The Anquoe family is still involved with planning this event.

## Intertribal Powwow

*Two events are held at the Fairgrounds annually, one in August and one in December. Call (918) 744-1113 or 836-1523 for information.*

In addition to the traditional dancing, each of these powwows has over180 arts and crafts booths. More than five hundred dancers from approximately twenty-five states compete for prizes and awards in twenty-four categories. Hosted by the Intertribal Indian Club of Tulsa, these powwows enjoys a reputation for being extremely well-organized.

## Kid's World/Children's International Festival

*Call ahead early in the year; this special event is sometimes held in the spring; other years it's held in the fall. A biannual event, the next Kid's World will be in 1998. Call Tulsa Global Alliance at (918) 596-7839 or the Fairgrounds (918) 744-1113 for festival hours and admissions. Held in the Expo Building at the Tulsa County Fairgrounds, 21st and Yale. From Yale turn west on 21st, and continue to Pittsburgh. The large building immediately behind the Golden Driller is the Expo building. Parking is available in the Fairgrounds or on adjacent streets.*

Sample the sights and sounds of selected countries when you visit Kid's World! Representing countries from around the world, more than a hundred exhibitors offer hands-on experiences in arts and crafts, music, games, storytelling, puppet shows, and holiday traditions. Listen to stories and music from different cultures; taste the cuisine of foreign lands. Create an Italian mask; practice the technique of Japanese origami. Learn about currencies and rates of exchange; travel through world time zones. To select that special souvenir, shop the aisles of the international marketplace. Visit each booth, adding stamps to your passport. You can even make new friends in faraway places as you chat with other young people through the Internet. The first day of the festival is usually reserved for group tours and school field trips. For group reservations, call the Tulsa Global Alliance. Concessions are available. Don't miss this wonderful opportunity to explore world cultures!

## Tulsa International Mayfest

*Held downtown on Main Mall from Thursday through Sunday during the third weekend in May. For more information, call Downtown Tulsa Unlimited, (918) 583-2617. The festival is held from the Williams Center Green at 3rd Street and Boston Avenue, to the area at 6th and Main. Park on side streets near Main Mall or in one of the fee-based lots. This event is free.*

Visit this spring celebration, and join with other Tulsans as they proclaim "I Love Downtown!" Visit the Invitational Art Gallery and enjoy the quality art of both local and national artists; shop the aisles of arts and crafts booths lining the downtown streets. Listen to both local and big-name entertainment featured on any one of three festival stages. Watch as local school organizations, dancers, cloggers, singing groups, and other entertainers perform. Arrive hungry; Mayfest offers some of the best festival food available.

The Family/Kidzone area provides engaging entertainment for children. Youngsters can listen to storytelling, see a puppet show, a mime, a magician, or jugglers. For a reasonable fee, they can create, decorate, paint, glue, glitter, and assemble a variety of arts and crafts. They can even tour a miniature museum!

Participate in one of the special activities offered in conjunction with Mayfest. In the past, activities have included a Big Band Dance, 5K Mayfest Run, and a guided tour of downtown Tulsa. Special demonstrations of quilting, woodworking, beading and other crafts are held throughout the festival.

### Helpful Hints

Downtown Tulsa Unlimited, an organization dedicated to the promotion and growth of downtown Tulsa, hosts several events and activities throughout the year. **Junteenth** is a four-day festival which has historically celebrated the end of slavery. It features jazz performances and cajun-style food. "**Summer in the City**" takes place in July and includes a '50s style dance. In September, the **Hispanic Fiesta** offers Mexican cuisine, clothing, arts and crafts. Music played by mariachi bands and acoustic guitarists are highlights of the fiesta. In December, the arrival of Santa Claus provides a dramatic conclusion to Tulsa's Christmas "**Parade of Lights**." For a complete calendar of events, call Downtown Tulsa Unlimited at (918) 583-2617

## Tulsa's Boom River Celebration

*Held July 4th at River Parks along the banks of the Arkansas River. For more information, call (918) 596-2001. Parking is available in several lots along Riverside Drive, on some streets adjacent to Riverside Drive, and from some entrepreneurial residents along the thoroughfare. The fireworks display can be seen from many different locations throughout the city. Admission is free. Festivities begin at 4 p.m.*

Celebrate our nation's birthday at this popular community party. Continuous entertainment is offered, beginning with local entertainers performing on the amphitheater's floating stage. At 8 p.m., Tulsa's own Starlight Bank performs their patriotic salute. Next, various aircrafts perform fly-bys, and parachutists fill the air with their demonstrations. Beginning at 9:45 p.m., the largest pyrotechnical display in Oklahoma begins. The aerial salute lasts twenty-five minutes and is staged from the 21st Street Bridge. The program is choreographed to music that is simulcast by a local radio station. You won't want to miss this spectacular birthday celebration!

### Helpful Hints

Be prepared for crowds at this annual celebration. Convenient parking is limited; you may have to walk quite a distance. Avoid the crowds by watching the festivities from an area facing 21st Street and Riverside. You may not see all the fireworks, but you'll see most of them.

Arrive early for the River Parks Fourth of July festivities; be sure to bring lawn chairs, sunscreen, blankets, coolers, and picnic baskets.

## Balloonfest

*Usually held the first weekend in August from Friday through Sunday. Sponsored by the Gatesway Foundation, (918) 251-2676, this festival is held in the southwest corner of 41st Street and 129th East Avenue. Parking is available for $5 per car. Shuttle service is $2 per person, children under age five are free. Shuttles regularly depart from Expo Square at the Fairgrounds and Broken Arrow High School. Parking and shuttle fees are an important source of funds for this non-profit organization that helps children and adults with developmental disabilities.*

Enjoy the beautiful sight as more than seventy-five colorful hot air balloons float in the blue Oklahoma sky. The balloons come in varieties such as solid color or striped, standard design or custom built. Smokey the Bear, Hagar the Horrible and Noah's Ark balloons add fun and whimsy to the festival. On Friday evening there is a balloon glow; tethered balloons are illuminated against the night's sky. On Saturday, there are special balloon races. Festival-goers will enjoy live entertainment on two different stages as well as a display of antique and collectible cars. Sky-divers can be seen throughout the day, and more than one hundred booths offer arts, crafts and refreshments to visitors. Special activities are available for children, with most being offered at no additional charge. Enjoy the activities and colors at Balloonfest!

### Helpful Hints

No ice chests, alcoholic beverages or pets are allowed on the grounds. For safety reasons, a "no smoking" policy is enforced on the balloon field.

## Jazz on Greenwood

*This four-day event is traditionally held the second or third weekend in August in downtown Tulsa, between Archer and Haskell Streets on Greenwood. From I-244 take the Detroit exit, going north one block on Detroit. Turn right (east) onto Haskell and park in the University Center at Tulsa parking lot. From the "bricktown" section of downtown, park along one of the adjacent streets and walk to Greenwood. For a nominal fee, parking is provided along the streets, and in small private lots. Call (918) 584-3378 for information. No admission fee.*

When you visit Jazz on Greenwood, stroll the streets of Tulsa near north downtown and listen to some of the country's best jazz artists. This outstanding event draws an estimated 80,000 enthusiasts. Once a thriving commercial center for Tulsa's black population, Greenwood was known as "America's Black Wall Street." This area was also known for its tremendous musical talent. In Bob Wills' song, "Take Me Back to Tulsa," he sang, "Let me off at Archer, and I'll walk down to Greenwood."

Since 1988, jazz greats have entertained crowds during the festival. Lou Rawls, Natalie Cole, Cab Calloway, and Dave Brubeck have all played here. Concerts begin nightly at 6 p.m. and feature more than forty local and regional bands performing on the festival's three stages. Headline acts begin at 9 p.m. on the Dreamland Stage. Music lovers are encouraged to bring their lawn chairs and cameras (it's fun to snap photos of little ones dancing in the street). Vendors offer all types of ethnic foods. Don't miss this cultural experience in a historic setting.

## Bluegrass and Chili Festival

*This event is usually held the second weekend in September at the downtown Main Mall. This area is located along Main Street (a brick street) between 2nd and 6th Street. For a small fee, parking for festivals staged in the downtown area is provided at area lots. Parking is also available on side streets adjacent to the festival. For more information, call Downtown Tulsa Unlimited at (918) 583-2617. This event is free.*

Savor the sights and smells of the Bluegrass and Chili Festival. What began in 1979 as a Bluegrass concert has grown to a three-day event drawing nearly 60,000 visitors. Bluegrass music, at one time exclusive to the Appalachian region, now draws a large and varied crowd. In addition to the music, entertainment includes exhibition dance teams who perform clogging and two-step routines.

Over ninety entrants try to outdo each other in several different categories of competition in the Mid-American Regional Chili Cook-Off. Although "Best Chili" is the coveted prize, awards are also offered for booth decoration and presentation. By purchasing a tasting kit, chili-lovers can sample the various recipes. Visiting with the often-flamboyant chefs and competitors can be as much fun as tasting the delicious chili!

Arts, crafts and food booths line the sidewalks of the Main Mall and the Kiddie Korral offers special activities for children. Local businesses sponsor games and entertainment for the little ones.

## Tulsa State Fair

*This event is held the last week of September to the first week of October at the Tulsa Fairgrounds. For information call (918) 744-1113. From Highway 51 take the Yale exit and go north to 21st Street. Turn west onto 21st to Pittsburgh. The entrance to the State Fair is on the north. Parking is available on-site, along adjacent streets and in the yards of residential entrepreneurs. A tractor-drawn shuttle service is available to fairgoers who use outlying on-site lots. Gate admission is adults $5, youth $2, children under six free. A variety of promotions and gate discounts are offered; watch the local media for details. This event is handicapped accessible.*

Plan ahead to attend the Tulsa State Fair, an all-American cultural event! In mid-September, begin watching the *Tulsa World* for information outlining the entertainers, what's new, and where to eat at the fair. A pullout section is published each year, featuring a ten-day calendar of events, or you may pick up one of the booklets distributed at the fair. Walk through the livestock barns along the northern perimeter of the fairgrounds. View farm critters such as cows, horses, sheep, and pigs that are exciting for city kids to see. Visit the Children's Barnyard nearby, where cats, dogs, goats, chickens, rabbits, donkeys, and other animals with their young can be seen up-close.

Stroll through the educational displays of the Oklahoma Wildlife Department, then tour the trade buildings where the latest gadgets are demonstrated. Watch educational displays, explore new products and services, collect campaign literature, or sign up for sweepstakes. You'll find a little bit of everything at the fair. Take a walk down the Midway and try your luck at one of the many games, or just watch others as they try to win large stuffed animals. Sample the endless variety of food—from sweet snacks to full meals! Ride the carousel, ferris wheel or one of the other amusements.

Take a break and rest your weary legs at one of the daily shows. The shows have something for everyone: singers, dancers, magicians, marionettes, high divers, sky divers, comedians, and actors. Special events include concerts, rodeos and the fantastic **Ice Capades**. Tickets for these events can be purchased at the Pavilion Ticket Office at (918) 747-0001 or the Grandstand box office.

### Helpful Hints

Special ride passes can be purchased on opening night for a substantial savings over other ride/gate packages. You can also purchase an all-you-can-ride bracelet, good for the duration of the fair. Watch for details in the Tulsa paper or call the Fairgrounds for more information. Other services available include a post office, first aid station, and automatic teller machine. Rent strollers and wheelchairs at the Pavilion. Sundry items may be purchased at the Comfort Zone on the Midway.

## Oktoberfest

*Usually held the third weekend in October along the west bank of the Arkansas River. Call the River Parks Authority at (918) 596-2001 for more information. From 21st Street, travel west over the 21st Street bridge. Turn left (south), following the signs to the Oktoberfest parking and entrance. This event is free. Parking is somewhat limited at the festival site. However, shuttle service is available for $1 from several convenient locations.*

Enjoy Tulsa's version of "Germany on the Arkansas!" This festival offers some of the most authentic German food and music around and ranks as one of the top ten German celebrations in the country. Visit Der Bier Garten, the largest and most spectacular tent at the celebration. This tent is the focal point of most activity during the four-day celebration, and it has some of the festival's best food. Visitors can eat, drink, listen to a German band, and dance the popular Chicken Dance! Other tents, with colorful German names such as Das Ess Zelt und Garten, host food and drink vendors and juried arts and crafts. At Der root Bier Garten, the children's tent, children are entertained with a German sing-along, a puppet show, and a storyteller. At Das Kinder Zelt, children can create numerous craft projects, ranging in price from fifty cents to $10. For the past

*Oompah at Tulsa's Oktoberfest.*

several years, a local television station has provided a news set where children are shown how to "televise" a newscast. Taped copies of these "little reporters" can be purchased, with proceeds benefiting a local charity. Purchase souvenirs in the outdoor Kunst Markt and Der Floh Markt. For a day of food and fun, take the whole family to Oktoberfest!

## Christmas in Tulsa

During the month of December, Christmas activities abound! Watch the *Tulsa World* for information on the special activities many churches sponsor during the holidays, and on the many areas in Tulsa that are particularly beautiful with special lighting displays. Load the kids in the car for a special "light-seeing" night tour. "Don't miss" spots on the tour include Utica Square at 21st and Utica, Warren Place at 61st and Yale, and Children's Medical Center between Yale and Sheridan on Skelly Drive.

The following lists other special holiday traditions in the Tulsa area.

Held the first weekend in December in downtown Tulsa, the **Festival of Lights** parade features area bands, organizations, and businesses, in addition to several seasonally-decorated floats. Lights adorn many of these creations; Cinderella's lighted coach is always a favorite. But most important to children, and many adults, is the annual appearance of Santa Claus on the last float of this traditional parade. For more information contact Downtown Tulsa Unlimited at (918) 583-2617.

Each year the First Lutheran Church of Tulsa (1244 S. Utica) presents Handel's **"The Messiah."** Usually held the first weekend in December, there are two performances on Saturday and two on Sunday. Plan to arrive early; the sanctuary seats only around 400. Performances are free. For more details, call the church at (918) 582-0917.

Drive through the **live nativity scene**, staged each year at Skelly Drive Baptist Church, 8504 E. Skelly Drive. The event is usually held for two consecutive weekends in December; for exact dates, call the church at (918) 627-4264. Visitors feel as though they've entered the ancient city of Bethlehem when they witness travelers, innkeepers, and soldiers, all dressed in the clothes of ancient Israel. An occasional live animal lends an air of authenticity to the scene. The culmination is the tableau of the birth of Jesus.

# Southeast Oklahoma

## Broken Bow

Broken Bow was established in 1911 by the Dierks brothers, who were pioneer lumbermen. Since then, the brothers' operations have merged with Weyerhaeuser; this company continues to be one of the area's major employers.

The Ouachita National Forest and Broken Bow Lake are a beautiful backdrop for family outdoor adventure. Make your reservations early for this popular area! No matter the season, there's much to enjoy here. Be a "leaf peeper" in the fall to enjoy cooler temperatures and colorful surroundings or, for a break from the winter doldrums, consider a trip to the area to enjoy the Beaver's Bend Resort Park when it's less crowded. You and your family will enjoy the cozy cabins, most of which have fireplaces, and, for a change of pace, winter hiking.

John Taylor

*Broken Bow Lake.*

*Broken Bow is 228 miles southeast of Oklahoma City. Take I-40 east to the Indian Nations Turnpike, then drive south to Antlers. If you are coming from Tulsa, take U.S. Highway 75 to Henryetta, then take the Indian Nations Turnpike. At the Antlers exit, take S.H. 3 to Broken Bow. Tulsa is 236 miles from Broken Bow. Broken Bow Chamber of Commerce (800) 52TREES.*

### Attractions

#### Beaver's Bend Resort Park

*Located north of Broken Bow, (405) 494-6300 or (800) 654-8240. From Broken*

*Children can't resist the allure of the rails at Beaver's Bend.*

Bow, go north on Highway 259 seven miles to the park entrance. *Forest Heritage Center Museum: Daily 8-5; Nature Center: Summer, Tuesday-Sunday 10-5; Winter, Saturday-Sunday 10-4:30. The Forest Heritage Center Museum and the Nature Center are both free.* ⑤ ★

Situated on the shores of the scenic Broken Bow Lake, the popular and beautiful Beaver's Bend Resort Park includes approximately 12,000 acres of forested land. This is one of the best parks for family fun. Families can rent paddle boats and canoes, take guided horseback rides through the park, and hike the many nature trails that wind through the park—among many other choices. The Mountain Fork River flows through the park and, twice a month, it is stocked with rainbow trout. (NOTE: Watch your children closely when they're around the river's edge; the river has a very strong current).

**Beaver's Bend Depot** (405-494-6613) offers many activities for families, such as guided trail rides, hayrides, and miniature train rides. **Beaver's Bend River Floats** offers seasonal ten-mile white water trips for $30 per canoe and two-and-a-half-mile float trips for $15. Eighteen holes of challenging golf is available at the scenic Cedar Creek Golf Course.

Self-guided tours are available through the park's Forest Heritage Center Museum. Highlighting the forestry industry, the museum houses antique forestry tools, wood art, homestead memorabilia, and historical documents. Taped narrations, along with fourteen dioramas, tell the story of Prehistoric forests, the Caddo Indians, Papermaking in the South, and the process of lumbering in the 1940s.

The park's outstanding **Nature Center** exhibits birds, small mammals and reptiles. (Your children will love the flying squirrel!) When you arrive, be sure to get a schedule of events for programs offered by the Nature Center and plan to participate in the hands-on instructional activities led by the knowledgeable park naturalists. Some of the programs featured are hawk and owl feedings, educational nature walks, campfire programs, nature crafts, and Bald Eagle watches.

Cabins are available year round, and reservations should be made as much as a year in advance, especially for holidays and weekends. You may have a better chance of renting a cabin during the week. (You may also ask the park staff for suggestions of privately-operated cabins and other accommodations that are located near the park.) Forty-seven cabins are available in the wood groves and overlooking the Mountain Fork River. Cabins range in price from $45-95, and they sleep two to six people. RV sites are available for $11-14 per night; some require reservations, and others are on a first-come, first-served basis. Eighty tent sites are available for $6 per night. Another option is the new and luxurious forty-room **Lakeview Lodge**, situated on the shore of Broken Bow Lake near Hochatown State Park. Each hotel-style room comes with a beautiful view and a continental breakfast. Prices range from $110-175.

Two events take place at Beaver's Bend. The **Owa-Chito Festival** (Festival of the Forest) is held the third weekend of June and usually runs from Thursday to Saturday. First held in the 1970s, this free festival celebrates McCurtain County's heritage, culture and forestry industry. Arts, crafts, food, and live entertainment (including a big-name celebrity concert on Saturday night) make this festival a real treat. Visitors are often asked to participate in games related to the forestry industry.

The **Fall Folk Festival and Craft Show** is held the second weekend of November. It features folk music, demonstrations, fall foliage, a petting zoo, and arts and crafts. For more information regarding this free educational festival, call (405) 494-6300.

# Hugo

The county seat of Choctaw County, Hugo was named after the novelist, Victor Hugo. In early statehood days, the town was important for its connection with the railroad. The town still enjoys its railroad heritage with an excursion train, a historic depot, and remnants of the Harvey House tradition. Hugo's other claim to fame is as a winter home for the circus. Three traveling circuses have winter headquarters in Hugo.

*Hugo is 208 miles southeast of Oklahoma City (I-40 to the Indian National Turnpike, then south to Hugo) and 169 miles from Tulsa (south on Highway 75, continuing south on the Indian Nation Turnpike). Hugo Chamber of Commerce (405) 326-7511.*

## *Attractions*

### Circus Winter Quarters

*(405) 326-3173. Turn north from U.S. Highway 70 onto State Highway 93 and go about a mile to East Kirk Road. Turn west and go to the circus wagon. Open seasonally, weekdays 9-5. Free. Handicapped accessible.*

Three circuses, the Carson and Barnes Circus, the Kelly Miller Circus, and the Chinese Imperial Circus, are in winter quarters here from mid-November until mid-March. The guided tour focuses on the animals; animals from all three circuses winter with the Carson and Barnes outfit. You'll also see circus trucks and equipment and, depending on the schedule, you may be able to see various performers practicing their skills.

It is imperative to call in advance for an appointment; your reception will depend on the circus schedule and who is available to show you around.

### Frisco Depot Museum

*300 West Jackson, (405) 326-6630. As you enter Hugo from Indian Nation Turnpike and travel east on Highway 70/271 (West Jackson Street), look for the sign for the museum immediately after crossing the railroad tracks. The museum/depot is located about one block north of West Jackson. The museum is open from April 1 to mid-November, Monday-Saturday 10-4. Admission for the museum is "by donation." Call to verify the hours of the museum.*

The original depot burned in 1913, and this replacement was built in 1915. At one time, the large depot serviced approximately fourteen passenger trains and 1,200 passengers per day. The depot includes a restored Harvey House diner, which is in the process of being renovated; plans are to serve full meals here.

The museum contains many diverse exhibits that children will enjoy. Exhibits include a handmade replica of a five-ring circus, an 1890s barber shop, an elaborate working railroad model, and a hands-on antique cash register. A tour conducted by the curator will bring Hugo's colorful history and interesting characters to life.

## Hugo Heritage Railroad

*Call (888) RR DEPOT (toll-free) or (405) 326-6630. The excursion train leaves from the Frisco Depot Museum and runs on Saturdays from the first Saturday of April until November 1. June, July, August, and October are the busiest months for*

*the train. Ticket prices and departure times vary throughout the season; calling ahead for details and reservations is an absolute must. Adult round-trip tickets range from $15 to $26, and trips are usually two hours in length. The train is available for large group charters.*

Experience a "ride on the rails" and relive history on the Hugo Heritage Railroad, the only regularly-operating excursion train in Oklahoma. This memory-making

*Tickets, please!*

trip is a pleasurable one as family members enjoy the comfortable, air-conditioned train and spend time looking for wildlife and admiring the countryside. In addition to the pleasures of the scenery, families will enjoy the history lesson presented by the train's conductor, a retired engineer with the Frisco Railroad. For your convenience, snacks are offered for sale during the ride.

## Mt. Olivet Cemetery

*Located at Trice and South 8th Street, (405) 326-7511. From the intersection of Jackson Street (also known as Highway 70/271) and 8th Street, turn south. The cemetery is past the railroad tracks on the left. Open dawn to dusk. Visitors should be sensitive to those people who are not here for sight-seeing.*

While in the area, you'll want to visit this most unique cemetery. It only takes about thirty minutes for a drive-through tour. An area called "Showmen's Rest" features beautiful monuments to circus showmen. The tombstones are shaped like tents, wagon wheels, ticket booths, and more. In another area are monuments to rodeo heroes, including Freckles Brown and Lane Frost. The monument to Lane Frost is inscribed "A Champion in the Arena, A Champion in Life."

# Idabel

Established in 1903 and the county seat of McCurtain County, Idabel was named to honor the sisters, Ida and Belle Purnell. The area's abundant history and beauty are the focus of many attractions and events.

*Located 225 miles south and east of Oklahoma City (I-40 east to Indian Nation turnpike south to Hugo, east forty-three miles on Highway 70), and 236 miles south and east of Tulsa (south on Highway 75/62 to Indian Nation Turnpike). Idabel Chamber of Commerce (405) 286-3305.*

## *Attractions*

### *Barnes-Stevenson Home*

*300 Southeast Adams, (405) 286-3616 or (405) 286-6314. From Southeast Washington (Highway 70/259) turn south on East Madison Street, then go one block to Southeast Adams. During the winter, the house is open by appointment only. From the first of May to the first of September, the house is open on Sundays from 2-4, other times by appointment. Admission is free. The house is not handicapped accessible.*

When Judge Barnes and his wife came to McCurtain County, they had few possessions other than his law books. When Oklahoma became a state in 1907, Barnes was elected as a county judge. In 1911, Barnes built this sixteen-room, three-story mansion, which now carries his name, along with its subsequent owner's. The house was constructed with indoor plumbing, electric lights, and central heating from a coal-fired furnace—all "fancy" amenities for that time and place. The home was purchased by the McCurtain County Historical Society in 1987, and has been furnished to accurately reflect life in the early 1900s.

### *Museum of the Red River*

*812 East Lincoln Road. Located on U.S. Highway 70 Truck Route, just east of U.S. Highway 259 South. (405) 286-3616. Tuesday-Saturday 10-5, closed Sundays, Mondays, Thanksgiving, Christmas and New Year's Day. Admission is free, but donations are encouraged.*

This museum houses items which interpret the prehistory of Native Americans in southeast Oklahoma (7000 BC to the 1800s) and the history of the local Choctaw tribe. In the museum's attempt to further the understanding of all Native American culture, exhibits of other North and South American tribes are included.

The Choctaw house exhibit is of special interest to visitors. It shows that, by the 1860s, the Choctaw had incorporated many of the "white man's ways" with their traditional life-style.

#### *Helpful Hints*

A problem-solving scavenger hunt or "Museum Detective" game has been developed by the museum. Be sure to ask for a copy for your school-aged children. Call one week ahead to schedule group tours for fifteen or more. Ask about Native American games for children that are led by the museum staff during tours.

## Events

### Dogwood Days

*This event is held the first Friday and Saturday of April at various locations in Idabel. For dates and a brochure, call (405) 286-3305. Admission is free.*

Held to coincide with the blooming of the dogwood, this festival includes a barbecue cook-off, a 5K run, and a soap box derby. There are also arts and crafts, entertainment, a special sale of dogwood seedlings, and suggested dogwood tours. Over 1,000 dogwood plants are sold each year, making each year's festival more colorful than the previous one.

## McAlester/Krebs

The many ethnic groups who worked in the coal mines near McAlester from 1873 to 1928 contributed greatly to the area. In fact, the main attractions in McAlester and Krebs center around authentic Italian food!

*Located approximately 121 miles southeast of Oklahoma City (I-40 east to Indian Nation Turnpike, south to McAlester). From Tulsa, travel approximately 106 miles south on Highway 75/62 to Indian Nation Turnpike. The small town of Krebs is located a mile east of McAlester on Highway 31. McAlester Chamber of Commerce (800) 879-2550.*

## Attractions

### Italian Restaurants

Reflecting the influence of the area's Italian immigrants, these restaurants have served delicious Italian food for generations! Treat your family to an authentic Italian dinner with all the trimmings at these fine restaurants. To avoid a wait, it is recommended to arrive early for weekend dinners. All of the following restaurants are handicapped accessible.

**Gia Como's Italian Cuisine**

*19th and Comanche, McAlester, (918) 423-2662. Located on U.S. Highway 69 Bypass South on the east side of town. Open Tuesday-Saturday 11:30-9:30, closed Sunday and Monday and most major holidays.*

This restaurant has been owned and operated by the same Italian family for four generations. In addition to delicious Italian specialties such as chicken florentine, veal parmigiana, and shrimp alfredo, this restaurant prides itself on serving outstanding steaks. All entrees come with plenty of "extras."

**Isle of Capri**

*150 Southwest 7th Street, Krebs, (918) 423-3062. Open Monday-Saturday 5-10:30.*

The Isle offers traditional Italian food and specializes in cornfed steer steaks prepared with a garlic and butter sauce. All entrees are served with antipasto, salad, spaghetti, ravioli, and garlic toast.

**Pete's Place**

*8th and Monroe (Highway 270 East), Krebs, (918) 423-2042. Open Monday-Thursday 4-9 p.m., Friday-Saturday 4-10, Sunday noon-9.*

Established in 1925 by Pietro Piegari (Anglicized to Pete Prichard), this famous restaurant is now run by grandson Joe Prichard. Family-style service includes entrees served with spaghetti, meatballs, ravioli, salad, and garlic bread. While you are at Pete's, notice the many photos on display featuring the celebrities who have eaten here.

### Roseanna's Italian Food

*205 East Washington (Highway 31 East), Krebs, (918) 423-2055. Open Tuesday-Wednesday 11-8, Thursday-Saturday 11-9.*

Roseanna's has an extensive Italian menu with half-order dinners available. This is a great idea, since the portions are more than ample. Devotees declare the lasagne "awesome."

## Lovera's Grocery

*95 West 6th Street, Krebs, (918) 423-2842 or (800) 854-1417. Monday-Saturday 7 a.m.-6 p.m.*

Lovera's Grocery.

This Italian grocery store was built in 1910, and it has been run by the same family since 1946. A shopping expedition at Lovera's is a bit like a trip back to Old Italy. The wonderful smell of Italian spices, the variety of Italian products on the shelves, the old-fashioned meat counter, and the festoons of hanging cheeses and ristras of peppers add to the "Old World" atmosphere. The factory processes up to a ton of sausage each week, as well as caciocavallo, provolone, parmesan, and mozzarella cheeses. The cheese plant produces 800 to 1,000 pounds of cheese each week. To add an educational element to the experience, be sure to call a week in advance to learn which days the sausage and cheese will be processed.

## McAlester Building Foundation, Inc.

*220 East Adams, (405) 423-2932. The museum is located in the Old McAlester High School, two blocks north of Carl Albert Parkway (U.S. Highway 270) and two blocks east of Main Street. Monday-Friday 8-2. Free.*

Fourteen rooms in this former school building are being used to house museum exhibits dealing with the area's history. Displays include the Native American Room which honors local tribes and the Coal Mine Room devoted to the history of the coal industry. Through period rooms such as the 1800s Historical Room, visitors find clothing and furniture typical of the era. Displays are well-organized, and the setting is unique. During the Christmas season, Christmas trees are decorated to carry out the theme of each room.

*McAlester Building Foundation, Inc.*

### Helpful Hints

All tours are guided. Walk-in guests are welcome, but groups should call in advance for reservations. Plan at least one hour to see everything.

## St. Joseph's Catholic Church

*290 N.W. Church Street, Krebs, (918) 423-6695.*

While you are in Krebs, take the time to visit the beautiful St. Joseph's Catholic Church. The church was built in 1903, and it is listed on the National Register of Historic Places. Notice the pressed tin ceiling and the exquisite stained glass windows.

Call a week in advance to schedule a short, informative tour that lasts about thirty minutes. The tour will include information regarding the symbols in the stained glass windows and a walk through the Trinity Garden located near the church.

# Events

## Italian Festival

*Held the Saturday and Sunday of Memorial Day Weekend. For a brochure and more information (including the festival's location) call (918) 423-2055. Open Saturday 10:30-8, Sunday 11-4. Admission is free, but food and some activities are extra.*

A tradition in this area since 1970, this festival celebrates the history, heritage and influence of Italian immigrants in the McAlester community. It features homemade Italian food such as Italian sausage, meatballs, spaghetti, and garlic bread. Activities at the festival include Italian games, traditional music and dancing, entertainment, an arts and crafts show, and carnival rides.

## Ethnic Festival

*Held the Saturday and Sunday of Labor Day weekend in Krebs. For more information, call (918) 423-2842. Admission is free.*

Learn about the cultures of other countries such as Germany, Italy, Greece, and Mexico while you experience ethnic foods and dancing at this friendly, family-oriented festival. The festival also includes an eclectic blend of musical entertainment such as Greek dancers and accordion players, as well as arts and crafts.

*The scenic Ouachita National Forest.*

## *Ouachita National Forest*

*The northern edge of the forest is located about twelve miles south of Poteau on Highway 59. You can enjoy the Ouachita National forest by traveling west/east on Highway 1 (the well-known, scenic Talimena Drive), or by traveling north/south on Highway 59/259. For more information about the forest, contact the Choctaw Ranger District in Heavener on the north side of the forest at (918) 653-2991, or the Kiamichi Ranger District in Talihina on the west side of the forest at (918) 567-2326. Visitor Information Stations are open April 1-November 15, daily 8-4:30. The Talihina Station is open November 16-March 31, Friday-Sunday 8-4:30.*

The Ouachita Mountains are the highest mountains between the Appalachians and the Rockies, and they are particularly unique because they run east and west, rather than north and south.

Enjoy beautiful sights along the Talimena Scenic Drive from Talihina east to the Arkansas state line (Highway 1), or along the north/south scenic drive (Highway 59/259) from Heavener to Beaver's Bend Resort Park. Visitor Information Stations are located at each end of the drive. Stop by for brochures, maps, and other information for your trip.

Thirty-two recreation areas are scattered throughout the forest. There are several activities for visitors, including swimming, wading, fishing, picnicking, hiking, and camping. There are many short, easy-to-walk nature trails with illustrated interpretive signs. The longest trail in the forest area is the Ouachita National Recreation Trail, which provides 186 miles of challenging trails for hiking and backpacking.

The breathtaking Talimena Scenic Drive winds along the crests of the mountains from east to west; this drive is particularly beautiful in the fall as the foliage colors change. Located midpoint along this fifty-four-mile drive is the **Robert S. Kerr Memorial Arboretum and Nature Center**. This complex encourages visitors to take an interest in the environment. A few self-guided trails near the nature center offer educational, scientific, cultural, and recreational experiences.

## Poteau

Established in 1887, Poteau boasts of being home to "the world's highest hill," Cavanal Hill, which tops out at 1,999 feet. The town is named after the Poteau River and the name Poteau comes from a French word meaning "post." The French influence in the names of rivers and other landmarks originates from the French traders who were in the area in the early 1800s.

*Poteau is 189 miles east of Oklahoma City. Take I-40 east to the west Sallisaw exit, ten turn south on Highway 59. To travel the 135 miles from Tulsa, take the Muskogee Turnpike south to I-40, then continue east to the Highway 59 exit. Poteau Chamber of Commerce (918) 647-9178.*

### Attractions

### Kerr Conference Center and Museum

*Located six miles south of Poteau near Highway 59, (918) 647-8221. Call ahead for directions to this facility. Signs help visitors find their way. Summer hours are Monday-Friday 9-5, closed Mondays. Winter hours are Tuesday-Sunday 1-4, closed Mondays and major holidays. The facility is open extended hours in April and May; special times are available by appointment. Admission for the museum is by donation.*

Overlooking the Poteau River Valley, the Kerr Conference Center was once the magnificent home of one of Oklahoma's most respected individuals. Designed in 1957 for Robert S. Kerr and his wife, the mansion stretches for 365 feet along the top of a bluff. Made of native stone and Oklahoma forest products (some gathered from the Kerr Ranch), the home cost $640,000 to complete. Be sure to notice the interesting architecture and decor. Regrettably, Kerr resided here only two years before his death. Notable guests that have visited the home include John F. Kennedy, Lyndon Johnson, Norman Schwarzkopf, Gerald Ford, and George Bush.

The museum is located close to the home, and it is operated by the Eastern Oklahoma Historical Society. It contains Indian artifacts, material regarding the famous Heavener Runestone, and items used by area pioneers.

The Kerr Conference Center is also available as a bed and breakfast facility. Overnight guests may use the grounds and facilities, such as the pool and sauna located on the patio. Also available are horseshoes, volleyball and basketball. Lake Wister and Kerr Lake are located nearby, providing visitors with a wide choice of water sports such as boating, skiing and fishing.

## In the Vicinity

## Heavener

Named around 1895, the town honored Joe Heavener, who owned the townsite. Said by some to be a Native American, by others a white man, Heavener had come from Virginia and settled among the Choctaws. The site was a stop on the Pittsburg and Gulf Railroad (later named the Kansas City Southern).

*The small town of Heavener is located approximately ten miles south of Poteau. Heavener Chamber of Commerce (918) 653-4303.*

## Heavener Runestone State Park

*Located two miles east of Heavener; follow the signs. (918) 653-2241. 8 a.m.-dark. Admission is free. Those with physical disabilities should not hike the trail.*

This small, fifty-acre park located on Poteau Mountain provides a breathtaking view of the valley below, but more important, especially to children and others with imagination, is the mysterious Runestone for which the park is named. The Runestone was first discovered in the 1830s by the Choctaw Indians. The native stone stands twelve feet high and is ten feet wide and sixteen inches thick. Once thought to bear the date November 11, 1012, it has recently been translated as a boundary marker with the inscription, GLOME VALLEY, meaning "Valley of (or belonging to) Glome." Experts hypothesize that the Runestone was inscribed by Scandinavian explorers more than one thousand years ago.

To see the Runestone, visitors must climb down a steep incline; walking shoes with nonskid soles are recommended. After visiting the Runestone, make use of the park's picnic areas and explore its hiking trails. There are five individual picnic shelters and fifteen open-area tables with grills. Two trails for adventurous hikers are available; each is about a mile long and has medium to steep grades. Watch for wildlife along the trails.

### Helpful Hints

Near the entrance to the park is the Gift Shop/Visitor Center/Park Office complex. Those with handicaps will especially appreciate the interpretive signs and materials about the Runestone that are located here. A booklet by Gloria Farley that explains the Runestone discovery and its translation is offered for sale in the gift shop. It makes interesting reading for families—before or after their viewing of the mysterious rock.

## Peter Conser Home Site

*This home is located four miles south of Heavener on Highway 59. (918) 653-2493. Open Wednesday-Saturday 10-5, Sunday 1-5, closed Monday and Tuesday. Admission is free. The restrooms are handicapped accessible, but the home is not.*

The 1894 home has been renovated to reflect the lives of the Peter Conser family during pre-statehood days. Born to a white trader and a Choctaw Indian woman, Peter Conser worked hard to become a successful farmer and businessman. He was also a well-respected captain of the Choctaw Lighthorse. The Choctaw Lighthorse were the mounted police of the Five Civilized Tribes. Operated by the Oklahoma Historical Society, the home will give children and adults an idea of what life was like during the state's Indian Territory days.

## Keota

### Overstreet-Kerr Historical Farm

*Located near Keota. (918) 966-3396 or (918) 966-3282. From Poteau, travel north for a few miles on Highway 59, then 1/4 mile west on Overstreet-Kerr Road. Open Tuesday-Saturday 10-4, or by appointment. Adults $3, children ages 6-18, $2. The price may increase during special events or exhibits. A tour of the house takes about twenty minutes; to include looking at outbuildings and livestock, plan to take forty-five minutes. Groups need to call for reservations. The ground floor is handicapped accessible.*

Completed in 1895 by Tom Overstreet, this house is a restored Choctaw pioneer home listed on the National Register of Historic Places. The facility is

*Overstreet-Kerr Historical Farm.*

dedicated to educating the public on the lives of farmers and ranchers in Choctaw territory during the late 1800s and early 1900s. It is maintained by the Kerr Center for Sustainable Agriculture. The two-story house contains only a few pieces of original furniture. However, most pieces are typical of the period. The home features original woodwork custom-made from local materials and four fireplaces. The attractive upstairs bedrooms are included on the tour.

The Overstreet family once controlled almost 3,000 acres, where they raised quality livestock. Family members are credited with bringing the first registered Hereford cattle to Indian Territory in 1902. The remaining 140 acres are being farmed much the same as they were at the turn of the century. In addition to experiencing pioneer life, children really enjoy petting and feeding the barnyard livestock.

### Helpful Hints

Held the second Saturday in October, the **Historical Fall Farm-Fest** is a wonderful, "hands-on" time to visit this historical farm. The highlight of the day is the sorghum milling and cooking. The house and livestock areas are open for self-guided tours, and throughout the day there are demonstrations of 1800s-style crafts such as basket weaving, rug making, broom making, and quilting. Live entertainment, food, and gift items add to the festivities. Admission is $5 for adults and $3 for children (under eighteen).

# Wilburton

Wilburton is the county seat of Latimer County, and is named after Elisha Wilbur, who was president of the Lehigh Valley Railroad. Its history dates back to the arrival of the Choctaw Coal and Railway line. After the Civil War, the area became known as an outlaw hangout. Some of the stories associated with the area make modern history seem tame.

*Located 153 miles southeast of Oklahoma City and 123 miles south and east of Tulsa. Go to McAlester, then take Highway 270 east to Wilburton. Wilburton Chamber of Commerce (918) 465-2759.*

## Attractions

### Robber's Cave State Park

*Located five miles north of Wilburton on State Highway 2, (918) 465-2565. Hours, rates and fees for activities vary. For more information, check with the Nature Center and the on-site grocery store.* 🏕

The beautiful terrain of the San Bois Mountains gives rise to large, rugged, stone outcroppings. One of these outcroppings contains Robber's Cave, the landmark for which the park was named. The French were the first to make use of the cave as a place to store provisions. Later, the cave became well-known as an outlaw hideout. Overlooking the entire valley, the cave has a narrow opening and, at one time, it had a freshwater spring flowing inside. The outlaws evaded lawmen for several years by making use of a hidden exit that allowed them to escape to a natural stone corral which held their horses.

Today, hikers climb steep inclines to reach the entrance of the cave, then descend steep trails to reach the stone corral. Youngsters will enjoy scrambling over the rocks, pretending to be famous outlaws making their escape. If you plan to participate in any of these activities, you are advised to wear proper shoes or boots.

The park also has less strenuous activities available such as **miniature golf** and **paddle boats**. During the summer, **swimming** in the pool or lake is re-freshing. **Fishing** is also available at the lake, with trout fishing offered from December to mid-March. Located in a restored Civilian Conservation Corps (CCC) bathhouse, the **Nature Center** offers special exhibits and programs for children. To get a schedule of events, call (918) 465-5154. Children also enjoy the abundant playground equipment with extra-high swings.

There are twenty-six cabins and 117 campsites in the park. Be sure to call in advance for cabin and campground reservations. This 8000-acre state park is often booked well in advance. Rates for cabins range from $48-88 per night. A new twenty-room lodge, **Belle Starr View Lodge**, provides motel-style accom-modations at $78 per night.

### Helpful Hints

An excellent time to visit the park is during the **Robber's Cave Fall Festival**. Held in the park and in nearby Wilburton on a mid-October weekend, the festival features a rod and custom car show, arts and crafts show, food booths, an old West show, gospel singing, and carnival rides. This well-attended festival is usually scheduled during Oklahoma public school's fall break weekend.

# Southcentral Oklahoma

## Ardmore

Ardmore is the county seat of Carter County. Once a railroad station on the Santa Fe line, Ardmore was named by a railroad official for his hometown of Ardmore, Pennsylvania. Early on, Ardmore suffered through two disasters. In 1895, a fire destroyed eighty-two homes and businesses. A railroad car blew up twenty years later, killing forty-four people and injuring 200. Through the years, Ardmore has benefitted from the discovery of oil nearby. Located halfway be-tween Oklahoma City and Dallas, Ardmore offers a wide variety of activities for a weekend getaway, especially antique shopping and outdoor recreation.

*Ardmore is located ninety-seven miles south of Oklahoma City on I-35 and 176 miles south and west of Tulsa. Ardmore Chamber of Commerce (405) 223-7765.*

### Attractions

#### Charles B. Goddard Center for Visual and Performing Arts

*Located at D Street and 1st Street SW, (405) 226-0909. From I-35, take exit 31 to*

*Highway 199, (Main Street) and travel east. Take a right onto D Street in downtown Ardmore; travel south one block to 1st Avenue NW. The Goddard Center is on the northwest corner; parking is available on the south side of 1st Avenue. The Art Museum is open Monday-Friday 9-4, Saturday-Sunday 1-4. Admission for the art museum is free; ticket prices vary for theater performances.*

Charles B. Goddard was the founder of the Humble Oil Company. The Goddard Center was dedicated in his memory by his wife, Ethel Goddard. An art museum and a theater are housed at the center. The art gallery hosts several traveling exhibits each year, and it has a permanent collection of contemporary paintings. The Little Theater offers five shows each year comprised of dramas, comedies, and/or musicals. Call ahead for information and tickets. Every year in March, the center hosts an all-school art exhibit.

## Eliza Cruce Hall Doll Museum

*Located in the Ardmore Public Library, 320 E Street N.W., (405) 223-8290. From I-35, take Exit 33 to Highway 142 east. At Commerce Street, take a right and travel south to 4th Avenue N.W. Take a left onto 4th Avenue N.W. (also known as Grand Avenue), and travel east again. This street runs into the parking lot of the library. Open Monday-Thursday 10-8:30, Friday-Saturday 10-4. Admission is free.*

The estate of Eliza Cruce Hall donated this collection of more than 300 antique and unusual dolls for the enjoyment of Ardmore residents and visitors. Girls of all ages will love to examine these dolls. The costume details and facial expressions are incredible. Arranged in cases for easy viewing, this collection contains dolls from the past, from around the world, and from modern times. You may purchase postcards of some of the more popular dolls.

## Greater Southwest Historical Museum

*35 Sunset Drive, (405) 226-3857. From I-35, take Highway 70 east. Turn north onto Sunset Drive (located just past the football stadium). The museum is on the west side of the street. Tuesday-Saturday 10-5, Sunday 1-5. To reserve a guided tour for large groups, call at least two weeks in advance. Admission is free.*

The Greater Southwest Historical Museum is housed in a 1936 Works Progress Administration-constructed building and focuses on area history from the Indian Territory days to the 1930s. The Sam Noble Hall houses replicas of a log cabin, a general store, and a blacksmith shop. A room devoted to children's toys, dolls and doll houses really captures children's interest. Other exhibits featured are old-time household items, clothes, jewelry, machinery, and military memorabilia.

Outdoor displays include farm and oil field equipment and the 700 Ranch House, Ardmore's first permanent structure. It was moved to the museum grounds and is authentically furnished to reflect the late 1800s.

## Lake Murray Resort Park

*Located southeast of Ardmore. Contact the park office at (405) 223-6600. From I-35, take Highway 70 east, then Highway 77S south to the lake. The park office is located at the intersection of Highways 70 and 77S. For lodge and cabin reservations, call (800) 654-8240.* ⑨ ★

Besides the obvious boating and water sports at Lake Murray, park visitors may look forward to many other activities. **Lake cruises** (no reservations required) are available as well as wave runners, paddle boats and canoes. For information concerning these activities call (405) 223-7483 or 223-7185. **Lake Murray Riding Stables** offers guided horseback riding. These rides last about an hour, and children must be at least two years old to ride; children from ages two to six must ride with an adult. The stables are located two miles east of the intersection of Exit 24 and I-35. An eighteen-hole **miniature golf** course is available from May to mid-September. The cost is $3 per person. The **swimming pool** is open from Memorial Day weekend to October 1 from 10-8 daily. The cost is $2 for adults; children ages twelve and under $1.

This resort park is very popular; if you plan to rent a cabin or lodge room, make your reservations for summer and holidays about one year in advance. Reservations for other times should be made at least two weeks in advance. Cabins and cottages ($43-78; larger cabins $128-225) that sleep from two to ten people are available. The lodge has guest rooms and suites ($40-75; suites are $150), a restaurant, recreation areas, and a gift shop. Tent camping and recreational vehicle sites are also available.

Several events are held at the park. On Saturday nights from Memorial Day weekend to Labor Day weekend, the lodge hosts **dances** from 7 to 11 p.m. on the recreation patio. There is no charge, and children are welcome. After sundown on the **Fourth of July**, there is a fireworks display. On Thanksgiving Day, a **Thanksgiving Feast** is held. Seating times are 11, 12:30 and 2. Adding to this family event are face painting, hayrides, and a visit from Tom the Turkey. The cost is $10.95 for adults and half-price for children under twelve.

**Tucker Tower and Nature Center** is the tall, distinctive rock building located along the lake. The tower was originally built in the 1930s for the National Park Service as a WPA project. The suggestion was made to have Tucker Tower serve as a summer residence for Oklahoma's governor. It was never used until 1950, when it became a museum. It now holds interpretive exhibits about the wildlife of the Lake Murray area. Highlights include hands-on exhibits and a large meteorite. Cassette tape players with headphones are available for more information. Hours for Tucker Tower and Nature Center are Monday-Saturday 9-5 and Sunday 1-5. Admission is fifty cents for ages two and up.

## *Events*

### The Ardmore Shrine Rodeo

*This event is held the first week of April at Hardy Murphy Coliseum. 600 Lake Murray Drive. For more information, call (405) 223-2672. Admission varies each year but is usually around $8-10, with children under age twelve being free.*

The Shrine Club sponsors a professional rodeo each year to raise money for handicapped children. Dances, a parade, a barbecue, and a chili cook-off are all part of the fun.

## SUMMERFEST!

*Weekends from the first of May through the fourth of July and held at various locations in Ardmore. For more information, call (405) 223-7765.*

Each weekend, family-oriented activities such as a bike rally, music festival, fireworks show, and more take place. Your family will love the fun!

### Ardmore's Birthday Celebration

*Held the last week of July at several city parks. For more information, call (405) 223-7765.*

Activities at this celebration include hot air balloon races, street dances, musical entertainment, retail Crazy Daze Sales, birthday cake, and more.

### Art in the Park

*Held the last weekend of September in Central Park, downtown Ardmore. For more information, call (405) 223-7765.*

This two-day festival features regional artists displaying and selling their artwork; children enjoy special activities such as face painting and other hands-on projects. Food booths, local musicians, and dancers add to the festivities.

# Davis

In the 1830s, Chickasaw Indians began moving to this location, but Davis didn't become a town until 1887. It was named after Samuel H. David, a prominent settler. Davis is a small, attractive place with clean-swept streets. The town is well-situated for the tourist trade, as it is located near Arbuckle Wilderness, the Chickasaw National Recreation Area, and Turner Falls.

*Davis is located 71 miles south of Oklahoma City on I-35. From the interstate, take Highway 7 east three miles to Davis. The town is about 150 miles from Tulsa. Davis Chamber of Commerce (405) 369-2402.*

## Attractions

### Arbuckle Wilderness

*South of Davis. From I-35 take exit 51 south of Davis. Travel 1/4 mile then follow the signs. Open every day except Christmas from 8 a.m. until one hour before sundown. Call ahead for information about special events held during evenings and on holiday and summer weekends. Adults $14.99, senior citizens $8.99, children ages three through ten $9.99, children under age three are admitted free. The "pay one price" admission enables visitors to enjoy the rides and attractions as many times as they want.*

Arbuckle Wilderness was Lake Country's #1 attraction in 1995 and 1996 and, in 1993, it was voted "Oklahoma's Most Outstanding Tourist Attraction" by the Oklahoma Tourism Department and the Oklahoma Travel Industry Association. Be prepared to spend the entire day here; children can easily fill their time between the drive-through zoo, walk-through zoo, rides, and attractions.

Take the eight-mile drive through the Arbuckle Mountains and observe wild animals up-close. Animals to look for on the drive include deer, elk, ostrich, giraffes, lions, tigers, buffalo, and zebras. Be sure to buy a bucket of food as you begin the drive; then watch the excitement when some of the animals come right up to your car when you stop. These animals are not shy; they've even been known to stick their heads in visitor's car windows!

Children will also delight in the **walk-through zoo**. It includes beautiful and exotic birds, an otter who likes to show off for visitors, twin chimpanzees, and several other animals. Throughout the day, entertaining and educational shows are performed. You don't want to miss feeding time at the lake. Watch as the hundreds of catfish come to the surface to get a snack.

The **Fun Park** is open daily during the summer season (Memorial Day weekend to mid-September); during other seasons, it is open on weekends, weather permitting. This area offers rides and attractions such as paddle boats, camel or llama rides, a moonbounce, bumper boats, an arcade, and go-karts. Kiddie bumper boats and a rookie go-cart track are available for younger children.

### Helpful Hints

Upon request, group programs can be customized by the tour guides for specific educational needs. Call for prices. Box lunches can be served, with prices for the program and lunch in the $7 range.

For groups of thirty-five or more, guided hayride tours are available. The hayride includes the eight-mile drive through the park accompanied by a park ranger; it is followed by a cookout. Reservations are required.

If you and your family plan to spend the day, you can pack a picnic lunch or buy meals at the park's two restaurants. Shaded picnic tables make this a perfect spot to enjoy the beauty of the Arbuckle Mountains.

## Canoeing the Washita River

*Rose Grocery. Located two miles south of Davis on Highway 77. (405) 369-2223. Cost is $15 per person for a ten-mile trip.*

Enjoy the beautiful scenery in this part of Oklahoma as you float down the Washita River. Pack a picnic lunch and spend a relaxing day exploring the shoreline. Call in advance to reserve your canoe. Life jackets are included in the cost of the trip or bring your own for a better fit.

### Helpful Hints

Children as young as four can go on the river. Before you go, it is necessary to check with the Rose Grocery staff about the water level of the river; the river could be too high or too low for a safe trip. The Washita River is a red-colored, muddy river but it is not polluted; wear old clothes. The trip down the river takes approximately three hours, but stops along the way for resting, exploring and picnicking could make this an all-day excursion.

## Cedervale Botanical Gardens

*From I-35 and Exit 51, travel south on U.S. Highway 77. Follow the signs. (405) 369-3224 or (405) 369-3658 for reservations. Open from April-October. Spring hours, daily 11-8, Summer (after Memorial Day) hours, 11-9. The tour is free with a meal, or $3 for the tour only.*

*Turner Falls is a favorite with Oklahoma families.*

Set on twelve acres of natural and landscaped beauty, Cedervale Botanical Gardens offers a most pleasurable evening of dining. Older children will appreciate the uniqueness of this place. While dining on the deck overlooking the gardens, enjoy the house specialty of fresh trout. After your dinner, you may walk through the gardens which have been growing for seventeen years; you may wish to stroll down one of the trails to the swinging bridge.

## Turner Falls Park

*South of Davis, (405) 369-2917 or (405) 369-2988. From I-35, take Exit 51 and turn south on U.S. Highway 77. The entrance is located 3.5 miles south of Davis. Follow the signs. Swimming areas are open daily from May to September; camping is available all year. Park admission: adults $6, children ages seven to twelve $4.50, senior citizens $4.50. Group rates are available. Per night camping rates: adults $7.50, children $5.50, senior citizens $6.50. Cabins are $45 per night. Parking is available at several areas in the park; keep following the paved road if you cannot find a place to park. Important note: No glass containers are allowed in the park.*

Turner Falls, Oklahoma's oldest park, is owned by the City of Davis. Mountain streams combine into a cascading seventy-seven-foot waterfall, then combine again to form another stream that meanders through the park. The swimming and wading at Turner Falls are irresistible! Two natural spring-fed swimming areas, Blue Hole and Falls Pool, along with several sandy beaches, make this a very exciting place to visit in the heat of the Oklahoma summer. Bring your bathing suit and sunscreen but, most importantly, bring shoes to wear in the water! You'll need them, especially when wading in Honey Creek, where rocks are rough on tender feet!

The **Blue Hole swimming area** is more appropriate for older children. Attached to the face of the mountain is an exciting slide that young people will want to try over and over again. There is also a diving board available. The **Falls Pool** is situated below the waterfall and it has both shallow and deep areas for swimming. Rocks located near the pool's edge make climbing great fun for everyone. During the summer, lifeguards are on duty at both swimming areas, but life jackets are still recommended.

Take the younger children to **Honey Creek**, where they will delight in exploring the shallow pools and mini-waterfalls. Grassy banks provide the perfect spot to enjoy the sun or to have a picnic. Fortunately, there are plenty of trees to provide shade. Hike the trails leading through the park; you may find a cave. On your way to the waterfall, visit the "castle" home perched on the mountainside. Built in the 1930s, it is the former summer home of a college professor. You may explore the buildings, stairs and patios of the home.

### Helpful Hints

Picnic areas and camping sites (both primitive and R.V. sites ) can be found throughout the park. There are two rustic cabins located on the grounds. Each includes a refrigerator and linens for the two double beds, but you must bring your own dishes. Grills and picnic tables are furnished outside the cabins. If you are picnicking and would like to find a less crowded area, try the picnic areas on top of the mountain.

You can bring your own lunch or buy it from the concession stands conveniently located by the swimming areas. Before you leave Turner Falls, take advantage of the showers in the bathhouse next to the Blue Hole; you won't want to bring the sand home with you!

Turner Fall sponsors several events throughout the year. There is a **car show** in June, and **arts and craft shows** in early April and early October. During December, the park hosts **Fantasyland**, a half-mile display of Christmas scenes.

# Sulphur

Indians knew of the "healing waters" found in mineral springs in this area long before the white man came to settle the area. This area was Indian land, but as more non-Indians moved into the area, the Indians became concerned for the preservation of the springs. In the early 1900s, they gave the area to the U.S. Government to be used as a park, forcing the two hundred or so settlers to move their town to the present site of Sulphur. The area around Sulphur Springs became Platt National Park, the smallest national park in the country. In the 1970s, the park and other nearby areas were incorporated into the Chickasaw National Recreation Area, and Platt National Park ceased to exist.

*Located 71 miles south of Oklahoma City off I-35. Take Highway 7 east through Davis, then nine miles further east to Sulphur. Sulphur is 144 miles from Tulsa. Sulphur Chamber of Commerce (405) 622-2824.*

## *Attractions*

### *Chickasaw National Recreation Area*

*From I-35, take Highway 7 east to Sulphur, then follow the signs. (405) 622-3165. Hours at Travertine Nature Center are summer (Memorial Day through Labor Day): Sunday-Thursday 8-7 and Friday-Saturday 8-9. Winter hours: daily 8-5. Admission is free.*

From early times, springs, streams and lakes have attracted people to the Chickasaw National Recreation Area. The water from the more than thirty mineral springs in the area was said to have magical healing powers. Because of the popularity of these mineral waters, a town called Sulphur Springs grew around them. The town was later moved to the present site of Sulphur when the Native Americans who owned the land donated it to the Federal Government as a preserve.

Visitors to this beautiful park find a variety of activities including camping, boating, fishing, swimming, and hiking. Begin your tour with a drink from the mineral springs. These mineral springs give off a very distinct aroma, but in the words of one young visitor, "the water tastes pretty good if you're holding your nose."

The park offers over twenty miles in hiking trails. Walking a trail along a stream, you may pass from an eastern forest into a prairie and back again. This unique combination of ecosystems makes Chickasaw National Recreation Area a "biological crossroads." Visitors may catch a glimpse of a roadrunner in the same area as a cardinal, or a sycamore, oak, and pecan tree alongside tall grasses and prickly pear cactus. Fox, squirrel, whitetail deer, armadillo, beaver, gray fox, skunk, bobcat, and wild turkey may also be seen. Hike along the trail with a ranger and learn about some of these interesting critters and how they interact in their unique environments. Bird watchers should bring their binoculars!

Visit the **Travertine Nature Center** to explore our natural world through exhibits, live animal displays, nature hikes, and other educational programs. During the summer months, nature movies are shown daily at 11 a.m., 12 noon and 1 p.m. Morning hikes, creek walks, and daily feeding demonstrations make for a fun-filled learning atmosphere! During the off-season, guided hikes and educational programs are available by appointment. Park Rangers are always available and ready to answer your questions.

Bring your swim suit; a dip in the water is always a good way to complete your visit. Little Niagara is the most popular swimming area, but anywhere along Travertine or Rock Creek is perfect for wading. **Veterans Lake**, a small lake located near Rock Creek Campground, offers fishing, boating (inquire about the lake's special regulations), swimming, hiking trails, and picnicking areas. A fishing dock designed for those with disabilities is available.

**Lake of the Arbuckles** is also located in the recreation area. This secluded lake offers fishing, picnicking, boating, hiking, and camping. For more information about lake activities, call (405) 622-3165.

### Helpful Hints

Park maps are available at the Travertine Nature Center and at Park Headquarters. For group picnics, covered pavilions are equipped with picnic tables and grills, and they are available on a reservation-only basis.

Call ahead to inquire about special ranger-led hikes, evening programs, and other activities available through the Travertine Nature Center. One of the best programs offered through the center are **Night Hikes**, held every Friday and Saturday during the summer season. During the hike, participants use their senses (aided by a flashlight) to identify wildlife. The hike lasts about ninety minutes and is recommended for children approximately six years and older. To participate in the hike, you must call or stop by the Nature Center early in the morning on the day you wish to go. Be sure to bring your flashlights!

If you are planning an overnight excursion, family and group camping sites are available throughout the park. Family campsites are $8 per night for primitive sites and $14 per night for sites with hookups. Hookup sites are located at Buckhorn campground located near the Lake of the Arbuckles. All camping sites (except for group camping) are available on a first-come, first-served basis. Group camping is $16 per site and can accommodate groups up to twenty-five people per site; call ahead for reservations.

# Southwest Oklahoma

## Anadarko

Anadarko is the county seat of Caddo County and is often thought of as the "most Indian" place in Oklahoma. The town is named for one of the Caddoan tribes, the Nadako clan, but sometime early in the town's history, the name was spelled incorrectly. In 1878, the agencies of the Kiowa, Apache and Comanche tribes consolidated with the Wichita Tribe. Even today, Anadarko is known as the "capital" of the Plains Indians.

Beadwork demonstration.

Start your tour of Anadarko at the National Hall of Fame for Famous American Indians and Anadarko Visitors Center. The people here will help customize your tour of the area. Include on your trip a stop in downtown Anadarko. With its many turn-of-the-century buildings, the downtown area is designated as a historic district on the National Register of Historic Places.

*Anadarko is sixty-five miles southwest of Oklahoma City, and about 242 miles southwest of Tulsa. From Oklahoma City, take the H.E. Bailey Turnpike (I-44) to the Highway 62 (Exit 83) exit at Chickasha, then go west to Anadarko. Anadarko Chamber of Commerce (405) 247-6651.*

### Attractions

### Indian City, U.S.A.

*From the intersection of Highway 62 and Highway 8, turn south on Highway 8. Travel approximately two miles, then turn east at the Indian City sign. (405) 247-5661 or (800) 433-5661. Open daily 9-6 during the summer and 9-5 during the winter. Adults $7, children ages six to eleven $4 and children under six free. (There is no charge if you don't take the tour.) The lodge and tours are handicapped accessible.*

Indian City, U.S.A. promotes itself as being "the only authentic restoration of Indian dwellings and way of life in America!" To insure the authenticity of the village, the Department of Anthropology at the University of Oklahoma supervised the planning and construction of the villages when they were built in the mid-1950s.

Indian City, U.S.A. is located on the site of the Tonkawa Massacre. During the Civil War, the Tonkawa Indians were attacked by a band of Shawnee Indians and other mercenaries. Now, a herd of buffalo roams this area.

To get the most from Indian City, take the guided tour of the seven different Indian Villages, available daily from 9:30-4:30 (the final tour begins at 4:30). Each tour is led by members of the same Native American tribes represented on the tour. Tours start at the lodge, and they are conducted every forty-five minutes. The villages are designed to give insight into the daily, religious and social lives of Native Americans and, although the villages are showing their age, they still provide an educational experience for families. As an added bonus, during summer days and on most Sundays, the Indian City dancers perform for each tour.

Located in the lodge, a three-room museum is included in the tour. The museum houses and preserves Native American artifacts such as artwork, baskets and clothing. A gift shop containing traditional jewelry, dolls, pottery, moccasins, and other items is also located here.

### Helpful Hints

Overnight camping is offered at Indian City. A campground offering a swimming pool, restrooms, showers, and drinking water is available for tents, campers and self-contained trailers.

Just north of Indian City is the Buffalo Gap Restaurant, which features Indian tacos and buffalo burgers. A free **petting zoo** filled with farm animals is located next to the restaurant. The **Buffalo Gap Exotic Animal Drive-Thru** contains buffalo, black buck antelope, fallow deer, whitetail deer, and llamas. The drive-thru costs $5.

*National Hall of Fame for Famous American Indians.*

## The National Hall of Fame for Famous American Indians

*Highway 62 East, (405) 247-5555. Monday-Saturday 9-5 and Sunday 1-5. Admission is free; donations are appreciated. The center is handicapped accessible.*

If you are planning to visit the many Native American museums and historical sites located in Anadarko, your first stop should be The National Hall of Fame for Famous American Indians and Anadarko Visitors Center. Here, you will receive the information necessary to visit local museums and attractions. The local ladies who staff the center are very friendly, and they will gladly help you with any questions regarding local attractions and anything else you may want to know about the town of Anadarko. Free literature and maps are available.

Inside the center, video presentations of past Hall of Fame dedication ceremonies may be viewed. There is also a brochure available for a self-guided walking tour of the forty-one bronze busts located at the center. Five of the busts are located inside; the other thirty-six are found outside in the lovely statuary garden. Viewing the busts and reading the accompanying information provides a great history lesson for everyone.

## Philomathic Pioneer Museum

*311 East Main, (405) 247-3240. As Highway 62 enters town, it becomes Central Boulevard. At the intersection of Central Boulevard and 3rd Street, turn north and travel three blocks to Main. Open daily 1-5, closed Mondays and legal holidays. Admission is free. The museum is not handicapped accessible.*

This museum was established in 1936 for "the historic preservation of regional antiques and Indian artifacts." Although originally housed at the old city hall, the collection was moved to the historic Rock Island Railroad Depot in 1976. The word "philomathic" means "love for the search of knowledge"; it is also the name of the women's club that started the collection.

Areas within the museum include railroad memorabilia displayed in an old ticket office, military equipment and uniforms, a Native American doll collection, garments and artifacts, a photograph exhibit, an early-day physician's office, and a country store. Life-size figures dressed authentically in period clothing are found throughout the museum, and these help the past come to life for visitors. The volunteers at the museum are very helpful, and they will be glad to answer any questions you may have.

## Southern Plains Indian Museum

*Highway 62, east of Anadarko, (405) 247-6221. June-September: Monday-Saturday 9-5 and Sunday 1-5, October-May: Tuesday-Saturday 9-5 and Sunday 1-5. Closed New Year's Day, Thanksgiving and Christmas. Adults $3 (groups of ten or more $1), children (ages six to twelve) $1, and under six free. If scheduled in advance, school groups are free; otherwise, there is a charge of $1 per student. The museum is handicapped accessible.*

Children of all ages will be interested in the colorful displays depicting the lives and traditions of the Southern Plains tribes, past and present. Especially interesting are the life-size figures of Southern Plains men, women and children wearing various traditional clothing, including warrior apparel, ceremonial dress, and dancers' regalia.

Another interesting display features cradleboards for babies. A rounded piece of wood placed on top protected the baby from the sun, and a wooden foot rest placed under the feet raised the baby up to keep it from developing a rash.

*Elaine Warner*

*Southern Plains Indian Museum.*

Yarn strung across the top supported mosquito netting in the summer and wool covers in the winter. While mothers were traveling, the cradleboard was carried on the back or shoulders; it was used until the baby was nine or ten months old.

Other significant displays include everything from household implements to hunting and fighting equipment. Games, smoking accessories, religious and ceremonial items are also available for viewing.

Children will enjoy the opportunity to see authentically-decorated tepees. Miniature tepees may be viewed year-round inside the museum, and full-scale painted tepees are set up outside the museum during the summer.

The Oklahoma Indian Arts and Crafts Cooperative operates a quality gift shop within the museum. The Cooperative maintains high standards of authenticity as it promotes Native American artists. Articles found in the gift shop include bead medallions, bead jewelry, silver jewelry, miniature tepees, dreamcatchers, artwork, dolls, Indian clothing, and more.

## Events

### American Indian Exposition

*Held during six days in early August at the Caddo County fairgrounds, N.E. 7th and Broadway, two blocks north of Highway 62 on the east side of town. For a brochure and schedule of events, call the Anadarko Chamber of Commerce. Entrance to the fairgrounds and arts and crafts exhibits are free, but there is a charge for the dancing, pageants and racing.*

Indian dance competitions, arts and crafts, games, pageant presentations, dog and horse racing, parades—all this adds up to an ideal opportunity for your family to experience Native American culture! Try Indian tacos, fry bread, corn soup, or Indian stew at the food booths. The entire town supports the Exposition, making it the perfect time to visit Anadarko!

### Holiday Celebration

*Held from dark to ten p.m. nightly beginning the Tuesday preceding Thanksgiving* through New Year's Eve. The festivities and lights are located in Randlett Park. Go west on Central (Highway 62). Continue west on Central several blocks past Mission Street (where 62 turns south), and you'll see signs to the celebration. For a brochure, call the Anadarko Chamber of Commerce at (405) 247-6651. Free.

This Christmas light festival began in 1995 with thirty-five light displays, and it's growing. Many of the displays have special significance to the donors; some exhibit a Native American influence. Hot chocolate and coffee are sold in the park. You can drive through, park and walk, or hire a horse and buggy when available.

# Clinton

Established as a railroad town, Clinton is now best known for its Route 66, "Mother Road" heritage. The town boasts a restored downtown with many quaint shops, and a community theater, the Southwest Playhouse, located in a 1930s WPA native stone building.

*Clinton is located eighty-four miles west of Oklahoma City on I-40, and 184 miles south and west of Tulsa. Clinton Chamber of Commerce (800) 759-1397 or locally 323-2222.*

## Attractions

### Mohawk Lodge Indian Store

*(405) 323-2360. One mile east of Clinton on Route 66. From I-40, take Exit 69 and go south. This will put you on old Route 66 through Clinton. Open Monday-Saturday 9-5.*

The oldest Indian store in Oklahoma, this place is part museum and part shop. It began in 1892 in Colony, Indian Territory, where it was situated next to the Indian Agency. Missionaries of the Dutch Reformed Church, anxious to provide opportunities for the Indians to sell their wares, started the store and even published a catalog. Back then, a pair of fully-beaded

*History for sale at Mohawk Lodge Indian Store.*

moccasins sold for $2, compared to $260 today.

In 1940, the store was moved to its present location on Route 66. Owner Pat Henry still sells or trades materials to the Indians and retails their finished products. New merchandise sits side by side with antiques, making this as much a history lesson as a shopping expedition.

### Oklahoma Route 66 Museum

*2229 W. Gary Boulevard, (405) 323-7866. From I-40, take Exit 65; the museum is*

Elaine Warner

*Oklahoma Route 66 Museum in Clinton.*

*about 1/4 mile north on the west side of the road. Winter hours: Labor Day-Memorial Day, Tuesday-Saturday 9-5, Sunday 1-5. Closed on Mondays. Summer Hours: Memorial Day-Labor Day, Monday-Saturday 9-7, Sunday 1-6. The museum is closed on state holidays and during the first week of January. Adults $3, children (ages six to ten) $1, children under six are free. This museum is handicapped accessible.*

Route 66, also known as the Main Street of America, the Mother Road, the Free Road, and sometimes the Will Rogers Highway, was dedicated on November 11, 1926, as the first of the nation's "super highways." Stretching across 2,440 miles from Chicago, Illinois, to Santa Monica, California, this road crossed eight states and three time zones, and it played a significant role in our nation's history. Oklahoma is an important part of the Mother Road's history; today, more of the original road is preserved in Oklahoma than in any other state.

Touring the Oklahoma Route 66 Museum includes listening to a 45-minute audio tape presentation by Michael Wallis, noted author of the book *Route 66, The Mother Road*. As you pass from room to room, the recording will signal when to stop and start your tape. Each room represents a particular decade, and a button at each entrance activates popular music from that era.

The museum's exhibits demonstrate how this incredible stretch of highway was utilized in each decade. During the 1920s, automobiles became more common, and a need for better, more interconnected roads developed. The 1930s brought the Depression, forcing many tenant farmers from Oklahoma and elsewhere to load their vehicles and move west to California. (These people were often referred to as "Okies," thus giving Oklahomans a new nickname.) World War II broke out during the 1940s; giving a ride to a GI hitchhiking his way home was considered a patriotic duty. The 1950s were a popular time for roadside diners, and the 1960s emerged as the decade of hippies and VW vans.

Over a period of three decades, Route 66 was replaced by five interstate highways. The last stretch of this famous road was closed in 1984 in Williams, Arizona.

As the tour ends, visitors sit at a replica of a drive-in theater and watch old film clips about Route 66. You'll be full of nostalgic feelings as Bobby Troup sings his hit song, "Get Your Kicks on Route 66."

### Helpful Hints

The museum has a nice gift shop featuring everything from T-shirts to fuzzy dice for your rearview mirror. Your length of stay will be determined by the age of your children; this museum is best for children who can read. To experience first hand an authentic Route 66 diner, try out Clinton's **Pop Hicks Restaurant** 🍴, located at 223 Gary Boulevard. Known for wonderful chicken-fried steak and homemade pie, this historic cafe has reasonably-priced food and provides a welcome relief from typical "fast food" family vacation meals.

# Duncan

In 1879, trader William Duncan settled in this area with his wife, a member of the Chickasaw Nation. In 1889, when the Chickasaws were given allotments, Mrs. Duncan selected a site where the Rock Island Railroad was intended to come through. Later, she divided the land and sold lots. The town was officially founded in 1893.

Duncan steadily grew and was largely dependent on farming until the early 1920s when oil became "big business" in the area. In 1924, Erle Halliburton started an oil-well cementing service; his worldwide company has greatly influenced the town of Duncan.

Duncan visitors will find wonderful parks (especially Fuqua Park), a one-of-a-kind community center, an educational museum, and a growing music festival. *Located ninety miles south and west of Oklahoma City, and two hundred miles south and west of Tulsa. Take I-44 (H.E. Bailey Turnpike) to Chickasha, then U.S. Highway 81 south to Duncan. Duncan Chamber of Commerce & Industry (405) 255-3644.*

## Attractions

### Simmons Center

*800 N. 29th Street, (405) 252-4386. If traveling south on U.S. Highway 81, turn west at Plato Street on the north edge of town. Go one mile to 29th Street, turn south and continue for about a mile and a half. Indoor facilities are open Monday-Friday 6 a.m.-10 p.m., Saturday 8-8, Sunday 1-6. The playground is open from daybreak until 11 p.m. Visitors can purchase day passes to the recreation area or temporary weekly memberships. Day-passes are $5; there is no charge for Centennial Park. Prices for cultural events vary. Handicapped accessible.*

The beautiful and extensive Simmons Center complex contains both recreational and cultural facilities. The recreation area includes a twenty-five meter swimming pool, walking/jogging track, whirlpool and saunas, racquetball courts equipped for squash, walleyball and handball, weight and aerobics rooms, a gym, a gameroom, and a nursery. There is also a children's pool and an area called "Exploration Station" for children ages three to eleven. This area has slides, tunnels and a ball pit.

Centennial Park is a fantastic outdoor playground which was designed with the needs of children of all abilities in mind. Giant dragons, swings, towers, sandboxes, mazes, slides—ten thousand square feet of pure fun. There are wheelchair ramps, braille games, accessible swingsets, and a number of adaptations to make this a space that all children can enjoy. Picnic tables are available on-site.

A theater at the center hosts numerous cultural events; for a complete schedule, call (405) 252-2900.

## Stephens County Historical Society Museum

*U.S. Highway 81 and Beech, (405) 252-0717. Open Thursday-Sunday 1-5. Admission is free. Handicapped accessible.*

Located in an old armory in Fuqua Park, this museum is larger than the average county historical museum. Through its extensive collection, visitors leave with a real sense of the area's history. The Boomer Room showcases pioneer life from 1877-1920. Displays include Indian artifacts, Chisholm Trail memorabilia, and replicas of a covered wagon and a surrey. Children will especially enjoy the recreated schoolroom and dentist's office. The Sooner Room highlights the history of Halliburton and the oil industry.

## Events

## American Music Festival

*Held in mid-July at the Simmons Center. For information, call (800) 255-0909. Tickets for evening performances cost $15-20, afternoon performances cost $20, children's concert costs $2.50. Series packages are available at a discounted price.*

This four-day fest features classical and popular American music and premiers a newly-commissioned work each year. As the festival builds, it is attracting more concert-goers and more big-name entertainers. In the past, guest artists have included guitarist Mason Williams and trumpeter Al Hirt. Popular American classical works like Barber's "Adagio for Strings" share the stage with big band compositions or Rodgers and Hammerstein favorites. A children's concert is held on the Saturday morning of the festival. In 1997, the concert is entitled "The Gift of the Eagle" and through an entertaining story, the concert shares the history of music with children. There's something for everyone's musical taste at this exciting and growing festival!

## Elk City

This town, like so many in Oklahoma, was established by the railroad. Elk City takes great pride in its western heritage. Families can learn about the area's pioneer days through the Old Town Museum which is conveniently located next to a large city park.

*Elk City is approximately 120 miles west of Oklahoma City on I-40 and 211 miles from Tulsa. Elk City Chamber of Commerce (800) 280-0207.*

## Attractions

### Ackley Park

*U.S. Highway 66 and Pioneer Road. Traveling from Oklahoma City, take Exit 41 from I-40 and go west through Elk City on old Route 66. The park and the Old Town Museum are on the west side of town. The only restrooms in the park are in the Aquatic Center, which is closed in the winter.*

Ackley Park was a favorite stopping place of travelers on Route 66 for years. It was a wonderful place for a picnic or just to get out of the car and stretch. The beautiful pond, old mill, playgrounds, and trees still make this a great place to visit. Children will enjoy fishing in the pond or feeding the ducks. On weekends, miniature golf and a mini-train are big attractions. The park also has an aquatic center, tennis court and fenced playground area.

### Old Town Museum

*U.S. Highway 66 and Pioneer Road (next to Ackley Park), (405) 225-2207. Tuesday-Saturday 9-5, Sunday 2-5. Adults $2.50, children under 12 free. The main floor of the museum and several of the Cowtown buildings are handicapped accessible (others may involve several steps).*

The main part of the Old Town Museum complex is located in an authentic turn-of-the-century home that belonged to an early-day Elk City merchant. Several rooms are decorated in Victorian style. In the museum, you'll find a variety of exhibits reflecting the lives and interests of the area people. A campaign button collection was contributed by one resident and Susan Powell, former Miss America and Elk City native, donated her crown, dress, trophy and earrings from her 1981 victory. Upstairs is the Beutler Brothers Rodeo Hall. It houses equipment and memorabilia donated by the Beutlers, rodeo cowboys, and producers of rodeo stock. "Cowtown" is located adjacent to the museum, and it includes both original and replicated structures. There is a one-room school, livery stable, chapel, depot, and a one-room house (Elk

*The Old Town Museum.*

City's first wooden home). If the buildings are locked, please make inquiries in the museum. Allow at least one hour to see the exhibits in the museum and to look around the old town.

## Hinton

### *Attractions*

### *Red Rock Canyon State Park*
*Located in Hinton, (405) 542-6344. From I-40, turn on U.S. Highway 281 (Exit 101) and travel five miles south, or drive one mile south of downtown Hinton. Various prices are charged for different activities; for more information, call the park office.* 🅂

Located in western Oklahoma, Red Rock Canyon was formed over 260 million years ago during the Permian geologic age. Water cutting into the soft sandstone formed this wonderful area where families can camp and enjoy the beauty of nature. A spring-fed creek which flows year round is responsible for creating this beautiful location; it is unlike any other place in this part of Oklahoma.

In the early 1800s, the Plains Indians used the canyon as a shelter during the winter; it was also a place to hunt for food. When gold was discovered in California, wagon trails were suddenly established. One such trail, named the California Road, passed through Red Rock Canyon. The canyon was used as a natural landmark and, many times, the travelers would stop here to repair their wagons and to stock up on fresh water.

Many family activities are available at Red Rock Canyon State Park. During the day, picnic sites are available in Area 2, which is also the location of the swimming pool and playground equipment. Additionally, unimproved campsites not being used for camping may be used for picnicking. Five group picnic areas located throughout the park are available all day on a first-come, first-served basis, or by reservation made through the park office. There is a fee for using the group picnic areas.

From Memorial Day to Labor Day, the **swimming pool** is open from Wednesday through Sunday 12-7 p.m. There is a minimal admission charge for the pool.

Two maintained **nature trails** are available for use. The one-eighth mile Rough Horsetail Interpretive Trail is located at the bottom of the steep entrance hill at the north end of the park, and it is an excellent place to examine the various plants and trees found in the canyon. On the south end of the park is the California Road Interpretive Trail. This three-quarter mile trail was once part of the trail that originated in Little Rock, Arkansas; it was traveled by pioneers heading west to seek their fortunes. Visitors are welcome to explore other parts of the canyon on their own; but they should be cautious, and they should always be on the lookout for snakes.

The park is a popular place for rock climbing and rappelling. This can be a great group activity; however, all safety procedures should be followed. Always use proper equipment and have someone with experience in your group; this activity can be very dangerous, and serious accidents are possible.

Overnight activities at the park include semi-modern and unimproved camp-sites and a group camp facility. For tent or recreation vehicle camping, the park maintains comfort stations with hot showers and an RV sanitary dump station. Use of the group camp facility is available by reservation only; the facility is available from April through October and can accommodate up to 160 people. Fees are charged for all overnight camping.

### Helpful Hints

For the safety of visitors, and in an effort to preserve the natural beauty of the park, a strict set of rules and regulations are maintained. These rules and regulations are posted throughout the park, and a complete copy is available of the park office.

# Lawton

The fourth largest town in Oklahoma, Lawton was born when a lottery was held in 1901, opening over two million acres of the Kiowa-Comanche-Apache reservation to white settlement. Lawton's growth and development had a "jump start" due to the earlier 1869 establishment of nearby Fort Sill. The fort still greatly influences Lawton and is now a noted tourist attraction as well as an active Army military base. With an active arts council and a full slate of arts activities, Lawton is the hub of an area containing fascinating museums, natural beauty, and places of historic importance and interest.

*Lawton is ninety-eight miles southwest of Oklahoma City on I-44 (H.E. Bailey Turnpike); it is 214 miles southwest of Tulsa. Lawton Chamber of Commerce (800) 872-4540.*

## Attractions

### Elmer Thomas Park

*Ferris and Second Streets. (405) 581-3400 or (405) 581-3410. From I-44, exit on Second Street, and travel south to Ferris. Open daily.*

Although there are many park activities here, the most popular involves a large prairie dog town. On nice days, the prairie dogs sun themselves at the entrance of their burrows while showing off for visitors and waiting for hand-outs. There is an informative sign showing a cross section of an underground prairie dog town. It also gives information about the animal's daily routine. Also available at the Elmer Thomas Park are a lake, playground equipment, a two-mile walking trail, pavilions, and picnic areas.

### Helpful Hints

This park is located near the Museum of the Great Plains and the Percussive Arts Society Museum, making it a perfect place to have a picnic and "run off" extra energy!

### Fort Sill Museum

*Located two miles north of Lawton. From I-44, take the Key Gate exit and follow the signs directing you to each of the museums. (405) 442-5123. Open daily 8:30-4:30, closed December 25-26, and January 1-2. Guided tours for large groups are available if you make prior arrangements. Admission is free.* ★

General Philip H. Sheridan founded Ft. Sill on January 8, 1869. It was constructed by the troops of the 9th and 10th U.S. Cavalry, also known as the famed "Buffalo Soldiers." There are actually three posts at the Fort. Made of limestone houses and barracks, the earliest post houses the museum complex, the largest of its kind in the Army's museum system. To start your tour, pick up a self-guided tour brochure at the Visitor's Center or at a map kiosk.

The Visitor's Center originally housed the Infantry barracks, although it was designed to serve as a warehouse. It now shows a chronological history of Fort Sill, from its early days as an Indian village to the present. "Cricket's Corner" is a small, hands-on area designed to help younger children imagine life during the frontier days. A replica of a soldier's barracks and an Indian village, including a brush arbor, are displayed in this area. Also featured is a kitchen complete with a butter churn, stove, and hand-operated washing machine. A schoolroom includes pictures of students who once attended school here.

Older children will enjoy visiting the **First School of Fire** to learn about the history of field artillery training. A trip to the **Geronimo Guardhouse** will instruct them about the lives of soldiers and Indian tribes. These well-arranged and informative exhibits help visitors relive the early days of Oklahoma history.

Built in 1870, the **Quartermaster Corral**, or "Old Stone Corral," once held horses, mules and oxen. Later, it was used to temporarily confine the "Boomers" (those men and women who attempted to settle Indian Territory before it was legal to do so), before the army escorted them out of the area. Current exhibits include horse-drawn vehicles and a blacksmith shop.

Those interested in artillery weapons should visit the Commissary Storehouse, where artillery exhibits from the colonial days to 1900 are housed. Outdoor exhibits called "Cannon Walk," "Missile Park," and "Desert Storm Artillery Park" include field artillery weapons collected from around the world.

### Helpful Hints

If you have questions, ask the knowledgeable staff at the Administrative Office, located in the Old Post Headquarters building. Plan to spend at least a half a day at the Fort. Fort Sill is a few miles from Lawton; you may want to pack a lunch or find the fast food restaurant located at the corner of Currie and Sheridan.

The famous Apache warrior, Geronimo, is buried in the Apache Prisoner of War Cemetery; people continue to bring tributes to his grave site. The interesting cemetery is just a short drive north of Fort Sill; follow the signs. With older children (ages six and up), reading the gravestones can provide a valuable history lesson.

Several special events are held each year at Fort Sill, including the **Candlelight Christmas Stroll** (held the second weekend in December) through the Old Post Quadrangle, and **A Tea in Time** in mid-June, a recreation of an old-time entertainment featuring authentic recipes of the chosen period. Occasionally, there are military parades and ceremonies. The biggest event is the **Heritage Fair**, held on Memorial Day weekend. This educational experience is designed to showcase traditional skills and life-styles of the military, civilian and Native American peoples of the nineteenth century. Call ahead for information on scheduled events.

## Mattie Beal Home

Elaine Warner

*Mattie Beal Home.*

*1006 Southwest 5th Street, (405) 353-6884. From I-44, take Lee Boulevard west to 5th Street. Turn north onto 5th Street and travel to Summit Avenue. The home is located at 5th and Summit Avenue. Open the second Sunday of each month, 2-4, and occasionally other Sundays. Often open the first Sunday in August for Lawton's birthday celebration, and some extra Sundays during the Christmas season. Adults $2, children ages twelve and under $1. The home has limited handicapped accessibility.*

Built in 1908, the Mattie Beal Home is now a National Historical Landmark. In 1901, Mattie Beal was twenty-two years old when she won 160 acres in the Oklahoma Territory land lottery. Because her land included downtown Lawton and was considered very valuable, Mattie received several marriage proposals. Just two weeks short of a year after winning the lottery, Mattie married C.W. Payne, a lumberman. Together, they built a Neoclassic Greek Revival mansion that had fourteen rooms. It was fashioned after the plantation home that belonged to Mattie's grandmother in southern Missouri. The home has since been restored to its Greek Revival beauty, and it now includes period antiques.

Visitors to the Mattie Beal Home will learn of her contributions to the city of Lawton; a generous land donation by Miss Beal resulted in the building of two parks, a school, and a church.

## Museum of the Great Plains

*601 Ferris Avenue, (405) 581-3460. From I-44, take the 2nd Street exit south to Ferris Avenue. Turn west onto Ferris Avenue and continue to the museum, located on the north side of the street. Open Monday-Friday 9-5, Saturday 10-5, Sunday 1-*

*5. Adults $2, children ages seven to eleven $1, children six and under free.* ★

One of the best museums in the region, the Museum of the Great Plains features over forty exhibits that focus on the Great Plains region dating from prehistoric times to modern times. Learn about Native Americans, particularly the Plains Indians, the role of the U.S. Cavalry, early settlement, turn-of-the-century businesses, and much more. If your children get restless, take them outside to enjoy the Elgin train steam engine and a replica of an 1830s trading post. Buffalo robe and fur trading was important to the area in the early 1800s. The Red River Trading Post includes a stockade fence, a trader's cabin, a corral, and a fur press; they are interesting to examine, especially when a curator is there to explain how the traders and the Native Americans lived at the time.

Opening in midsummer, 1997, is a 27,000-square-foot wing. The new addition will primarily feature the over 3200 items from the Tingley Indian Store of Anadarko. This outstanding collection will help museum visitors understand more about twentieth-century Native American culture and history. The new addition will also house the Domebo Site Mammoth exhibit. Found at the Domebo archeological site in present-day Caddo County were the remains of a Columbian mammoth and several weapons. Archeologists have dated these items to be 11,200 years old. (For more information about the Domebo site, see the "Oklahoma Archeology" article on page 14 of this book.)

*The Domebo Mammoth.*

Illustration by Ron Ford

### Helpful Hints

The museum offers special educational programs for school groups. Subjects include "One-Room Schoolhouse" and "Children on the Frontier." The programs cost $1 per student and average one hour in length. Supplemental materials may be rented for these programs. Call ahead for a schedule of the museum's two special events, usually held in October and May. Among other activities, re-enactors portray life during the frontier days and illustrate skills such as blacksmithing. These types of events provide a more "hands-on" experience and are very educational to children and adults.

## Percussive Arts Society Museum

*701 Northwest Ferris, (405) 353-1455. This museum is located west of the Museum of the Great Plains and opens to Elmer Thomas Park. Look for the sign; the building is tucked behind McMahon Auditorium. Monday-Friday 8-5, Saturday 10-6, Sunday 1-6. Adults $1, children eleven and under free. This museum is handicapped accessible.* ★

The Percussive Arts Society Museum is home to anything you can bang, shake or hit together. More than 250 musical instruments from over fifteen countries are on display. Six hands-on nooks are available with instruments from an African thumb piano to an ocean drum. There are also instruments that belonged to famous percussionists, such as a broken drumstick owned by Buddy Rich and a xylophone played by Haskell Harr, author of the most-widely-used percussion instruction series. A research library contains periodicals and books on the subject and copies of solos that will inspire percussion students. Occasional concerts are held at the museum.

This museum is one of the best in Oklahoma. How can you resist the urge to strike the ten-foot wind chime hanging from the ceiling or bang the gong and play the xylophone!

### Helpful Hints

Be aware that on crowded days the noise can reach ear-shattering levels. (Ear plugs are recommended!) During the school year, groups keep the museum busy between the hours of ten and three on weekdays. Allow at least thirty minutes for the visit, but be prepared to stay longer! The appeal of the prairie dogs at Elmer Thomas Park may help your family to "move along" when your ears are tired!

## Wichita Mountains Wildlife Refuge

*Northwest of Lawton, (405) 429-3222. From I-44 (H.E. Bailey Turnpike), take Exit 45 and drive seven miles west on Highway 49. The Refuge is open daily from daylight to dark. The Mount Scott Road is open from 9 a.m. until one hour after sunset.*

Nature lovers will delight in the beauty of this combination of native grassland and low-rising mountains. This is a perfect place for a day (or a weekend) of family fun experiencing "Native America."

Approximately one-third of the 60,000 acres in the Wichita Mountain Wildlife Refuge is open to the public. Self-guided tour maps are available in map kiosks at park entrances. Use the map to plan your visit.

Mount Scott is located near the entrance to the refuge and offers a panoramic view of the wildlife refuge. Children love to climb the huge boulders and hike the trails around the parking areas at the top. Bring a camera, binoculars, and wind jackets (it's always windy on Mount Scott). A drive through the park provides an opportunity to see the herds of bison, longhorn cattle and

Sarah Taylor

*View from Mount Scott.*

other animals which roam the refuge freely. Visitors are encouraged to observe these animals but are reminded not to get too close; bison and other wild animals are very unpredictable.

A new 22,000-square-foot **Visitor Center** offers informative and hands-on exhibits about the wildlife at the refuge. Located near the intersection of State Highways 115 and 49, the center is an excellent resource for current information about wildlife sightings. Hours are Wednesday-Monday 10-5:30 (closed Tuesday); there is no admission fee.

**Hiking trails** of all lengths wind through the refuge; most children can handle the Dog Run Hollow Trail. Fishing is available at the twenty-eight lakes in the refuge. Other activities including camping at the Doris Campground and picnicking.

### Helpful Hints

Several nature and wildlife-related programs are held at the refuge. Call ahead to get a schedule. Children must be eight years old to attend the **Elk Bugling Tours**, held the second week of September through mid-October. **Bald Eagle Tours** are held during January. For either tour, the cost is $3 per person and reservations are required. Call one week ahead. The buses for the tours are handicapped accessible. Handicapped accessible restrooms are located in the Visitor Center and at several of the campsites.

## Events

### Prince of Peace Easter Pageant

*Held on Easter Eve at 9 p.m. at the Holy City in the Wichita Mountains. For date and brochure call (405) 248-4043. Admission is free, but donations are appreciated. The restrooms are handicapped accessible.*

Watch and listen as the story of Jesus Christ's life, from birth to resurrection, is presented. This dramatic presentation lasts approximately three-and-a-half hours and takes place in the picturesque Wichita Mountains.

No seating is provided; arrive early and spread your blanket out on a good spot. In order for everyone to have a good view, lawn chairs are not allowed during the performance. You may bring a picnic, but concessions are available. Wear warm clothing; it can become very cold at night.

### Armed Forces Day Parade

*Held the second Friday in May at 5 p.m. in downtown Lawton. For more information, call (405) 355-3541 or (800) 872-4540.*

More than one hundred entries make this the largest Armed Forces Day parade in the United States. Entries include horse riders, bands, military equipment, and antique cars. Keep your eyes and ears open, and be prepared for the military aircraft flyovers!

Be sure to arrive early to insure a good view of the parade. Bring a lawn chair, an umbrella, and sunscreen. The day following the parade, military equipment, tanks, and helicopters are displayed at various locations around town.

## International Festival

*Held the last full weekend in September in Library Plaza at 4th and B Avenue. For dates and brochure, call (405) 581-3470. Admission is free.*

The entertaining International Festival offers over fifty performances. Adding to the excitement is food from around the world and arts and crafts. Street dances and concerts are held in the evening. On Saturday and Sunday, beautiful and informative displays from other countries are available for viewing. The children's activity area includes face-painting, special foods, a moonwalk, and more.

## In the Vicinity

### Meers Store

*From I-44 (H.E. Bailey Turnpike), take Highway 49 west to Highway 115. Turn north on Highway 115 to Meers. The Meers Store is located on the edge of the Wichita Mountains Wildlife Refuge. (405) 429-8051. Open Monday-Friday 8 a.m.-9 p.m., Saturday-Sunday 7 a.m.-9:30 p.m.*

The mining town of Meers thrived in the early part of the century; now the population of Meers is four, and the Meers Store is all that remains. Listed as a National Historical Site, the restaurant was once the town's grocery store. Although it also serves burgers, fries, barbecue, delicious cobbler, and more, the restaurant is best known for its Meersburger, made from Longhorn beef; it is seven inches in diameter.

*The Meers Store.*

While you are visiting the restaurant, ask the staff for directions to the fifteen-mile crack in the earth's crust. Seismologists believe this crack could produce a major earthquake.

# Weatherford

The college town of Weatherford has drastically changed from its auspicious "wild and wooly" beginning, when saloons and dance halls almost outnumbered wagonyards and lumberyards. In 1901, Weatherford was chosen as the site for a teacher training school. The town is justifiably proud of its most honored native son, General Thomas P. Stafford, and the accomplishments of Southwestern State University. When near this town, families should make the effort to visit a small but outstanding museum at the airport.

*Weatherford is seventy miles west of Oklahoma City on I-40, and 179 miles southwest of Tulsa. Weatherford Chamber of Commerce (800) 725-7744.*

## Attractions

### General Thomas P. Stafford Museum

*3000 Logan Road. From I-40, take the Airport Road exit on the east side of Weatherford. Continue west on the access road to Lyle Road. Go north to Logan Road, then east to the airport. Open daily 8-6. Admission is free. The museum is handicapped accessible.*

*Stafford Museum.*

Thomas P. Stafford was born in 1930 at Weatherford, Oklahoma. Living by the motto "higher and faster," Stafford became an extraordinary astronaut, and he is now known as America's space ambassador. In 1993, he received the Congressional Space Medal of Honor from Vice-President Dan Quayle.

Memorabilia spanning Stafford's early school days to his days spent in space is housed in this small museum. Comments from Stafford's school teachers, along with his fourth grade penmanship papers, are displayed. These displays prove that, with hard work and determination, dreams can come true.

In a separate room dedicated to Stafford's NASA career, a video presents Stafford's space explorations. In May, 1969, Stafford was part of the crew aboard Apollo 10, which established altitude and speed milestones that will be unbreakable for decades. During reentry, 4,000 feet above the Pacific Ocean, the Apollo 10 spacecraft set a speed record of 24,791 miles per hour; this record will be broken only when someone returns from a trip to Mars.

In June, 1969, Stafford succeeded astronaut Alan Sheppard as the new Chief of Astronauts. After the Apollo 14 mission in 1971, he was promoted to Deputy Director of Flight Crew Operations.

He concluded his space career in 1975 in a joint mission with Russia. As part of the Apollo 18 crew, Stafford participated in the first international space link-up.

Children, especially those fascinated with space, will enjoy seeing everything from uniforms worn by Stafford to the actual ejection seat from the Gemini Spacecraft. Plan to spend thirty minutes to an hour at this small but information-packed museum.

# Central Oklahoma (Frontier Country)

## Chandler

A small, charming town located along Route 66, Chandler offers visitors a well-established museum (read on to learn of its exciting programs for children), a long-standing baseball camp, and a guest ranch complete with horseback riding and Western outdoor adventure.

*From Tulsa, drive west approximately sixty-six miles on I-44 (the Turner Turnpike), and from Oklahoma City travel about forty-eight miles east to the Chandler exit. Chandler Chamber of Commerce (405) 258-0673.*

## Attractions

### Bo Belcher Baseball Camp

*2000 W. Park Road, (405) 258-1720. From Highway 18 in Chandler, turn west on 6th Street. Look for the camp on the right at the top of the hill. The office is open year round; camps are held in the summer.*

Opened in 1958 and internationally known for its quality baseball instruction, this camp brings hundred of boys together each summer to learn the skills of baseball. Each year boys ages 8 to 18 attend this rustic camp facility, carved out of Oklahoma's wooded hills. Tours are available anytime; feel free to drop by.

### Museum of Pioneer History

*719 Manvel Avenue, (405) 258-2425. Open Monday-Friday, 9:30-4. Free admission.*

This museum features exhibits of early-day Oklahoma for all ages. Children will learn about Route 66 history, see an outstanding collection of antique dolls, and view military history exhibits. Of special interest is the replica of an early-day Oklahoma schoolroom filled with antique desks that children may sit in.

"Hung by a String" is a special exhibit of marionettes made by Chandler teacher Miss Fay Armstrong, known to those who admired her as "Miss Fay." Using her marionettes, Miss Fay would teach manners and morals to her students.

A program of the museum, "Miss Fay's Touring Historical Marionette Theater," revives Miss Fay's legacy of traditional marionette theater while focusing on Oklahoma history. Joan McMillan, portraying Miss Fay, travels the state using handcarved wooden marionettes to present her unique program to elementary schools. This hit program features plays with titles such as "The Last Land Run: Opening of Kickapoo Territory." Each play lasts about forty minutes and is followed by a question and answer session.

Other performances of the marionettes are held throughout the year. For example, on the Fourth of July at Chandler's Tilghman Park, marionette performances of "The Life and Times of U.S. Marshal William Tilghman" will be presented. Call the museum for a schedule and for information about puppet camps.

On the last Saturday of September each year, the Lincoln County Arts Council sponsors children's art activities at the annual **Indian Summer Arts Festival**. This event is held on the lawn of the Lincoln County courthouse in downtown Chandler. For more information, call (405) 258-3131.

### Read Ranch

*Located approximately five miles west of Chandler on Route 66. Well-placed road signs make the ranch easy to find. (405) 258-2999. Open Tuesday-Saturday at 10 a.m. and Sunday at noon. Admission is free; activity costs vary.*

Opened in 1992 as a 240-acre guest ranch, Read Ranch includes a petting zoo, a pavilion for special events, longhorn cattle, bison, ponds, bunkhouses, and RV sites with electrical hookups. Western activities abound, including individual guided trail rides (for ages seven and older) and group hay rides. There are moonlight rides, breakfast rides, chuck wagon rides, haywagon rides, and trolley rides. Of special interest to families are the pony rides for children under age seven, the roping corral, playground equipment, and a catch-and-release fishing pond stocked with perch and catfish. Every Labor Day, Read Ranch hosts a **Talent Contest and Music Jamboree**. Musicians, trick ropers, fiddlers, cowboy poets, and others compete for prizes.

## In the Vicinity

### Stroud

Since the 1890s, Stroud has been known as a retail trade center. The oil industry provided another stable economic source for the community. Its ideal location halfway between Tulsa and Oklahoma City along I-44 (the Turner Turnpike) led to the development of Tanger Outlet Center. Visitors will also want to visit the **Paramount Apparel Manufacturing** at 414 W. 4th; this T-shirt manufacturing plant provides another bargain for families shopping in the area. Children can create their own shirts, choosing the color and transfer they prefer, usually for about $5. The factory is open during regular business hours.

*Stroud is located fifty miles west of Tulsa and fifty miles east of Oklahoma City on I-44, the Turner Turnpike. Stroud Chamber of Commerce (918) 968-3321.*

## Attractions

### Stroud Lake

*Located three miles north on Highway 99 and three miles east of Stroud. For more information, contact the Stroud Chamber of Commerce.*

Stroud Lake offers 621 surface acres of water for boating, fishing, water skiing, camping, and swimming. The east side of the lake has picnic tables, barbecue grills, a pavilion, and a boat ramp; the west side features a pavilion, boat ramp and a fishing dock. Seventy-two campsites (twenty-eight with electricity) are available on a first-come, first-served basis.

### Tanger Outlet Center

*Located on I-44, east of Highway 99. (918) 968-3566 or (800) 4-Tanger to verify hours. (Hours are subject to change depending on the season; they are open extended hours during the holidays.) Open Monday-Saturday, 10 a.m.-9 p.m., Sunday noon-6 p.m.* 🖉

Tanger Outlet Center features over fifty brand name manufacturers' and designers' outlets. Shoppers find almost anything they want here—men's, women's, and children's apparel, housewares and home furnishings, toys, hardware, gifts, books, fishing equipment, and more. Two fast food establishments are located on the premises. At the end of each major season, the center hosts bargain days sales.

# Edmond

In 1887, the railroad originally named this area Summit, but after the land run in 1889, the townsite committee decided to call the area Birge City. Upon review of the papers filed at the land office in Guthrie, the name Birge City had been crossed off and mysteriously the word "Edmond" had been written in. It wasn't until recently that anyone knew who the mysterious "Edmond" was; he was a freight agent for the Santa Fe Railroad.

This wooded community located north of Oklahoma City is growing at a phenomenal rate. Situated in the center of a great tourism area, Edmond offers shopping, golf, elegant and casual dining, live theater, and beautiful parks. A family-oriented city, Edmond celebrates families with an "awesome" festival in October, the Celebration of Children.

*Edmond is approximately fifteen miles north of Oklahoma City and may be reached by U.S. Highway 77 (Broadway Extension) or by Interstate 35. If you are traveling the approximately 115 miles from Tulsa, exit north onto I-35, or continue on the turnpike (in Oklahoma City named the Kilpatrick Turnpike), and take the Edmond exit north. For more information, contact the Edmond Convention and Visitors Bureau at (405) 341-2808. ⬛*

## Attractions

### Arcadia Lake

*Located east of Edmond, (405) 396-8122. From I-35, exit at Route 66 (2nd Street) and go east three miles. The entrance to Central State Park is on the south side of the road, and further east on 2nd Street is the Project Office Building. Central State Park and Campground are open 24 hours, seven days a week, year round. Edmond Park, Spring Creek Park, and Scissortail Campground are open seasonally. Seasonal park operations hours and dates are subject to change; call ahead or check at the entrances for posted dates and times. Daily entrance fees are Pedestrian/ Bicycle $1, Passenger Vehicle $6, Watercraft $6, Motorcycle $2. Annual passes are $45. Edmond residents receive a 20% discount on annual passes. Camping fees: Primitive $8, Regular $13, full hookup $15. Various discounts are available. Ask at the fee collection station.*

Arcadia Lake is a great place to take the family exploring. As you hike the trails, look for animal tracks, native plants, and (in the winter) bald eagles. Throw a fishing line in the stocked lake and catch a bluegill, redear sunfish, channel catfish, blue catfish, or a largemouth bass. Arcadia Lake has 679 acres of developed park area and twenty-six miles of shoreline. There are many shaded picnic areas in the woods or near the water.

For swimming, try the popular beaches and designated areas available at Edmond Park, Central State Park, and Spring Creek Park. A U.S. Coast Guard-approved flotation device of proper size and fit must be worn by children under the age of thirteen while they are in the water. Each swimming area has twenty vests available to borrow, but they go quickly; it's always best to bring your own. The beaches are closed from sunset to sunrise, and no lifeguards are available.

Biking enthusiasts will want to try the fifteen-mile multiuse trail. Have fun as you exercise and watch for deer, raccoons, opossums, and other wildlife along the trail. Other trails are available for hiking; ask at the Project Office or consult the lake's map.

Bring your own recreational "disk" and try the thirty-six-hole disc golf course, located in Spring Creek Park. Children of all ages will enjoy this game. No reservations are required. The course operates on a first-come, first-served basis with no extra fee required.

Bird and animal lovers will want to come to the park early in the day to get the best view of the wildlife. Bring your binoculars or a bird book, and visit the Bird Watching Blind in Central State Park. You may see hawks, woodpeckers, red-winged blackbirds, ducks, kites, pelicans, and even the Oklahoma state bird, the scissortail flycatcher.

Camping is permitted on numbered sites in designated areas on a first-come, first-served basis. Cottonwood Campground has the most accessible showers. RV camping with full hookups is available in Central State Park. Picnic pavilions are available to rent for $35 plus a $40 damage deposit.

Watercrafts are welcome on the lake. Jet Skis, Wet Bikes, Wave Runners, or similar crafts are restricted to the designated Jet Ski Area in Spring Creek Park.

### Helpful Hints

Many programs and events are sponsored at Lake Arcadia for children and families. Groups of children preschool age and up may take advantage of the special **nature programs**; programs last from thirty minutes to two hours and they are free. Make reservations two weeks in advance for groups of eight or more. Program subjects include the animals that live in the park (includes some live animals), forestry, pond life, field trips, ground water, and more. Young people ages seven to twelve may participate in fishing clinics; everything but the bait is provided.

On the first weekend after the New Year, an **Eagle Watch** is held. Visit with the game rangers, and they will inform you about the eagles and recommend a place to watch for the birds. Bring your binoculars. The eagles arrive in November and stay until mid-March. During the Eagle Watch, all parks are open to the public at no charge.

A **Kids Fishing Derby** takes place at the Spring Creek Park the first Saturday in June. Registration begins about 7:30-8, and fishing lasts from 8-11. At noon, prizes are awarded. Children from five to fifteen may participate in the Derby, and no license is required for these ages. Participants should bring their own fishing tackle and equipment. Admission to the park and the event is free for adults accompanying children to the derby.

The Edmond Chamber of Commerce hosts the **Arcadia Lake Regatta** during the first weekend in August.

Other rules and regulations exist at Arcadia Lake. Get a list of rules when you enter the park. However, if you plan to take your dog, you should know that all animals must be caged, penned, or be on a leash no longer than six feet.

## Arctic Edge Ice Arena

*14613 North Kelly Avenue, (405) 748-5454. From the intersection of the Broadway Extension (Highway 77) and Kelly, go north on Kelly less than a mile. The arena is located on the west side of Kelly. Skating: Adults $5, children twelve and under $1.50. Skate rental: $1.50. Hours vary for public skating, call ahead to confirm.*

Try something different this weekend and take the kids to the Arctic Edge—it's the "coolest place in town." Daytime skating sessions are exciting, perfect for parents and young children to give ice skating a try. Evening sessions feature music videos and theme nights. Everyone will love this new alternative for family fun!

### Helpful Hints

The Arctic Edge also offers hockey leagues for youth and adults. Cost for the program ranges from $165 to $175 and includes one rating session, ten games and five practices plus playoffs, certified coaches, a team jersey, and a party and awards for first and second place teams.

Also available at the Arctic Edge is a beginners ice skating program, a beginners hockey program, and figure skating lessons. You may rent the ice arena for a private party at a rate of $225 per hour.

Birthday parties at the Arctic Edge start at $125 for up to ten party members and $12 for each additional member. The rate for twenty party members is $225 and $10 for each additional member. Party participants receive skate rental, pizza, soda, and birthday cake, all served in a special room with paper goods provided. The only thing you have to do is supply the birthday child!

## Edmond Historical Museum

*431 South Boulevard, (405) 340-0078. From I-35 take 2nd Street west to Boulevard. Turn south on Boulevard. Follow Boulevard to the museum, located on the west side of the street. Open Tuesday-Friday 10-4 and Saturday 1-4. Admission is free; donations are appreciated.*

The small but informative Edmond Historical Museum is housed in an armory built in 1936 and listed on the National Register of Historic Places. Many exhibits include artifacts, old photographs, and documents that tell the story about the development of Edmond and the surrounding area. Children will particularly enjoy the replica of an 1890s rustic family home located in what became known as the town of Edmond. Although the house and its typical family residents are well-described through exhibit labels, a thirty-minute guided tour for children ages four and up will further explain what life was like for this family. Call two days

*89er Homestead Fair.*

in advance to schedule a tour.

On a weekend near April 22nd, the museum hosts an **89er Homestead Fair** that is particularly geared to children and their families. The fair highlights life in the early days of Oklahoma and features clothing and tools from this era as well as an early-day schoolroom. Admission is $1.

Occasionally, children's programs are held, and traveling exhibits such as "The Diary of Anne Frank" are on display. Call ahead for a schedule of events.

## Hafer Park

*9th Street and Bryant Avenue. From Broadway Extension go east on 15th Street to Bryant Avenue. Go north on Bryant to 9th Street. Turn east into the park.*

Visit this lovely, tree-filled park and go for a walk, feed the ducks, or turn the little ones loose on the many playgrounds. The extensive playground equipment is always well-maintained and provides a real treat for children; they can bounce, slide, swing, crawl, climb, drive a toy car, and much more. Enjoy the flower gardens or bring fishing equipment for the "children-only" fishing pond.

Many Edmond events and festivals take place at Hafer Park. On Memorial Day weekend, the park hosts the **Edmond Blues and Jazz Festival** and, during the summer, **concerts** are presented on Thursday nights. Music styles range from big band to rock 'n roll. Audience members are invited to bring their own blankets or chairs to sit under the trees and enjoy the program.

## Oklahoma Shakespeare in the Park

*Held at Hafer Park, 9th Street and Bryant Avenue, (405) 340-1222. See above for directions to the park. Once you enter the park, continue driving east and watch for signs. The season runs from May through August. All performances are held Thursday through Sunday beginning at 8 p.m. (pre-show at 7:30 p.m.). Regular tickets may be purchased for $6 at the gate. (Prices are subject to change.) Children ages twelve and under are free. Students and senior citizens are $5. Special rates are available for groups of ten.*

Since 1985, Shakespeare in the Park has thrilled audiences of all ages with performances of the classic Shakespearean stories. Held in a natural amphitheater, the plays are performed by semiprofessional actors.

Shakespeare in the Park is a delight for the entire family. The outdoor setting (with plenty of room for spreading out) is perfect for children. While young children may not follow every scene, they will take more interest when the jesters appear or the sword fights begin.

### Helpful Hints

Expect to walk down the paved and lighted path to the theater area. Take lawn chairs or blankets to sit on, or you may rent chairs for a nominal fee; bring a picnic or purchase the snack items that are available. Arrive early if you like to sit close to the stage. However, no matter where you sit, you will be able to hear the lines; a new speaker system has helped acoustics. Performances are held regardless of the weather, and they are cancelled only at the last minute because of extreme circumstances.

## Paint'n Station

*3419 Wynn (located near the southeast corner of 33rd and Broadway, aka Highway 77, behind the Pepperoni Grill restaurant), (405) 330-6530. Also located at 6444 N.W. Expressway #430 (Peppertree Square Shopping Center), (405) 720-7900. Wednesday-Saturday 11-4, Thursday 11-7, Sunday 1:30-4. Summer hours are extended to Tuesday-Sunday. Prices range from $5-7. Some specialty pieces are $8-12.*

Do you have a potential Michelangelo or Leonardo living in your house? Bring your young artist to the Paint'n Station and find out just how creative he/she can be! Plastercraft and ceramic pieces shaped like animals, sport items, and more are available for selection by your child. Brushes, paints and paint shirts are provided. No reservations are required for this fun activity and children ages five and up can be dropped off long enough to create a masterpiece while mom runs her errands.

Programs offered at the Paint'n Station encourage children to explore their creativity. A special class offered is Kindermusik, an arts enrichment program for ages eighteen months to seven years. The program includes art, movement, dance, drama, music, percussion instruments, and games. Kinderfit is a program offered for children ages two through approximately ten to encourage physical development. Qualified instructors lead weekly classes, held each Tuesday, for six-week sessions. The classes last forty-five minutes and help develop skills such as balance, movement, and rhythm through developmental gymnastics and tumbling.

The Paint'n Station provides programs for day cares, after-school groups, church groups and others, either in the studio or at the location of your choice. Young people will have fun while creating decorations for their rooms or gifts for others. Birthday parties are always a big hit at the Paint'n Station; call for details.

A "Kids Nite Out" is scheduled once a month from 6:30-9; call for the next date. Children (ages five and older) spend the evening painting, watching movies, playing games, and having snacks. Cost is $12 per child and reservations are necessary.

## Sorghum Mill Christmas Tree Farm

*7121 Midwest Lane, (405) 340-5488. From I-35 take 2nd Street east to Midwest Boulevard. Follow Midwest Boulevard north to Sorghum Mill Road, then travel east 1/8 mile to the Farm. Opens the day after Thanksgiving and remains open until Christmas Eve. Monday-Friday 1-8, Saturday-Sunday 10-8.*

Start a family tradition by visiting the Sorghum Mill Christmas Tree Farm. Select the perfect tree for your family, then cut it down yourself! The farm also offers pre-cut Christmas trees, wreaths, tree stands, and balled and burlapped live Christmas trees that can be planted in your yard after the holidays. Have a cup of hot chocolate or hot cider, and then ask for ideas on how to recycle your tree after the season is over.

## University of Central Oklahoma Theater

*Mitchell Hall. From Broadway Extension go east on 2nd Street to University Drive,* *then go north. Mitchell Hall will be on your right. (405) 341-2980, extension 3375. Adults $7, students from other schools $2, UCO students free and senior citizens $3.*

The University of Central Oklahoma Theater presents several shows each year. In the past, they have performed family favorites such as *Hansel and Gretel.* Call the box office for shows and dates available. Children should be at least school age to view the performances. Call ahead to determine if the shows are appropriate for children.

While on campus of the University of Central Oklahoma, take time to see the many improvements and new buildings as well as the old favorites, such as the **Old North** building. Located near Mitchell Hall, Old North is the oldest school building in Oklahoma still in use; it has been continuously occupied since 1893.

## Events

### LibertyFest

*Held during the first week of July at various lo-cations around Edmond. For date and brochure, call (405) 340-2527. Most activities are free.*

Bring your family to LibertyFest and cel-ebrate our nation's birthday in grand style. Many activities are held throughout the week leading up to the big parade and fire-works show on July 4th. Kite competitions, exhibitions, and education are just part of the fun at the annual **KiteFest**. Everyone from beginners to pros can participate in

*LibertyFest parade.*

this festival which is sanctioned by the American Kite Association. Watching the kites is free, but a $15 registration fee is required to enter the event. In 1997, the event will be held at Arcadia Lake.

The family-oriented **Road Rally** is organized like a scavenger hunt, and it is an exciting way to spend the day. Once you register for the rally, you will re-ceive a map and instructions. Be the first to finish, and you will win a prize!

The **PRCA Rodeo** has been a highlight of LibertyFest for more than twenty years. The rodeo is held at an out-door arena on Kelly, just north of 2nd Street. More than 400 con-testants from around the world participate in seven events. Tick-ets are available at the gate.

Air up your tires and hop on your bike for a day of touring the Oklahoma countryside. The **Clas-sic Bike Tour** allows everyone, young or old, novice or experi-enced, a chance to participate. A

*The Green Angels entertain the crowd.*

registration fee is required, and all proceeds go to The Epilepsy Association of the Sooner State and LibertyFest.

Everyone loves a parade! Considered one of the best in the state, the **LibertyFest parade** starts at 10 a.m. on July 4th and travels from the University of Central Oklahoma through downtown Edmond. Watch as celebrities, drill teams, cheerleaders, bands, floats, clowns—even the "Green Angels," a group of Elvis imitators pushing lawnmowers —entertain the crowd for almost two hours. Although this parade is free, arrive early to get a good spot. Be sure to bring your own shade (an umbrella) and plenty of sunscreen.

When the parade is over, head to Hafer Park for **ParkFest**. It begins at noon and features games, clowns, trolley rides, a Kid's Talent Review, and a costume contest. Free watermelon for everyone helps make ParkFest great family fun!

End your day by attending the extensive fireworks display at UCO's Wantland Stadium. Entertainment starts at 7 p.m., and refreshments are available for purchase at the stadium.

## Celebration of Children Festival

*Held the second weekend in October in Hafer Park. 9th Street and Bryant Avenue.*

*From Broadway Extension go east on 15th Street to Bryant Avenue. Go north on Bryant to 9th Street. Turn east into the park. For date and brochure, call (405) 359-4630. Admission for children ages one to fourteen is $5; adults are free.*

Children become part of a magical world at the two-day Celebration of Children Festival. Smiles abound as children experience storytelling, theatrical groups, clowns, dancers and singers, and numerous hands-on art projects. The festival allows children the opportunity to grow and learn through open-ended creativity. Whether they are learning about other cultures, enjoying the challenge of the "Climb the Wall" area, or creating an artistic masterpiece, children must adhere to only one rule: Have Fun!

*Creativity at work at Celebration of Children.*

# Edmond/Guthrie

## Helpful Hints

All ages enjoy this festival. There are toddler play areas as well as challenging areas for preteens. Plan to have more than one adult with your group if you have varying ages of children. A limited number of tickets are available each half-hour for the wall climb, so be in line early; the tickets are free, but children must be forty-two inches tall to participate. An "Ouch Station" is conveniently available for any minor mishaps. Parking is available, but lots are usually overflowing. Look for an area to the northwest of the park for extra parking, then ride the trolley to the festival. If you park at the nearby Aquatic Center, simply walk across the bridge to the festival.

Dress for a "messy" day, and be prepared for lots of merriment and laughter. Concessions are available.

## Guthrie

On April 22, 1889, Guthrie went from a population of zero to 10,000 through the first of Oklahoma's land runs, the run of the Unassigned Lands. Out of dirty tents grew a charming Victorian town. Guthrie was the capital of Oklahoma from statehood in 1907, until 1910, when it was moved to Oklahoma City by a controversial vote.

Today, Guthrie has one of the largest urban National Register Historic Districts in the United States; it covers 1,400 acres and 400 city blocks. Step back in time when you visit Guthrie, a town steeped in history, architectural beauty, and fun family attractions.

*Located thirty-two miles north of Oklahoma City on I-35. Located ninety-one miles southwest of Tulsa. From Tulsa, take I-44 west to I-35 north to Guthrie. Guthrie Chamber of Commerce (800) 299-1889.*

## Attractions

### Beacon Drive-In Theater

*2404 South Division, (405) 282-4512. From I-35 take Guthrie Exit 153 and follow it north. Watch for the drive-in on the east side of the road. Show time is at dusk. Open Friday, Saturday and Sunday evenings from April through mid-October. Open daily when school is out in May through August. Adults $4, children eleven and under free. Look for discount coupons in local newspapers. Call to hear a recording about which movie is playing.*

Watch movies under the stars! There are not many drive-in theaters left; take your family to Beacon and relive the days of your youth. Bring lawn chairs and blankets to sit outside and enjoy the summer air. You may bring your own snacks, or you may buy them at the concession stand.

### First Capital Trolley

*1st Street and Vilas Avenue, (405) 282-6000. From I-35, take Exit 153 to Guthrie. Go north to Harrison and turn west. Park in the city parking lot on the southwest corner of 1st and Harrison. Walk south along 1st Street to Vilas. Open March-*

December, weekdays and Saturdays 9-4, Sunday 1-4; December Candlelight tours at 6, 7 and 8 p.m.; January-February weekdays noon until 2, Saturdays 9-4, Sundays 1-3. All tours leave on the hour. Adults $2, children ages twelve and under $1. All seats for the candlelight tours are $2. The trolleys are not handicapped accessible; however, there are buses available that are. Call ahead for more information.

When the brass bell rings, it's time to board the mahogany, hunter green and brass trolley for a tour of historic Guthrie. Travel past buildings that date back to 1893 as you listen to a tape that explains the history of Oklahoma's first state capital. You'll even hear about a humorous old law prohibiting people from eating an ice cream cone while walking backwards down the sidewalk. This forty-five minute tour is a fun way to begin your visit in Guthrie.

## Guthrie Scottish Rite Masonic Temple

900 East Oklahoma Avenue, (405) 282-1281. From the intersection of Highway 77 and Oklahoma Avenue, turn east. The Temple is at the end of Oklahoma Avenue. Guided tours are given Monday-Friday at 10 and 2, Saturday at 10 (schedule may vary during festivals). Adults $2, no charge for Masons or students. The handicapped accessible entrance is on the south side of the building.

You'll be amazed at the incredible variety of architectural designs as you tour the largest Scottish Rite Temple in the world. Built in the 1920s, the elaborate temple has a Gothic library, a Roman atrium, a Pompeiian Room, an Italian Renaissance Lounge, and a 3700 B.C. Egyptian Room. A kaleidoscope of color reflects through the 396 stained glass windows adorning the walls. Still being used by the Masons, the temple provides the backdrop for a fascinating tour.

### Helpful Hints

Be sure your children are prepared and ready for a long tour; the tour takes about ninety minutes, which is a long time for young children. Self-guided tours are no longer offered.

### Honey Hill Farm

(405) 969-3236 or 341-5499. Located five miles northwest of Guthrie. Ask for directions when you make reservations. Tours are $2 per person, with a minimum of twelve required.

Take a tour of Honey Hill Farm and learn how deer are raised. The beautiful farm consists of 320 acres of land, of which about forty acres is used for a deer pasture. Tours of the farm last approximately one hour and include visiting various paddocks, walking the raceway to the deer barn, and learning how the deer are caught and worked at various times throughout the year. Besides learning about deer, there is an educational honey bee exhibit that children particularly enjoy. The farm has its own bee hives which produce fresh honey; the honey is offered for sale in early fall.

While you're at the farm, try one of the venison lunches prepared fresh in the farm kitchen. Lunch includes a brief talk on cooking with farmed venison and you may eat at the picnic tables near the lake. Lunch is served at about 12 noon and averages $7-8 per person. Choices include venison burgers, venison lasagna, venison & wild rice, venison meatball stew, and venison chili. Each meal includes salad, bread, vegetables, dessert, and drinks.

An "**Open House**" is held annually, on the first Saturday and Sunday in May. Take a free tour, attend the venison cooking demonstration and tasting, visit the lake to see Canadian geese and swans, or take a hike and play horseshoes.

## Lazy E Arena

*From Oklahoma City, take I-35 north to the Seward Road exit. Follow Seward Road four miles east (drive carefully on this winding road) to the Lazy E Arena. (405) 282-3004 or (800) 234-3393. Call ahead for the arena's event schedule. There is no charge for tours. Admission to events varies. Be sure to ask about special discounts such as children twelve and under receiving free general admission with an empty pop can. The arena is handicapped accessible.*

Enjoy America's cowboy sport in the comfort of this completely enclosed and climate-controlled arena. Built in 1984, the Lazy E Arena seats 7,300 people and is the home to the only National Finals Rodeo event still held in Oklahoma, the **National Finals Steer Roping** in late November.

Each year, more than twenty-five championship events are held at the Lazy E Arena, including the **Timed Event Championship of the World** in March, the popular **Bullnanza** in late January/early February, the **Reba McEntire Pro Celebrity Rodeo** in May, and more. Contestants from Oklahoma, Kansas and Nebraska compete in the **Prairie Circuit Finals** in October.

Children particularly enjoy the **Children's Western Jamboree** in mid-February. This indoor event allows children to enjoy Western activities such as stagecoach rides and more. Another family favorite is the **Oklahoma Cattlemen's Association Range Roundup** held the last weekend in May. At this rodeo, working cowboys from Oklahoma compete in unusual rodeo events such as wild cow milking, wild horse racing, bronc riding, and branding.

## Mineral Wells Park

*From I-35, take Guthrie exit 153 (Highway 77) and go north. Watch for Mineral Wells Park sign on the west side of the road. (405) 282-1947. The restrooms are not handicapped accessible.*

When your children need a break from the many historic activities in Guthrie, visit tree-shaded Mineral Wells Park for a rest or to run off energy. Bring a picnic and enjoy lunch at one of the picnic tables. Before you leave, take the children to the pond and let them feed the ducks or, if time permits, go fishing.

## National Lighter Museum

*107 South 2nd Street, (405) 282-3025. From State Highway 33 and Division, turn south on Division to Oklahoma Avenue, then go west to 2nd Street. Take 2nd Street south to the museum, which is located next to the Fire Station. Open daily 10-6. Admission is free; however, a $2 donation is suggested.*

Lighters precede the discovery of tobacco by 4500 years. Ted Ballard, the museum's owner, is a nonsmoker, and he wants everyone to know this museum isn't about smoking; it's about "mechanical pyrotechnical apparatuses."

He was only seven-years-old when he started his collection; children will be amazed to see how a collection can grow.

This small museum is the only one of its kind in North or South America, and there's only one other like it in the world. There are nearly 20,000 lighters in this collection, but only about one-third of those are on display at one time. Some lighters look like dogs and some lighters have clocks in them. Commercial lighters date back to the 1750s, but one of the old flint and steel type lighters is five hundred years old.

### Helpful Hints

This is not a hands-on museum, and it doesn't take much time to tour. Stop by the fire station located next door. If the firemen aren't busy, they are happy to show children a real fire engine and tell them about fire safety.

## Oklahoma Frontier Drug Store Museum

*212 West Oklahoma Avenue, (405) 282-1895. From the corner of Division and Oklahoma Avenue, turn west on Oklahoma and go two blocks. The museum is across the street from the Post Office. Open Tuesday-Friday 10-5, Saturday 10-4, and Sunday 1-4. Closed Monday and legal holidays. Admission is free; donations are appreciated. This museum is handicapped accessible; upon arrival, you can request that a ramp be set up.*

F.B. Lillie was the first licensed pharmacist in Oklahoma, and F.B. Lillie Drugs is one of the two oldest pharmacies in the state. Established on the day of the Land Run, April 22, 1889, the pharmacy was once housed in the same building that the Drug Store Museum occupies today.

*Oklahoma Frontier Drug Store Museum.*

This museum looks more like a real drug store than a typical museum. The floor is made of wood, and the ceiling is covered with pressed tin. It is furnished with antique counters and cases.

What would you do if your doctor prescribed "Swamp Chill and Fever Tonic" or asthma cigarettes? How about an electric belt to improve your health? These are just a few of the unusual remedies displayed at this museum. It's a wonder that patients survived these prescriptions.

### Helpful Hints

Small children like the old-fashioned soda fountain. Although it doesn't work, you can buy a bottle of sarsaparilla or creme soda.

Guided tours are available for groups if you call in advance for reservations. The tours take about thirty minutes. Self-guided tours take approximately twenty minutes. A twenty-two minute tape (free of charge) describes the exhibits while you tour.

## Oklahoma Territorial Museum and Carnegie Library

*406 East Oklahoma Avenue, (405) 282-1889. From Highway 77 and Oklahoma Avenue, turn east. The museum is located on the northeast corner of Ash and Oklahoma Avenue. Tuesday-Friday 9-5, Saturday 10-4, Sunday 1-4. Closed Mondays and legal holidays. The last entry is thirty minutes before closing. Admission is free; donations are appreciated. This museum is handicapped accessible.*

For a good history lesson on Oklahoma since the late nineteenth century, take your family to the Oklahoma Territorial Museum. Through the use of photographs, artwork and artifacts, the museum gives a vivid account of territorial Oklahoma and the Land Run. Carrie Nation's axe, turn-of-the-century toys, and a reproduction of a jail with a "prisoner" inside are just a few of the exhibits. You will even learn the true story about the removal of the capitol from Guthrie to Oklahoma City. The museum is best for children ages seven and up, but younger children will find plenty to interest them.

Accessed through the museum is the **Carnegie Library**, which has been restored to its 1902 splendor. The Library was built at a cost of approximately $25,000 and housed 2,439 books when it opened. It is the oldest Carnegie Library remaining in Oklahoma, and it is probably the most elegant. On November 16, 1907, the first governor of Oklahoma was inaugurated on the steps of the Library. A symbolic wedding took place prior to the inauguration, uniting Mr. Oklahoma and Miss Indian Territory. Nearly 20,000 people watched the historic ceremony. This ceremony is recreated several times around the anniversary of Statehood Day (November 16th). Call for the exact days and times.

Another "fun fact" about the beautiful library is that Tom Mix, the Hollywood cowboy star, used to teach boxing in the lower floor gymnasium.

### Helpful Hints

A small gift shop is located on the first floor of the library. There is also a research library open from 1-4 p.m. weekdays or by appointment.

This museum and the State Capital Publishing Museum in Guthrie offer numerous inexpensive, educational programs for 1st through 12th graders. Classes offered range from Living History classes such as "Printer Pete" and "A Chat with an Old Codger" to hands-on programs such as "Victorian Fun & Games," a class that allows the students to make their own game to take home. Minimum class size is ten; maximum size is seventy. Call ahead for a list of educational programs available. It is best to schedule these programs about two to three weeks ahead.

## Pollard Theater

*126 West Harrison, (405) 282-2800. From the corner of Highway 77 and Harrison, turn east. The theater will be on the north side of the street. Curtain times are Thursday-Saturday 8 p.m., Sunday matinee 2 p.m. Ticket prices range from $12 to $16, with higher prices for musicals. Ask about senior or student discounts. The theater is handicapped accessible.*

Built around the turn of the century, this building was originally a furniture store as well as a funeral home. It was converted into a vaudeville theatre in 1919; it later became Oklahoma's first all-sound movie theater. Today, it is home to Oklahoma's only year-round professional acting group. Plays include period farces, contemporary dramas, musicals, and more. One holiday family tradition is the production of *A Territorial Christmas Carol*, held annually during the Christmas holidays. When calling for information or to get tickets, inquire about the productions that are most suitable for children.

## State Capital Publishing Museum

*301 West Harrison Avenue, (405) 282-4123. Take I-35 to Guthrie exit 153 (Highway 77). Go north to Harrison and turn west. The museum is located on the southwest corner of Harrison and 2nd. Tuesday-Friday 9-5, Saturday 10-4, Sunday 1-4. Last entry is fifteen minutes prior to close. Closed Mondays and legal holidays. Admission is free, but suggested donations are $1 adults and fifty cents for children. The museum is not air-conditioned, and the basement is not handicapped accessible.*

Elaine Warner

*State Capital Publishing Museum.*

Built in 1902, the State Capital Publishing Company building was home to the first newspaper in Guthrie, *The State Capital*. Turn-of-the-century printing equipment is located in the basement, and a demonstration of its printing capabilities can be arranged for groups of ten or more with reservations made a week in advance. You will be amazed to see how much work was required to print each page of early-day newspapers.

During the Christmas holidays, the museum is decorated with themed Christmas trees, with a new one added each year. A button tree, a patriotic tree, and a musical tree are just a few of the trees on display.

## Territorial Surrey Company

*107 West Oklahoma, (405) 282-0534. From the intersection of Division and Oklahoma Avenue, turn south. Located in the King Antique Mall. Monday, Wednesday, Thursday 10-4, Friday 10-4 and 6-7, Saturday 9-7 and Sunday 12-5. Four-passenger surreys: $14 for half an hour and $20 for a full hour. Two-passenger surrey: $7 for half an hour and $12 for a full hour.*

See the historic sites of Guthrie while you are peddling a bicycle surrey. There are two four-passenger surreys and one two-passenger surrey. All three can accommodate two additional small children. The surreys are street-approved, are equipped with safety belts, and are covered to provide shade from the sun.

### Helpful Hints

Be sure to ask about a suggested route through the historic district. The surreys are available only during good weather.

## Events

## '89er Celebration

*Held the week closest to April 22nd in downtown Guthrie, at the fairgrounds, and at other venues. For date and brochure, call (405) 282-1947. Admission is free.*

Celebrate the Land Run of 1889 in historic Guthrie with food, fun and history. Browse through the arts and crafts or attend the chuckwagon feed featuring live entertainment. Attend the carnival at the fairgrounds, the antique airplane fly-in at the airport, and a rodeo at Lazy E. Be sure to stay for the longest parade in Oklahoma!

## Jazz Banjo Festival

*Held Memorial Day weekend in downtown Guthrie. For date and brochure, call (405) 282-1947. Admission is free.*

Jazz Banjo players from all over the country congregate in downtown Guthrie to perform Dixie Land and other types of music. This festival features a parade, the world's largest Banjo Band Concert, jam sessions, a picnic, and banjo workshops. It was proclaimed the "1993 Oklahoma New Event of the Year" by the Oklahoma Department of Tourism and the Oklahoma Travel Industry Association.

## Sand Plum Festival

*Held the last weekend in June in downtown Guthrie. For date and brochure, call (405) 282-1947. Admission is free.*

This festival celebrates the delicious prairie fruit known as the Sand Plum. Activities for the weekend include a fine art show, bed races, a pet parade, and live entertainment. The Childrens' Area is full of Victorian crafts and games, puppets, clowns, and more.

## Autumn Magic/Tom Mix Festival

*Usually held in September in downtown Guthrie. For date and brochure, call (405) 282-1947. Admission is free.*

Tom Mix was always the "good guy in a white hat" in cowboy movies. Guthrie pays tribute to Tom Mix and other Oklahoma movie stars during this celebration. Activities include a western memorabilia market, a film festival, and a living history reenactment. Children will enjoy the Old West gunfights, but they may need several reminders that the gunfights are not real. There's also music, antiques and a car show.

## Territorial Christmas Celebration

*Held from Thanksgiving weekend through New Year's Eve in various locations throughout Guthrie. For dates and brochure, call (405) 282-1947. Most events are free; however, a few charge admission.*

Take your family to Guthrie and experience a Victorian-style Christmas during the Territorial Christmas Celebration. Take a tour of historic Victorian homes, listen to the strolling Christmas carolers, enjoy the Christmas parade, listen to special concerts, and take your family to see *A Territorial Christmas Carol* at the Pollard Theater. A Christmas Ball featuring Victorian dress, ballroom dancing and a silent auction is held in the Scottish Rite Temple. Your family will want to make this celebration a tradition.

*The Territorial Christmas Celebration in Guthrie involves the entire community.*

Fred Marvel/Oklahoma Tourism

# Norman

Norman is the county seat of Cleveland County. The town was settled during the Land Run of 1889; it was named after Abner Norman, a railroad surveyor who came to the area in 1886.

Today, more than 87,000 people call Norman home. This growing, family-oriented community is the third largest city in Oklahoma. Although perhaps best known for the University of Oklahoma, one of the state's first institutions of higher education, Norman also boasts a number of recreational, cultural, and historical events and attractions.

*Norman is located nineteen miles south of Oklahoma City on I-35. From Tulsa, take I-44 west to I-35, then south to Norman for a total of about 130 miles. For more information, contact the Norman Convention and Visitors Bureau (800) 767-7260 or (405) 366-8095.* 🚹

## Attractions

### Duck Pond

*Located on the east side of the University of Oklahoma campus, behind the athletic dorms. From I-35 exit Lindsey Street and go east past the football stadium. The park is on the north side of Lindsey.*

There is so much to do and see in Norman that children can get overwhelmed. Take a break from the hectic pace and enjoy O.U.'s Duck Pond park. Watch the wildlife or take a stroll down the walking trail. For those more energetic, take the exercise trail for a sports workout. Bring a picnic lunch and just enjoy being outside!

For a real treat, feed the ducks their favorite snack of whole corn. The owners of Ellison Feed and Seed at 115 South Porter in Norman will sell you a fifty-pound bag of whole corn at cost (approximately $5) if you tell them you intend to feed the ducks.

### Firehouse Art Center

*444 South Flood, (405) 329-4523. From I-35 take the Main Street exit. Follow Main Street east to Flood. Turn south on Flood, and look for the art center on the west side of the street. Admission is free; donations are appreciated. Costs for classes vary. Hours for the gallery are Tuesday-Friday 9-5, Saturday 10-4, Sunday 1-5. Closed Mondays and major holidays. The center is handicapped accessible.*

The Firehouse Art Center was originally used as a firehouse but, when it became outdated, it was converted into a wonderful art center. Drop-in visitors will enjoy rotating month-long exhibits featuring a wide variety of contemporary artists' works such as sculptures, paintings, photographs, and mixed media works. These artists come from around the nation to display their work. The popular gift shop will be expanded by midsummer, 1997; it features numerous works by Oklahoma artists.

Art classes of all types are available for adults and children. Beginning at age five, children can enroll in classes such as puppet making and clay working. Children ages ten to thirteen can participate in courses such as pottery, mask-making and sculpture. Classes for adults include jewelry making, photography, drawing, and painting. Classes may last for several days; summer sessions run two weeks. Call for a brochure about current class offerings.

The Firehouse Art Center sponsors the Chocolate Festival and the Mid-Summer Night's Fair, both ideal for family fun. See below for more information.

## Fred Jones, Jr. Museum of Art

*410 West Boyd, (405) 325-3272. Located on the University of Oklahoma campus. From I-35, exit onto Lindsey Street. Follow Lindsey east to Elm Avenue. Take Elm north to Boyd Street. The museum will be on your right. Regular and summer hours: Tuesday, Wednesday and Friday, 10-4:30, Thursday 10-9, and Saturday and Sunday 1-4:30. During O.U. school breaks, hours are Tuesday-Sunday, 12-4. Closed Mondays and major holidays. Call ahead to confirm hours. To schedule a group tour, make reservations two weeks in advance. The tour takes approximately one hour. Admission is free; donations are appreciated. Free parking passes are available at the museum's security desk.*

Established in 1936, the Fred Jones, Jr. Museum of Art houses an extensive collection of contemporary and traditional art. The permanent collection includes Mexican masks, Native American paintings, graphic arts, ceramics, and photographs. The newest addition to the permanent collection is the Fleischaker collection of Southwest art. Plan to visit this museum frequently; every six to eight weeks, the museum presents a new exhibit, either a traveling exhibit or an exhibit using the museum's permanent collection.

### Helpful Hints

The museum schedules **"family days"** periodically. These free events include hands-on activities for children.

The diverse collection of art at this museum lends itself to entertaining family games and discussions about the work. To involve your children in the art and to help them have fun studying the work, encourage each family member to pick his or her own personal favorites or try discussing how the art makes you feel (happy, sad, introspective, melancholy, etc.). Bring an empty paper towel holder tube to play "I Spy"; decide which painting or other art work best represents your family; or take paper and pencil and try to duplicate the artists' techniques. These games make a visit to any art museum or gallery more fun and meaningful for children.

## Jacobson Foundation

*609 Chautauqua, (405) 366-1667. Take I-35 to Lindsey Street; travel east to Chautauqua. Turn north on Chautauqua; look for the Jacobson House on the east side of the street. Open Tuesday-Saturday, 1-5. Closed Sunday, Monday and holidays. Call one week in advance to schedule tours for groups of more than eight people. Educational entertainment by dancers, singers, flute players, and others are available for a $50 fee. Adults $1.50, children ages eleven and under and members* *are free. The Foundation is handicapped accessible.*

The Jacobson Foundation is located in the Jacobson House, which is listed on the National Register of Historic Places. The Foundation focuses on the traditional art, music, poetry, and crafts of the Native American tribes of Oklahoma. Outstanding works of art are displayed, and traveling exhibits rotate every three months.

A tour of the home takes about thirty minutes. The Foundation also offers public education programs. Classes available include beadwork, featherwork, drum, bow making, tepee etiquette, and others. Call for more information.

## Little River Zoo

*Located east of Norman, eight-tenths of a mile south of State Highway 9 on S.E. 120th. Open daily 10-5 by appointment only. Adults $4, children ages eleven and under $2. Call for group rates.*

Janet Schmid, co-owner of the zoo with her husband Bill, has always been an animal lover. Her interest grew to the point that she gave up a career in the health field to become a zookeeper. Her collection includes over 400 animals ranging from domestic species such as the chicken to more exotic animals like the serval. You can pet the domesticated farm animals in the petting zoo or, with Janet's guidance, touch several "wild" animals while listening to information about the species. The Schmid's goal is to give visitors an appreciation of each individual animal.

### Helpful Hints

It is imperative that you make an appointment. Visit on a dry day, especially with wheelchairs. A concession stand, a picnic area, and a gift shop are available.

## Moore-Lindsay House

*508 North Peters, (405) 321-0156. Exit I-35 at Robinson Street. Take Robinson east to Peters and turn south. The house is on the west side of the street. Open Wednesday 10-12 and 1-4; Saturday 10-4:30. Individuals and small groups are admitted free; large groups will be charged a small fee per person. Donations are always welcome. The upstairs portion of the house is not handicapped accessible.*

In 1900, Mr. Moore, an investor, built this Queen Anne-style home at a cost of $5,000. The average cost for a home at this time was $400. It was the first house built on what would become known as "Silk Stocking Row." In 1908, the Lindsay family purchased the home, and it remained in their family until 1951. The house had two other owners between 1951 and 1973, when it was purchased by the City of Norman and restored for use as a historical museum.

### Helpful Hints

Visitors can tour the home alone or with a guide. Particularly impressive is the lovely 1900s-style furnishings and the woodwork of the "fancy" home. Antique toys are displayed during December and January. Guided tours last from fifteen minutes to an hour.

## Norman Children's Chorus Concerts

*First Christian Church, (405) 329-0170. From I-35, exit Main Street and go east to Webster near downtown Norman. Go south on Webster; the church is on the northwest corner of Webster and Eufaula. Admission is free.*

When seventy children, ages eight to fourteen years old, join together to sing praises, the room is filled with angelic harmony. The whole family will enjoy listening to the Norman Children's Chorus. Public performances are held in late April and early December.

## Perfect Swing Family Fun Center

*Located four miles east of I-35 on Highway 9, (405) 360-0800. Summer and school break hours: Monday through Thursday 10-10, Friday and Saturday 10-11 and Sunday 12-10. School year hours: Monday through Thursday 12-10, Friday 12-11, Saturday 10-11, and Sunday 12-10. Charged by venue, prices range from twenty-five cents to $4.95. Special rates are available for groups of eight or more. For $10.85 on Friday, Saturday, and Sunday, guests may participate in numerous activities; ask about their value packages when you arrive.*

The Perfect Swing Family Fun Center offers just about everything that excites a child. There are bumper boats, kiddie cars, go-karts, and a moon walk. Stay inside and play video games or step outside to the batting cages, driving range, and miniature golf course. If you get hungry, there's even pizza available!

Along with the regular activities, groups may make use of the covered pavilions, softball field, sand volleyball court, horseshoe pit, and barbecue grills. Catering is also available for groups.

## Sam Noble Oklahoma Museum of Natural History

*This museum is currently closed to the public; however, parts of the current museum may be opened to the public on an infrequent basis. Call the museum at (405) 325-4711 to ask about the possibility of drop-in hours or tours.*

The exciting news is that the museum will be expanding into a new 190,000-square-foot building at the corner of Chautauqua and Timberdale in the fall of 1999. The amount of gallery space will increase ten times, providing room for many more of the five million objects in the museum's collection to be displayed. It is anticipated that, with the new building and an extensive, valuable collection, the Sam Noble Oklahoma Museum of Natural History will quickly become a favorite destination for families across the state and nation.

Presently, interesting and educational traveling exhibits are available to schools, museums, libraries, cultural centers, nature centers, shopping malls, and other places. Call for more information.

## Shaklee Corporation

*300 Marshal Avenue, (405) 360-3300. From the intersection of I-35 and Highway 9, travel east on Highway 9 to Marshal Avenue. Look for the Shaklee sign. Tours are given Monday-Friday 9-2, on the hour. Closed major holidays. Admission is free. This facility is handicapped accessible.*

Take the forty-five minute tour of the production facility and you will see vitamins and other Shaklee health products being manufactured. Children will even get a hat and glove like the technicians wear.

### Helpful Hints

You'll see more activity if you take a morning tour. No reservations are necessary unless there are over twelve in your group. It is advised to call ahead to confirm that tours are being conducted on the day you plan to visit.

## Sooner Theatre

*101 East Main Street, (405) 321-8091. From I-35 and Main Street, travel east approximately 3 1/3 miles. The theater is located on the northeast corner of Jones and Main (past the railroad tracks). Prices vary with each performance. The theater is handicapped accessible.*

The Sooner Theatre is a restored vaudeville theater that features dance, jazz, classical music, drama, and other performances. Past performances have included music by the Moscow Boys Choir and *Cinderella*, a live musical production performed by the American Family Theater Broadway for Kids Series. Call to receive a listing of upcoming productions and performances.

## Thunderbird Riding Stables

*Located twelve miles east of Norman on Highway 9. (405) 321-5768. Hours are by reservation only, and you must call a day ahead. Available riding time is daily from 9 a.m. to dusk (closed Tuesday in the winter). Prices: miniature golf $2.50 per person, horseback rides $10 per hour (free miniature golf for everyone if the entire group goes horseback riding). Hayrides are $150 minimum.*

Located on 500 acres of wooded countryside, Thunderbird Riding Stables overlooks Lake Thunderbird; riding trails wind through deer and turkey country. From beginners to experts, everyone will love seeing nature from this view. For safety reasons, wear long pants and hard-soled shoes while riding. When your ride is complete, enjoy a round of miniature golf.

### Helpful Hints

Hayrides are available for groups. Bring your own food and ride to a cozy campsite with an open pit fire for a cookout under the open sky (electricity is available upon request). Spend the rest of the evening gathered around the fire, telling tall tales and singing.

During the last two weeks of October, Thunderbird Riding Stables offers a haunted walk through the forest to the "Black Hole." Cost is $7 per person.

## United Design Corporation

*Located in Noble at 1600 N. Main (Highway 77). Take I-35 south to Highway 9, then take Highway 9 east to Highway 77. Go south on Highway 77 approximately two miles; the factory is on the west side of the road. The gift shop is open Monday-Friday 9-5, and on the first Saturday of the month from 10-4. Plant tours are conducted Monday-Friday at 10 and 1:30. No reservation is necessary unless there are more than six in a group or handicapped routes are needed. Closed most Saturdays, Sundays and major holidays. Admission is free. United Design is handicapped accessible.*

United Design has grown from humble beginnings to become the largest animal figurine manufacturing company in the country. More than 2,000 designs are handmade here with more than 200 new designs created yearly. The company now employs seven hundred fifty people producing as many as twenty-five thousand pieces a day—everything from little figurine animals to picture frames, refrigerator magnets, large garden sculptures, and collector's Christmas figures. Plant tours show the whole process.

After the thirty-minute tour, stop by the gift shop; it has an excellent selection of figurines.

## University of Oklahoma

*Visitor Center-Jacobson Hall, 550 Parrington Oval, (800) 234-6868. From I-35, exit on Main Street. Go east to Flood, then south to Boyd. Turn east on Boyd to the light at the Parrington Oval. Jacobson Hall is on the northeast side of the Oval.*

This should be your first stop when you and your family visit O.U. Call in advance about a specific interest or to arrange for a tour of the campus customized for your family members. Parking is available anywhere not designated as faculty, staff or handicapped, and you'll need to know your car license number in order to get a visitor's parking permit. Be sure to pick up maps and directions for self-guided tours of the campus.

Major renovations have taken place at Jacobson Hall with University President David Boren's taking a personal interest in this "front door of the University." The reception area is filled with colorful Southwest rugs, Mission-style furniture, and Tiffany lamps.

Homeward Bound *by Allan Houser at O.U.*

The Oklahoma Tourism and Recreation Department has designated the University Visitor Center as a Local Tourism Information Center; you'll also be able to find information regarding state and local attractions here.

## University of Oklahoma Sports

*From I-35, exit at Lindsey Street and go east. Turn into Gate 15 at the football stadium, and you will see the ticket office. The Sports Information line is (405) 325-8231 and the Ticket Office is (405) 325-2424. Ticket prices range from $2 to $30.*

The University of Oklahoma offers a wide variety of spectator sporting events. Football games are held in Memorial Stadium from September-November. Men's and women's basketball is played from November-March at the Lloyd Noble Arena. Gymnastics meets are held from January-April in the Sam Viersen Center. Wrestling (November-February) and volleyball (September-December) matches are held in the O.U. Field House and occasionally at Lloyd Noble Center. Baseball is played at the L. Dale Mitchell Park from February-April. Softball is played at the Reaves Park Softball Complex from February-May.

## Events

### Chocolate Festival

*Held the weekend before Valentine's Day in the O.C.C.E. building on the University of Oklahoma campus. For date and brochure, call (405) 329-4523. Tasting sessions are held from 11-3, with the last entry at 2:30. Daytime session $12. Handicapped accessible.*

This festival is a chocoholic's delight! There is everything from chocolate gum to chocolate painting. You'll be amazed at the ways chocolate can be used. Edible masterpieces displayed in the past include chocolate boats, chocolate animals, and chocolate headdresses. Tasting sessions can create a problem: how does one select only ten pieces of chocolate from the dozens of delights displayed?

#### Helpful Hints

Several people can share a ticket for the samples. This helps children (and adults) not to "overload" on the sweet concoctions. Advance tickets are advised; this popular event has a limited number of tickets per tasting session. You may call ahead for tickets, and secure your order with a credit card.

### Medieval Fair

*Usually held the second weekend in April at the Duck Pond on the University of Oklahoma campus. From I-35, exit at Lindsay Street and go east past the football stadium. The park is on the north side of Lindsey. Friday-Saturday 10-7 and Sunday 10-6. Admission is free. Parking is available east of the Duck Pond and at O.U. parking lots. On Saturday and Sunday, campus buses run between the Lloyd Noble Center and the Fair. Admission is free. Handicapped parking is available.*

Medieval Fair by Carter

Be prepared to step back in time at O.U.'s annual living-history fair. The fair began in 1976, and it is presently attended by more than 70,000 people annually. Be on the lookout for sorcerers, gypsies, and even Sir Lancelot as you roam through the crowd. Enjoy "hearty food and drynk" while you

*Performer at the Medieval Fair.*

watch jugglers in bright costumes and listen to traditional music. Other thrilling activities include knights in medieval combat and a human chess game. Jousting tournaments are always a weekend favorite.

Children will love the Medieval Fair. Where else can they ride a unicorn or be knighted? A petting zoo and "games of yore" will fill their afternoon.

## 89er Day

*Held on a Friday and Saturday near April 22nd in downtown Norman. For date and brochure, call (405) 321-7621. Admission is free.*

Attend this festival and help celebrate the achievements of the early-day pioneers. You will see a reenactment of the 1889 Great Land Run crossing of the South Canadian River and a parade. A barbecue is held but the location varies each year; call ahead for more information.

## May Fair

*Held the second Saturday in May at Reaves Park. From I-35, exit on Highway 9 and travel east to Jenkins. At Jenkins, go north; the park is on the east side. For date and brochure, call (405) 321-7260. Admission is free. This site is handicapped accessible.*

Celebrate spring with your family at the May Fair festival. Children will appreciate making crafts and painting pictures, and everyone will laugh at the clowns with their silly acts. Enjoy the festive music and watch the talented dancers as they perform in the park. Browse through the artwork and make a purchase, then stop at one of the concession stands for some refreshments.

## Jazz in June

*Held the last weekend in June at various locations around Norman. Call KGOU radio at (405) 325-3388 or (405) 325-5468 for more information. All concerts are free, and all venues are handicapped accessible.*

Treat you and your family to a range of jazz performances at this popular festival. Jazz performances range from nationally-known artists to new and local groups. To not miss anything at this festival, call ahead for a schedule.

## SummerWind Festival

*Held in early July on the University of Oklahoma campus, (405) 325-0711. Because there are many events during the week of the festival, calling ahead for a brochure is important. Most events are free, but some activities have a minimum charge. Handicapped accessible.*

This six-day event is sponsored by the University of Oklahoma, and it features theater, dance performances, storytelling, performances by well-known artists, food, and more. Children will enjoy participating in their own opera, plays, and workshops. In the past, the forty-five minute workshops have included juggling, dancing, kite making, as well as Japanese culture and art. Workshops in storytelling and musical exploration are designed for children as young as three-years-old. Children from ages five to twelve can participate in camps for theater, visual arts, and dance offered through the University in conjunction with the festival.

In the evenings, families may bring a picnic or try the multicultural food available. Be sure to bring a blanket; you will enjoy the musical entertainment.

## Midsummer Night's Fair

*Usually held in mid-July at Lions Park, 400 South Flood. For date and a brochure, call the Firehouse Art Center at (405) 329-4523. Admission is free.*

The whole family, even the pet dog, will have fun at this event. Bring a lawn chair or blanket to this evening event and enjoy musical performances, mimes, food, an art show, pottery, and crafts for the whole family. Don't miss the dalmation mascot contest!

# Oklahoma City

Oklahoma City was settled on April 22, 1889, by 10,000 pioneers in the great Oklahoma Land Run. At noon, men and women raced on horseback, by trains, on bicycles, or in wagons across the plains to stake their claims to a part of what was once known as Oklahoma Station. On this one day, Oklahoma City went from being a small village with a Land Run office to a bustling tent town.

Fred Marvel/Oklahoma Tourism

In 1907, Oklahoma became a state and Guthrie was named the state capital; however, a vote of the people moved the capital from Guthrie to Oklahoma City in 1910. Rumor has it that the state seal was moved from Guthrie in a laundry basket. Oklahoma City was a thriving town from the beginning but, in 1928, something happened that would cause a major population expansion; a test well was drilled in the city. The well hit oil and gushed more than 110,000 barrels before it could be capped. This was the beginning of prosperity for Oklahoma City.

Oklahoma City has something for every member of the family with its world-class sporting events, festivals, performing arts, art galleries, museums, beautiful parks, and lakes.

*Oklahoma City is located in the heart of Oklahoma. It is 115 miles southwest of Tulsa and 200 miles north of Dallas. Take I-44 west from Tulsa or I-35 north from Dallas. Oklahoma City Conventions and Visitors Bureau, (405) 297-8912 or (800) 225-5652.* 🛈

## Attractions

### Aerospace Science and Technology Education Center

*2501 North Blackwelder, (405) 521-5898 or (800) 633-7242. Programs and camps are being held at Oklahoma City University and Shepherd Mall until a permanent facility is constructed on campus. From I-235, take the Northwest 23rd Street West exit; go approximately four miles to Shepherd Mall. The mall is located between Pennsylvania Avenue and Villa on the north side of the road. Programs are offered throughout the year. Reservations are required. Camps and programs are handicapped accessible.*

Exciting hands-on activities help educate children from preschool age and up in the areas of aerospace, science and technology. Specialized activities give children the opportunity to develop skills in leadership, problem solving, teamwork, communication, and responsible decision-making. Call for a schedule of their regularly-scheduled classes or to make arrangements for a special group visit.

### Helpful Hints

In June and July, five-day camps are conducted for children from ages eight to eighteen. The camps include opportunities for children to participate in activities such as rocketry, robotics, astronomy, and air space mission training. Participants also have access to a full-scale shuttle, a computerized mission control, a high-tech space station, and much more. Each class is specifically customized by grade level. A gifted and talented camp is also available.

Campers meet Monday through Friday from 9 to 4. Lodging in the OCU dorms is provided for campers who need housing. The cost varies with each program, and some discounts are available. Meals are included in the cost. Registration begins in January, and early reservations receive reduced fees. Several classes with high teacher/student ratio are conducted simultaneously. Sleep-overs, outreach programs and tours can be reserved, but try to call two months in advance. Be sure to stop by the gift shop named "The Space Place."

## Ballet Oklahoma

*(405) 848-TOES. Performances are held at Civic Center. From I-40 East, exit at Walker, and go north (or from I-40 West, exit at Robinson and go north. At Reno, go west to Walker, and turn north). At Colcord, go west. The Civic Center will be on your left. Ticket prices vary with each performance. Season tickets are available.* ★

Ballet Oklahoma has been thrilling audiences for over twenty-five years. Of special interest to families is a new program begun in conjunction with each Sunday matinee performance. Twenty minutes before the ballet begins, a professional storyteller will explain to children of all ages the story behind the ballet to be performed. Discount tickets are available for the Sunday matinee.

### Helpful Hints

Children always enjoy the holiday classic, **"The Nutcracker,"** performed during the two weekends prior to Christmas. Be sure to make reservations to attend the **Sugar Plum Tea Party,** held after each Sunday matinee performance. The cost is $10 for children and $6 for adults. Children will enjoy meeting the Sugar Plum Fairy, visiting with Santa, decorating cookies, and making special bags of food for the reindeer.

Free parking is available at the Civic Center in the evenings. The best seating for children is in Zone 2.

## Billy Balloo's

*8371 North Rockwell, (405) 728-7760. Exit I-44 at Northwest Expressway and travel west four miles to Rockwell. Turn into the Rockwell Plaza Shopping Center on the southwest corner; Billy Balloo's is located in the far southwest corner of the shopping center. Sunday-Thursday 4-12, Friday-Saturday 11-2. Food service stops at 10.*

Take the whole family to Billy Balloo's for an evening of fun for everyone. This 54,000-square-foot building has everything from billiards to in-line skating and arcade games to a golf simulator. Children will love the world's largest candy dispenser! When you work up an appetite, try the Waverly Avenue Grille. It serves pasta, pizza, salads, sandwiches, and burgers. Fountain Balloo is available for those needing just a small snack.

## Helpful Hints

Billie Balloo's is perfect for families with preteens and teens. You are allowed to bring your own in-line skates, or you may rent them from Billy Balloo's. A private area for birthday parties and other special events can be reserved. Gourmet chefs are available to serve an appetizer buffet, full course buffet, or a formal dinner. For children, birthday parties include pizza, soft drinks, cake, and tokens for the arcade games. Call for prices.

## Bricktown

*Located near downtown Oklahoma City on Sheridan. (405) 236-8666. From I-40 west, exit at Harvey and go north to S.W. 2nd Street. Go east to E.K. Gaylord, then north to Sheridan. Turn east on Sheridan. From I-40 east, exit at Robinson and stay in the left lane that leads directly to S.W. 2nd. Follow S.W. 2nd Street to E.K. Gaylord and turn north. At Sheridan, turn east. Hours vary with each business.*

Begun in the 1890s, Bricktown was once Oklahoma City's prime industrial area housing hardware, farm implements, groceries, print shops, hotels, and more. Although once a deteriorating area, the charm of the many brick buildings, its ideal location, and a concentration of shopping and eating establishments have brought crowds of people back to the area.

Located near popular downtown attractions such as the Myriad Convention Center and sports arena and the Myriad Gardens and Crystal Bridge, Bricktown is the ideal location to spend the evening after a hockey game or an excursion to the Botanical Gardens. Among the choices of restaurants are family-style eateries, offering a range of choices from Mexican food at Chelino's or Abuelo's to Chicago-style pizza at Windy City. Spaghetti Warehouse is family oriented, as are several other restaurants in Bricktown.

Other activities in Bricktown include shopping or, for a special treat, take a refreshing carriage ride around the area.

If you have problems parking, try the new trolley available in Bricktown. The trolley runs from various downtown Oklahoma City stops to Bricktown, weekdays from 11 a.m. to 2 p.m., and weekends from 6 p.m. to 2 a.m. There is a fifty-cent charge to ride one way, but most restaurants give free tokens to patrons for return trips.

Bricktown also hosts several events. The **St. Patrick's Day Parade** is always fun for children as it winds its way through Bricktown. The **Bricktown Fourth of July** activities include popular children's performers, a petting zoo, pony rides, and more. The December **Festival of Lights parade** ends in Bricktown with Santa handing out candy. **Opening Night** is celebrated in Bricktown with live entertainment, fireworks, and more. New events are added all the time; call ahead so you won't miss out on anything. (See page 235 for more information.)

## Celebration Station

*509 Westline Drive, (405) 942-7888. From I-40, exit at Meridian and make your way to the south-side service road. Celebration Station is on the southeast corner of Meridian and the service road. Summer hours are Monday through Thursday 10-10, Friday and Saturday 10-11, and Sunday 12-10. Winter hours are Monday through Thursday 3-9, Friday 3-10, Saturday 10-10, and Sunday 12-9. Call ahead to confirm. A play pass for children fifty-six inches and taller is $13.99. A play pass for children under fifty-six inches tall is $7.99.*

Children can play here all year! For older kids (including dad!), there are bumper boats, go-carts, miniature golf, and batting cages. When they're not riding the coin-operated rides such as a carousel or a boat, younger children will enjoy the new three-story play structure featuring tubes, tunnels and slides.

Enjoy the pizza in the animated-theater dining room. The mascot, Harry Hound, walks about visiting with children, while Daniel and the Dixie Diggers, the life-sized animated band, performs on stage. Birthday packages are available, as are group rates for parties of fifteen or more.

## City Arts Center

*3000 Pershing Boulevard, (405) 951-0000. Located on the State Fairgrounds. From I-44, exit at Northeast 10th, and drive east to May. Turn south to gate 2-26. City Arts Center is straight ahead. Register early; class sizes are limited. Six one-hour classes held on Saturdays for five to seven-year-olds cost $30. The same session for eight to twelve-year-olds costs $60 and includes two hours of instruction per week. Enroll early to receive a discount. The center is handicapped accessible.*

The City Arts Center provides art instruction for children of all ages. For children five to seven years old, classes include acting, creative movement, painting, and drawing. For children eight to twelve years old, classes are offered for acting, painting, drawing, paper and book making, photography, and pottery. During October, a special Halloween class is held for little goblins featuring art projects, games and stories. The Holiday Camp for Kids, held in December, offers holiday gift making, creative movement to the tunes of the season, games, and fun times with friends.

Weekend classes for children ages five to twelve are held in the fall, spring and summer. During the summer, week-long camps are held.

Special temporary exhibits are held in the art center's Eleanor Kirkpatrick Gallery. Past exhibits have included a Georgia O'Keefe exhibit and a Book as Art exhibit.

## Daily Oklahoman

*9000 North Broadway, (405) 475-3540. From the Broadway Extension (Highway 77), exit at Britton. The Daily Oklahoman building is on the southeast corner of Britton and Broadway. The tour is free, but reservations must be made one week in advance. Children should be at least ten years old or in the fourth grade. There must be six in a group but no more than forty. Groups of six to twenty-five are preferred. There must be one adult for every five students. Monday-Friday 9-4:30. The tour is handicapped accessible.*

This informative tour begins by watching the journalists at work, and it follows their finished product through the plant. The tour ends at the dock area, where the papers are made ready for delivery. According to the press run schedule, the paper usually completes printing around 3:30 a.m.; then it is sorted and bundled for delivery. Children will be amazed at sights such as the 7,000-gallon tanks containing ink and the large paper warehouse (the size of a football field!), which can hold up to 9,000 rolls of newsprint weighing a ton each. One full roll of newsprint can print 120,000 pages.

### Helpful Hints

The best days to see the presses running are Monday, Wednesday and Friday. Be aware that the presses are very noisy, and be sure to wear comfortable walking shoes for this sixty- to ninety-minute tour. This tour works well for groups of Boy Scouts, Girl Scouts, Camp Fire girls and boys, and other groups.

## Diamond B Farm

*(405) 359-1004. Located 1.1 mile north of Waterloo Road on Pennsylvania Avenue. Look for a sign on the west side of Penn. Available by reservation year-round except for the colder months of January to mid-March. $3 per person. The farm is handicapped accessible.*

A trip to the Diamond B Farm in northwest Oklahoma City will be both fun and informative for any child. The learning process begins as the host acquaints the children with various farm animals such as chickens, pigs, calves, and sheep; the guide explains how each is a source for our food and/or clothing. A delightful trip to the garden reveals seasonal crops. Be sure to take the tractor-pulled hayride. During the ride, look for wildlife such as deer and turkey that also inhabit the farm. After the tour, enjoy the picnic area and the hay bale playground.

### Helpful Hints

This is a working farm; dress appropriately, and remind children that the animals may not be friendly. In the hot summertime, visits should be limited to mornings. The Diamond B can accommodate groups as large as 120. Weiner roasting areas are available for groups; you bring the food, and Diamond B will provide the fire and the atmosphere.

## Discovery Zone

*Two locations: 7110 South I-35 Service Road, (405) 634-3866. Located near Cross-*

roads Mall, I-240 and I-35. This DZ is open Monday-Thursday 10-8, Friday and Saturday 10-9, Sunday 11-7. 2501 West Memorial Road, #105 (405) 755-5437. Located near the southwest entrance to Quail Springs Mall, May Avenue and Memorial Road. The Quail Springs DZ is open Monday-Saturday 10-9, Sunday 12-6. Children ages three to twelve $5.99, toddlers two and under $2.99. For organized groups of ten or more, admission is $3.99. Call ahead to confirm prices.

Children ages twelve and under can swing, hang, crawl, climb, slide, and more at Discovery Zone. It's great exercise, but all they care about is that it's fun. DZ is a wonderful place for children under twelve. When accompanied by a parent, even toddlers less than forty-inches tall can enjoy their own mini-zone with pint-size equipment.

### Helpful Hints

Safety is most important at DZ, and there are highly-trained, friendly Zone Coaches who help supervise the children. When you arrive, you and your child are given wristbands with matching numbers that are checked for a match when you leave.

Outside food is not allowed, but a full-service snack bar sells favorites like pizza, ice cream and soft drinks.

Organized groups of ten or more should call one week ahead for reservations. Participants are required to wear socks, and knee pads are available for adults who are brave enough to crawl through the maze of tunnels. Arcade games (not video games) and lockers are available. Expect to stay about ninety minutes; weekends and rainy days are the busiest.

*Lost in the ball pit at Discovery Zone.*

## El Dorado Ranch Inc.

*10400 North Sooner Road, (405) 771-4004. From I-35, exit on Sooner Road and go east. The ranch is located on the east side of Sooner Road, between Hefner and Britton. Reservations are required. Closed Mondays. Guided trail rides are $8 for one-half hour, $12 for one hour.*

Even "city kids" can conveniently enjoy a Western experience. Mosey on over to the friendly El Dorado Ranch for guided trail rides that are customized for the rider, whether experienced or a "tenderfoot." Your ride will take you through the woods and across the prairie of the forty-three acre ranch.

Hayrides are available for all ages. Cost is $5 per person with a $50 minimum. Parties can be customized to suit any group. Volleyball and horseshoes are always favorites, and cookouts or barbecues can be arranged for an additional charge.

Call ahead for reservations. From giving instructions on how to ride to helping you make plans for your next party, the kind folks at El Dorado Ranch are always helpful.

### Helpful Hints

Try a Western-theme birthday party complete with horses at El Dorado Ranch! For children seven and older, parties include a thirty-minute ride and a cookout with hotdogs, chips, and drinks. The cost is $12 per child; there is no minimum number of children necessary. For children six and under, parties include handled pony rides along with a cookout. Parties last approximately two hours and they cost $10 per child.

Approved safety helmets are furnished upon request. El Dorado offers basic Western riding lessons for $25 per lesson. Boy Scouts or Girl Scouts can also earn their horsemanship badges here.

## Enterprise Square, USA

*2501 East Memorial Road, (405) 425-5030. Located on the campus of Oklahoma Christian University. Take I-35, exit at Memorial Road, and go west, just past Bryant. Enterprise Square, USA will be on your right. Look for the building with giants peering out of the windows. From Broadway Extension, take the Memorial Road exit, and go east past Eastern to Enterprise Square on your left. Open Thursday through Saturday from 9 a.m. to 5 p.m. Hours are subject to change; call ahead for the latest information. Adults $4, senior citizens $3, students $2.50, and children under five are free. Discounts are available for groups of fifteen or more. Enterprise Square is handicapped accessible.*

The creators of Enterprise Square, USA realized a need to educate children about the free enterprise system. Utilizing sophisticated technology, they created entertaining exhibits as part of an educational center that teaches children how to be efficient consumers, better producers, and more informed voters.

As your tour begins, you will enter a large glass-walled elevator and travel three floors up as you watch a presentation concerning the free market economy. As your tour progresses, you will see digital counters (tracking changes such as the U.S. population), the Achiever's corner, and sixteen-foot figures of famous Americans in the Hall of Giants.

You will tour areas such as the Remarkable Supply Shop for Demanding Donut Dunkers and the Great American Marketplace. You may visit with a robot named D.O.C., watch the giant working cash register, or sing along with the dollar bills in praise of the free market. Be sure to listen to the Talking Face of Government as it explains our free market society.

In the Economics Arcade, children may choose one of thirty-two game stations to take an economic adventure. They may drill for oil and gas, build houses, or set up a lemonade stand.

The last stop is Venture, a place to test your business skills. Using touch-screen technology, visitors select one of six occupations, then guide that business through various economic stages over a period of time to see how successful it might be.

### Helpful Hints

Exhibits are designed for children of reading age. Tours begin every fifteen minutes, and they last approximately one to two hours. After the last tour begins, you may remain in the building one hour. If you need to leave before the tour is over, ask for help.

During the summer, special camps are held for children of various ages. Youngsters ages two to ten attend **Kid's Days,** which includes a space bounce and games on the lawn, and a tour of Enterprise Square. Children from first to sixth grade may attend week-long business camps where they will learn how to run a business, promote a product, and make a profit. They will tour Enterprise Square as well as community businesses. This camp costs $65. Near the end of October, the **Funny Face Festival Halloween Party** is held after regular hours for kids in preschool through fifth grade. Children will listen to a storyteller, play games, watch a movie, and enjoy lots of treats. Cost for children is $3; adults are free. During December, **Trim-a-Tree and Light up the Square** is held. Oklahoma school children decorate thirteen Christmas trees that are displayed. Guests may take a tour and enjoy cookies and cider with the staff.

## 45th Infantry Division Museum

*2145 N.E. 36th Street, (405) 424-5313. Located between I-35 and Martin Luther King Boulevard off N.E. 36th Street, approximately one mile south of the Remington Park area. Open Tuesday-Friday 9-5, Saturday 10-5, and Sunday 1-5. Admission is free; donations are appreciated. Call one week ahead for tour reservations. Each group must have ten or more, and high adult/child ratios are required; children under twelve must have a one-to-four ratio, and ages twelve to sixteen must have a one-to-six ratio. Upon request, group tours can be arranged to cover specialty topics. This museum is handicapped accessible.*

Military history featuring Oklahoma citizen soldiers from 1841 to Desert Storm is exhibited in this museum. Two exhibits of particular interest are the Jordan B. Reaves weapons collection and Pulitzer Prize-winner Bill Mauldin's original World War II cartoons. Outside the museum is an extensive collection of military equipment including tanks, aircraft and big guns. These items can be dangerous; be sure your children see them, but do not let them climb on the weapons.

Special ceremonies are held on Memorial Day and Veteran's Day to honor the men and women of Oklahoma's military. Each hour-long ceremony begins at 10 a.m. Ceremonies include the massing of the colors, a fly-over by the Oklahoma Air National Guard, and the presence of many dignitaries.

"Citizen Soldier-Oklahoma Military and Guard," a twenty-four minute slide/tape program is available on request. Also, there is a special exhibits room that features exhibits on a rotating basis.

### Helpful Hints

The 45th Infantry Division Museum is a wonderful place for grandparents to visit with their grandchildren. Grandchildren will have the opportunity to ask questions regarding their grandparents' role in military history.

Please be aware that some children may be bothered by a few of the pictures and exhibits here. Parents should use discretion at this museum.

## Frontier City

*11501 Northeast Expressway, (405) 478-2412. Located in northeast Oklahoma City on the west-side service road to I-35, between 122nd Street and Hefner. Parking is $4 per car. 1997 prices are $20.99 for adults, $15.99 for children under 48 inches tall; children under three are free. Admission includes all rides, live entertainment shows, and attractions in the park, with the exception of limited-capacity activities such as Geronimo Skycoaster flights and Thunder-road NASCAR-styled go-carts. If you leave and plan to return that day, be sure to have your hand stamped. Check page 269 in this book for a valuable coupon. Special discount offers are also available through local convenience stores, grocery chains, restaurants, and soft drink distributors. These are advertised regularly via radio and television. Group rates are available for party sizes of fifteen or more. Call (405) 478-2140, extension 214 for more information. Double Park Season Passes are available for $59.99 plus tax. The pass entitles guests to unlimited visits to both Frontier City and its sister park, White Water Bay. In addition, both parks include double park perks such as in-park discounts at select food and retail locations, "buddy day" discounts, and more. Frontier City is open from Easter weekend until the last weekend before Halloween, but sometimes only on weekends. Hours vary; call ahead to verify.* ▧ ★

This Western theme park features over sixty rides, shows, shops, and other attractions—something to interest and excite every member of your family!

Frontier City has five different roller coasters ranging from "easy" to "exciting." For the little ones, the Wild Kitty is located in the Kids Corral. Older children may prefer the Nightmare, which is ridden in total darkness. Bigger roller coasters include the Wildcat or Silver Bullet; the Silver Bullet is incredibly fast. The newest roller coaster, the Diamond Back, goes forward and backward in excess of sixty miles per hour. Other popular and thrilling rides include the Time Warp and the Geronimo Skycoaster.

In the heat of the afternoon, head for the Log Flume or Renegade Rapids. The Log Ride is a casual, relaxing float until the end, when you plunge down into the water. The Renegade Rapids is comparable to white water river rafting.

The Kids Korral and the new Paul Bunyan Tiny Timber Town offer a variety of rides and exciting hands-on activities for children and parents to enjoy together. Included are Babe's Barnyard Buddies petting zoo, Teeny's Tea Time tea cup ride, and Tippecanoes at Tadpole Creek. The highlight of the area is Buzz Saw Company, a four-story, interactive adventure set that is perfect for family participation.

Several restaurants serving a variety of foods are located in the park. Hot-dogs, hamburgers, chicken, barbecue, deli sandwiches, as well as Mexican and Italian food, are available. A child's meal costs about $3, and an adult's meal can range from $4 to $7. Water is available at most restaurants and snack shops for a quarter. No outside food or drinks are allowed in the park, but picnic areas are provided outside the front gate.

After dinner, browse through the Frontier Trading Company for that special Oklahoma or western souvenir. You may even dress up in western-style costumes and take a family portrait at the Old Time Photography Studio. Be sure to enjoy all rides and shows (including a "Wild West gunfight stunt show, a magic illusion show, plus musical revues), then head to the Log Flume Lagoon for a good view of the fireworks display. The fireworks show is held most every night around 9:30 from Memorial Day through Labor Day. What a spectacular way to end your day at Frontier City!

### Helpful Hints

For details such as a map of the park and times and locations of shows being offered, be sure to pick up a brochure as you enter the park. This would also be

Frontier City

*Renegade Rapids at Frontier City.*

a good time to decide which shows you would like to see and set any meeting times that might be necessary for your group.

Weekdays (particularly Mondays) before five are typically not as crowded; Saturdays and evenings are the most popular. Check your child's height before you go. Frontier City strictly enforces height requirement rules. If you have children in different height categories, you should plan to have at least two adults in your group.

To avoid spending time in long lines, ride the popular rides during off-peak times, such as early to mid-afternoon. Rarely are there lines for the kiddy rides which are found in the Kids Corral (northeast corner of the park) and in the northwest corner of the park. A train provides easy transportation from the Kids Corral area to the far west side of the park. The Kids Corral also has playground equipment for those energetic little ones.

Located next to the Silver Bullet Rollercoaster is the first aid area, complete with trained EMT's. A nursing area is located near first aid, and a diaper-changing area is provided in the restrooms near the Kids Corral (northeast corner of the park). Inquire at the front entrance about strollers which are available for $5 each. An ATM is located near the southeast corner of the Trading Post retail store.

Frontier City offers several special events throughout the season. **Summer concerts** are offered for guests at no additional charge. Upcoming performers include the Little River Band, Three Dog Night, and Lesley Gore and the Coasters. Call ahead for information. On July 4th, Frontier City celebrates our nation's birthday with the **Old-Fashioned American Celebration**. This celebration features concerts and an extended fireworks display. **Oktoberfest** is held during the first three weekends during October. Enjoy Bavarian foods, decorations, polka bands, and local talent performing throughout the park. A special low admission rate allows guests to enjoy the special event, but a ride pass is extra.

**HallowScream** is held during the last two weekends of October. This spooktacular event features a nightly Trick or Treat Trail with free candy and bags for children twelve and under, six different Halloween live entertainment shows, plus the notorious Trail of Terror Haunted Campground for those brave enough to enter after dark. Special pay-one-price admission also includes unlimited thrill-filled rides.

## Harn Homestead

*313 Northeast 16th Street, (405) 235-4058. Located south of the Capitol, west of Lincoln Boulevard, on Northeast 16th Street. Look for the sign along Lincoln Boulevard. Adults $3, children twelve and under, $1.50. If scheduled in advance, group rates are available for fifteen or more: adults $3, children $1.50. Tour reservations are required two weeks in advance. Tuesday-Saturday, 10-4.* ★

Harn Homestead helps explore the question, "What was life like for the settlers of Oklahoma after the exciting 1889 Land Run and before statehood?" The museum includes a one-room schoolhouse, the restored and furnished Harn Home (a typical middle-class home), a furnished farmhouse, a working barn, an exhibit barn, and working gardens. Tours of the Harn Home are given on the hour until 3 p.m., and they last about one hour. Visitors may explore other areas by following the map/brochure.

### Helpful Hints

Located on the grounds are tree-shaded picnic areas, an old-fashioned swing, drinking fountains, and public restrooms. Most of the museum is wheelchair accessible. Harn Homestead offers educational programs for school classes. Teachers should schedule visits months in advance. Harn Homestead will send a brochure in advance. Nearby attractions include the Oklahoma State Capitol and the State Museum of History.

You may call Harn Homestead to receive information about workshops for adults and youths and special family events offered at various times of the year. Held in October, the **Harvest Festival** provides an excellent opportunity for hands-on family fun. Spinners, weavers, blacksmiths, and storytellers gather to enlighten and entertain visitors. A petting zoo featuring farm animals, sack races, cake walks, and stilt walking are available for everyone to enjoy.

## International Gymnastics Hall of Fame

*120 N. Robinson (First National Center-East Concourse) in downtown Oklahoma City, (405) 235-5600. Traveling west on I-40, take the Robinson Street exit and go north. At Sheridan go one block east, then north on Broadway for two blocks. Park in the Main Street Parking Garage on Main, just north of the Medallion Hotel. Find the elevator and take it to the first floor, which is the main level of the concourse. Keep turning right to find the escalator; go down the escalator, and you will see the museum. It is suggested that visitors call before visiting the museum; curators can customize the tour to their interests. Monday-Friday 10-5, Saturday (for groups and by appointment only) 9-noon.* ▣

Originally located in Oceanside, California, this gymnastics museum has an extensive collection of memorabilia relating to the sport. These items include uniforms, bronze sculptures, prized medals, original art, and a reduced-size replica of "The Gymnast," a twenty-one-foot sculpture that is outside the Georgia Dome in Atlanta. Notable items include the 1976 Olympic parade uniform worn by one of gymnastics' first "darlings," Nadia Comaneci, apparel worn by gymnast-superstar and Oklahoman Bart Conner, the 1984 Olympic torch, on loan from the Olympic committee, and a 1984 Olympic flag.

The museum has an extensive collection of gymnastics-related books and magazines dating from 1904, and videos of men's and women's events, World Cups, and Olympic Games from as early as 1930.

Oklahoma City has pledged property in the southeast corner of Bricktown for the permanent home of the Gymnastics Hall of Fame. When completed, the proposed 20,000 square-foot building will feature a small gymnasium in addition to museum exhibits. See how far the sport of gymnastics has come, and become aware of the contributions to the sport of Oklahomans such as Conner, Comaneci (an adopted Oklahoman), and two-time World Champion Shannon Miller of Edmond.

# Oklahoma City

## Lake Hefner Trails

*Lake Hefner, Northwest Oklahoma City. Travel west on Britton Road from North May Avenue until the road ends at the lake. Turn right into the parking area. (405) 525-8822. Open daily. Admission is free.*

Known as a wonderful lake for sailing, Lake Hefner has two paved and well-utilized trails that follow the shoreline. One trail is for bicycling and skating, and the other is for walking and jogging. Benches are available for those needing a break. A nearby duck pond is the perfect place for young children to feed the waterfowl. To find the pond, turn west on Wilshire from May Avenue and continue until the road ends at Lake Hefner.

### Helpful Hints

Visit the Ranger's Station, located by the boat ramp on the south side of the lake, for information on water activities. Stop by Wheeler Dealer Bicycle Shop, 2729 Northwest 50th, (405) 947-6260, for a free map of the trails and the lake.

Be aware that some of the trails offer no shade. Bring your water bottle and, during the summer, go early in the morning or late in the evening. Always wear your helmet when skating or bicycling!

## Library for the Blind and Physically Handicapped

*300 Northeast 18th Street, (405) 521-3514. From I-44, exit Lincoln Boulevard going south past State Capitol building to Northeast 18th Street. Turn west and look for the Travis Leon Harris Building, which houses the library on the south side of the road. Open Monday-Friday 8-5. Admission is free.*

At the Library for the Blind and Physically Handicapped, children can experience how life would be different if they were blind or physically disabled. Just as important, they will discover what adjustments would be necessary for simple everyday living. Not only will they learn about Braille and be given an alphabet sheet to take home, but they will also learn how the visually-impaired handle other situations. For example, a hands-on lesson demonstrates the use of a plate, numbered like a clock, that helps the visually-impaired organize their food.

Although reservations are not required, calling ahead will allow the library staff to be better prepared. They will make name tags in print and braille and be ready to give a tour. The tour includes a twelve-minute video showing how handicapped children attend school. The entire tour takes about an hour.

Recently, an area featuring a garden and walking path specially designed for those with disabilities was opened. A braille tactile map located at the entrance identifies the layout and features of the garden. Trees, shrubs and flowers were selected based on fragrance, texture and beauty. Three different paving textures help visitors identify their surroundings; two semicircle sitting areas paved with brick and rough-textured concrete are identified and used as walking paths; a smooth concrete surface covers the ground where eating areas with picnic tables are located. The garden and the walking path are filled with chimes, bird feeders, bird baths, and bird houses. Let all your senses enjoy this special area!

## Lion's Fun Park

*13801 North Eastern, (405) 359-0081. From I-35, exit at Memorial Road and travel three miles to Eastern. Turn north on Eastern to the entrance on the west side of the road. Admission is free, but the cost for activities varies with the number of people and dates. Hours vary with the season; call ahead to confirm.*

Lion's Fun Park is a great place for family fun. Activities include miniature golf courses, go-carts, batting cages, a large arcade area, volleyball courts, bumper boats, and bank-shot basketball.

For Easter, Lion's Fun Park sponsors an **Easter Egg Hunt** and, on Father's Day, the park hosts a **father/son golf tournament**; the golf tournament is held on the challenging nine-hole, par-three golf course. To practice on the driving range, arrive early.

Birthday parties with a minimum of eight children can be arranged one week in advance. Group discounts are available for groups of eight or more. Snack food and indoor/outdoor eating areas are available.

## Martin Park Nature Center

*5000 West Memorial Road, (405) 755-0676. Located in northwestern Oklahoma City on Memorial Road between Northwest 122nd Street and Northwest 150th Street. The park is on the south side of Memorial Road between Meridian and MacArthur. Open March-November: Tuesday-Sunday 9-6; December-February: Wednesday-Sunday 9-6. Closed on major holidays. ★*

At Martin Park Nature Center, you may take a nature hike, watch a turtle sunbathe, or catch a glimpse of a deer. Make a game of trying to identify the raccoon and opossum tracks found in the park. Be sure to watch for prairie dogs and hawks. This 140-acre park is home to several different types of wildlife and plant life.

A nature center featuring many hands-on displays for children is located at the park. Here, children learn about wildlife and ways to protect it.

### Helpful Hints

On pretty days, the park may be crowded. For a change, visit on a snowy day and look for animal tracks. In the summer, wildlife may be easier to spot in the cooler part of the day. Picnic tables are available. One well-graveled trail is wheelchair accessible, and the Nature Center and restrooms are handicapped accessible as well.

Every Sunday afternoon at 2 p.m., the staff offers a **nature program.** You

*A naturalist at Martin Park*

can learn about bird watching, edible plants, or play a nature game for $1 (more if additional supplies are needed). Or, for $1 (10 person minimum), you can participate in a customized, guided nature hike. Bring dry dog food or cat food to feed the water turtles.

A seasonal program guide and map of all of the Oklahoma City parks can be obtained by calling (405) 297-2211.

## *Myriad Botanical Gardens*

*100 Myriad Gardens, (405) 297-3995. Located near downtown at Reno and Robinson. Westbound on I-40, take the Robinson exit and follow Robinson north. Turn west on Reno. Parking will be on your right. Eastbound on I-40, take the Walker exit and follow Walker north to Reno. Turn east on Reno. Parking will be on your left past Hudson Avenue. Admission (subject to change) is adults $3, children (ages four to twelve) $1.25, children under age four are free, reduced rates for senior citizens. Guided tours are available seven days a week; reservations should be made at least a week in advance. Tours average thirty minutes and can be specialized for any age group. Special exhibits, nature classes, and celebrations are held throughout the year. The gardens and Crystal Bridge are handicapped accessible. ★*

Did you know there is a rain forest in downtown Oklahoma City? Visit the Myriad Botanical Gardens and see "Dinosaur plants," colorful butterflies, camouflaged lizards, and a cascading waterfall. Look for Pony Tail trees, Sea Grapes, Mickey Mouse plants, and Antelope Ears in the garden. Take a walk under the waterfall or look for lizards among the plants. Notice how the temperature changes as you pass from one region to another.

Stroll through the seventeen acres of native landscaping surrounding the Crystal Bridge and watch the Japanese Koi and Goldfish in the spring-fed lake. In the spring and summer, you can buy fish food in the gift shop or bring puppy food to feed the fish.

Myriad Botanical Gardens

*View of the falls inside the Crystal Bridge at Myriad Gardens.*

Explore this brilliant environment and discover many intriguing secrets of nature. Learn how important it is to preserve the balance of nature.

### Helpful Hints

The Crystal Bridge gets very hot and humid during the summer months. The cooler days of fall and winter provide a more comfortable temperature and bigger, more colorful blooms from the plants.

Each year, several "free" days are scheduled. Guests may visit free on the Garden's anniversary date (March 25); mothers visit free on Mother's Day, and senior citizens visit free on Senior's Day. The gift shop offers an excellent selection of items that will educate visitors about our environment and the need to protect it.

*The Crystal Bridge at Myriad Gardens.*

## National Cowboy Hall of Fame

*1700 Northeast 63rd Street, (405) 478-2250. Take I-44 to Martin Luther (M.L.) King Boulevard, exit and go north a short distance to Northeast 63rd Street. Turn west on Northeast 63rd Street. The museum will be on the south. From Labor Day to Memorial Day, open daily 9-5; from Memorial Day to Labor Day, open daily 8:30-6. Closed Thanksgiving, Christmas and New Year's Day. Adults $6.50, senior citizens $5.50, children ages six to twelve $3.25, and children under six are free. Memberships are available. Call for group tours and special prices. Tour guides are available by appointment only; call or write the tour director two weeks in advance. The museum is handicapped accessible.* ⑤ ★

Dedicated to preserving the history and legends of the West, the National Cowboy Hall of Fame and Western Heritage Center features a renowned collection of classic and contemporary Western art and artifacts. A heroic-sized bronze statue of a weary cowboy facing the sunset welcomes visitors to the museum. Inside, James Earle Fraser's moving sculpture, "End of the Trail," and Gerald Balciar's marble masterpiece, "Canyon Princess," grace broad corridors.

National Cowboy Hall of Fame

*The National Cowboy Hall of Fame has something for all ages.*

The vast permanent collections of the museum, considered to be a "national treasure," reflect the breadth of America's frontier past from Native Americans and cowboys to miners, soldiers, and homesteaders. Breathtaking art works by famous Western artists such as Remington, Russell, and Moran provide visitors an inspiring view of the Old West.

Located inside the 1,200 seat Sam Noble Special Events Center are the magnificent "Windows to the West" murals painted by contemporary Western artist, Wilson Hurley. The five scenes include the California coast, the Grand Canyon, Monument Valley, New Mexico's Sandia Mountains, and Yellowstone Falls.

The "Hall of Great Westerners" honors men and women who embody the spirit of the West. This honor is the highest bestowed by the Hall of Fame. A large plaque contains the names of more than two hundred people who helped settle the American West. Names listed include Teddy Roosevelt, Charles Goodnight, Kit Carson, and Sacajawea.

The "Hall of Great Western Performers" is the most popular hall. This gallery honors famous Western stars and contains portraits of favorites such as Roy Rogers and Dale Evans, Barbara Stanwyck, Gene Autry, and even the cast of "Gunsmoke." Another room is filled with John Wayne memorabilia.

A new and exciting area is the Children's Cowboy Corral, dedicated "to those young in years and those young at heart." It relates the history of the cowboy from 1860-1900. As children enter, they will first notice the natural-looking rock cliffs resembling the famous Camel Rock Cliffs, located in New

Cowboy Hall of Fame

*Good eats at the Chuckwagon Gathering, National Cowboy Hall of Fame.*

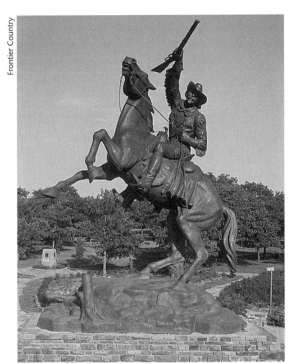

*National Cowboy Hall of Fame.*

Mexico, which have been used as the background for many western movies. Perched on the cliff are howling coyotes, and nestled in a crevice is a snake waiting to strike. Located in the cliffs are various dioramas that light up at the touch of a button to reveal scenes from the western days. This museum is "hands-on," with everyone from children to parents participating.

The bunkhouse area is filled with western clothes and boots. With just a little effort, anyone can look like John Wayne! Three "log horses" are saddled and ready to ride, and a stuffed Texas longhorn waits for young children to pet his nose.

Learn how cowboys survived on the range. Climb into the small tent, better known as a range tepee, or get into a bedroll and pretend to fall asleep under the stars. A covered chuck wagon, complete with authentic cookware, will give children an idea of what meals were like on the trail. They can even ring the dinner bell!

The highlight of the Corral is an animatronic cowboy sitting atop his horse. Watch as his eyes realistically move while he tells stories about ways of the Old West. Push a button to hear about cowboy songs, tall tales, life on the trail, and more. This is sure to be a hit with small children!

Work is currently under way on a branding pit specially designed for children. With the help of a docent, a child can use a real branding iron to brand a plywood calf.

### Helpful Hints

There is an indoor snack bar at the museum. The museum's beautiful gift shop, "Trappings of the West," includes inexpensive souvenirs and Native American jewelry, among other items.

The Hall hosts several outstanding events throughout the year. The most notable events for families are the **Chuckwagon Gathering** and **National Children's Cowboy Festival**; both are held in mid-May. Authentic wagons, traditional western food cooked by chuck wagon cooks, games, living history demonstrations, pony rides, and covered wagon rides are just a few of the unique experiences at this popular event. Create a special holiday family memory by attending the **Cowboy Christmas Ball** in early December. Call early for reservations.

## Oklahoma Children's Theater

*3000 Pershing Boulevard. Located on the State Fairgrounds. From I-40, exit at May Avenue and drive north. Enter at gate 2-26 on the west side of the street. (405) 951-0000 or (405) 948-6408. Adults and children (ages two and older) $4. Season tickets are $20 for seven admissions. ★*

Enjoy wonderful performances of children's favorites like *The Velveteen Rabbit*, *The Tortoise and the Hare*, *Treasure Island*, and more, performed by professional adult actors. Productions are often zany, and all are easily-understood by children as young as three. Children can sit on mats up close to the performance or sit on bleachers. On weekends, children can meet the cast after the show. This is a "must do" event for the family!

### Helpful Hints

In addition, summer and spring-break acting camps, classes, and workshop productions are held. In the summer, two shows are held that feature intermediate-level child actors who take lessons at the facility.

The Grandparents Club costs $30 and allows both grandparents and one grandchild to attend four plays with receptions following each one. Each additional grandchild costs $10. Make reservations one month in advance for birthday celebrations held during Saturday or Sunday performances. Children can see the play and meet the cast. Cost is $25 for the party room (you furnish the cake and birthday supplies), plus $3 per person for ten or more.

## Oklahoma City Art Museum

*3113 Pershing Boulevard, (405) 946-4477. Located on the State Fairgrounds. From I-44 take Northwest 10th East exit, and go to May Avenue. Turn south on May to the first fairgrounds gate and go west. The museum will be the first building on your left. Tuesday, Wednesday, Friday, and Saturday 10-5, Thursday 10-9, Sunday 1-5. Adults $3.50, seniors/students $2.50, children under age twelve are free. Membership information is available upon request. Members of the museum are admitted free. This museum is handicapped accessible.*

The Oklahoma City Art Museum contains over three thousand works of art. Up to twelve rotating exhibits featuring works from the museum collection and on-loan pieces are displayed each year. A significant portion of the museum's art pieces came from the Washington Gallery of Modern Art Collection, which was active in the nation's capital from 1961 to 1968.

### Helpful Hints

**Family Days** are held during the winter months. You might see a puppet show, hear a folktale, or create art. Call for information concerning dates and times. The **Children's Art Festival** is usually held the first weekend in September. Artists assist children in making kites, puppets, masks, and more. There are jugglers, musicians, craftsmen, and dancers. This is a very entertaining event for families; don't miss it!

## Oklahoma City Blazers Hockey

*Myriad Convention Center. From I-40 exit at Walker and go north to Sheridan. Turn east on Sheridan to the Myriad. (405) 235-PUCK. The season runs October through April. Games usually begin at 7:30 p.m., but call ahead; there are exceptions. Admission for lower level seating is $12; upper level seating is $8. Discounts are available for senior citizens and children under twelve. Inquire about group rates.*

Bundle up the children and plan to spend an exciting evening with the Oklahoma City Blazers, champions of the 1995-96 Central Hockey League. The action is fast and furious as the Blazers take to the ice and prepare to rumble! Children will get a kick out of watching the boisterous fans as well as the hardworking Blazer players. They will especially love the St. Bernard mascot, Doc Blades. In the southwest corner of the concourse, there is a special stand that sells children's souvenirs such as hats, clothes and pucks.

The Blazers have the distinction of being the fastest team in the minor hockey league to reach the 1,000,000 fan mark. Everyone enjoys a Blazers game!

## Oklahoma City 89ers Baseball

*Games are played at All-Sports Stadium, State Fairgrounds, (405) 946-8989. From I-44, go east on N.W. 10th Street to the fairgrounds and follow the signs to All Sports Stadium. NOTE: A new ballpark in Bricktown is scheduled to open for the 1998 season. The 89ers season runs from April-August. Game times vary depending on the month, but they are generally around 7 p.m. for weekday and Saturday nights and around 1:30 on Sundays. Lower Box Seats $6, Upper Box Seats $5, Reserved seats $3, General Admission $2. Children age four and under are free. Ticket packages and season tickets are available. Call for more information. ★*

Take your family out to the ball game to see the Oklahoma City 89ers, a Triple A baseball team and the Texas Rangers' top farm club. Join the excitement on Monday nights, when the 89ers have premium giveaways and entertainment such as sumo wrestling or celebrity concerts. Special nights include Wednesday Season Ticket Holder Nights, Thursday Family Nights, and Sunday Kid's Festivals.

### Helpful Hints

A popular area for families is the grassy slope; bring a blanket and enjoy extra room for roaming. Grab a bag of peanuts and a ballpark hotdog and start your own family tradition!

## Oklahoma City Philharmonic

*Performances are held at the Civic Center Music Hall. From I-40 east, exit at Walker and go north to Colcord. At Colcord, go west. The Civic Center will be on your left. From I-40 west, exit at Robinson, and go north to Reno. At Reno, go west to Walker. At Walker, go north and turn west on Colcord. The Civic Center will be on your left. Ticket prices vary, but they generally range from $9 for adults to $6 for children.*

Enjoy an evening of beautiful and inspiring music with the Philharmonic. During the season, nine performances are held, each featuring a different guest artist. Children will especially enjoy the Family Series. In the past, Family Series performances have starred noted children entertainers such as Fred Penner and have featured ever-popular favorite shows such as *Peter and the Wolf*.

Another "favorite" for families is the **Yuletide Festival**, held in early December. Children will laugh at the skits featuring Santa and the Nutcracker as well as be inspired by the beautiful Christmas music. This highly-recommended event gets families in the holiday spirit!

## Oklahoma City Zoological Park

*2101 N.E. 50th Street, (405) 424-3344. From I-35, exit N.E. 50th Street, travel west one mile and follow the signs to the entrance. From I-44, exit on Martin Luther King Boulevard, go south to Remington Place (N.E. 50th), turn east and follow signs to zoo entrance. From April-September, the zoo is open daily 9-6. From October-March, the zoo is open daily 9-5. Exhibit buildings close fifteen minutes before the zoo closes. Guests are welcome to remain on the grounds until dusk. Adults $6, children ages three to eleven and seniors ages sixty-five and older $3. Children under three are free. For groups of fifteen or more, children $1.50, adults $3. (To receive the special group rate, you must pay as a group; no reservations are needed but reservations are recommended to speed up the group's entry.) Aquaticus show $2. Seasonal Sky Safari $1 per person one way, children under three free. Seasonal safari train guided tours $1.50 per person. This facility is handicapped accessible.*

Consistently rated as one of the top zoos in the country, the Oklahoma City Zoo provides quality educational entertainment for all ages. From the Children's Zoo to the new Cat Forest/Lion Overlook, exciting exhibits and interesting animals are discovered at every turn.

As you enter, obtain a free Safari map and plan your route. To save time, pay for the Aquaticus show as your pay your admission fee. The most common route taken by visitors is to turn left (east) upon entering and enjoy the Children's Zoo and Discovery Area. Located nearby is the **Butterfly Garden**. The butterflys are most active from mid-spring to early fall. Continue on to the Island Life exhibit building, the **Herpetarium** (reptiles and amphibians), the bears, and finally the show at **Aquaticus** to take a rest and enjoy the delightful dolphins and other sea animals.

The **Island Life** exhibit building features many Galapagos tortoises, parrots that hang upside down, ducks that whistle, many endangered species, as well as interactive educational exhibits. Children will enjoy activities that provide hands-on learning, such as trying to lift an empty Galapagos tortoise shell.

In the **Herpetarium** are reptiles and amphibians from all over the world. View rattlesnakes, a boa constrictor, tree frogs, and eyelash vipers up-close but safely through the glass windows.

At **Aquaticus**, the dolphins are the stars of the show, and the sea lions amuse the crowd with their funny antics. After the show, visit the exhibits down the ramp to view more fresh and seawater animal life.

Fred Marvel/Oklahoma Tourism

*The amazing dolphins at Aquaticus.*

When the dolphin show is over, and you've viewed the Aquaticus exhibits, return to the main entrance area. Take advantage of the refreshment areas and playground along the way.

Next, take the train (runs April through September and October weekends) for a guided tour of the hoofed-stock animals. (During the off-season or bad weather when the train isn't running, take a nice stroll through this area and see some of the rarest animals in the zoo.) The train stops in the southeast corner of the zoo at the Great EscApe exhibit, a must-see highlight of the zoo.

Oklahoma City Zoo

The **Great EscApe** exhibit features a major collection of great apes (gorillas, chimpanzees and orangutans). It was the first exhibit in the United States to reproduce three and one half acres of tropical forest, meadows and streams. Visitors truly feel a part of a misty tropical forest as they view the gorillas through large glass windows. Mothers and baby gorillas are often within close view. Watch as mothers groom their babies and note how they interact with one another. Sometimes as visitors study these creatures, they find themselves the object of much scrutiny by the gorillas! Cool days will almost always insure good viewing because the gorillas crowd around the heated rocks near the windows.

*The Great Escape.*

Central to the exhibit is education about the great apes. For example, children can better comprehend the enormous size of the gorilla by placing their hand on the gorilla's handprint in the exhibit. If visitors are lucky, the intelligent chimpanzee will be seen using tools. Sometimes zookeepers place treats such as yogurt inside fake termite mounds, thus challenging the chimps to use willow branches to get their reward. Look for single orangutans using their human-like, large hands to swing from branch to branch in the treetops. As you observe these animals, closely watch for signs of emotion such as joy, curiosity, grief, fear, and anger.

Children learn by imitating and, after seeing the apes, they may want to copy them on the unique playground, complete with swing ropes, a jungle walk, and a fake termite mound. This is a good time to let them run off some energy!

After the Great EscApe, stop by the newest addition to the zoo, the magnificent **Cat Forest/Lion Overlook**. This exhibit covers more than four acres and cost $8.4 million. Special efforts have been made to simulate the natural habitats of the many cats living at the zoo. Sumatran tigers live in an area with bamboo, snow leopards enjoy rock outcroppings similar to those in the Himalayas, and the web-footed fishing cat wades through the exhibit's pool. Many other small and large wild cats can be seen in this extraordinary exhibit.

As you leave this area, head north to view a favorite of many children, the elephants. The trail past the elephants leads to the entrance area/exit. What a wonderful way to spend the day—at everyone's favorite, the zoo!

### Helpful Hints

Numerous outstanding educational programs are available both to school and afterschool groups and to individuals through special classes that are available year round. There are special spring and summer classes, too. Some classes offer parent classes at the same time as the children's programs. Teachers and other adult leaders should book their special program at least two weeks in advance. To get the brochure on classes for children (and adults), call the zoo in May. Highlights of the zoo's special events are the Summer Season Celebration and Haunt the Zoo for Halloween. For more information about these and other zoo events, call the zoo phone number for a recording.

The **Summer Season Celebration**, held the first or second weekend in April, features a scavenger hunt for kids, health and well-being exhibits, and more.

**Haunt the Zoo for Halloween** is the biggest special event at the zoo and features safe trick or treating for Halloween. Held October 26-31 from 6:30-

*Hands-on education at the Oklahoma City Zoo.*

8:30, the event features 700 carved and lighted pumpkins, numerous fantasy booths with candy, and the sounds of the zoo animals in the background. Admission is $4 per child, and discount coupons are available at local restaurants (call zoo information line for specific details). For two weeks before Haunt the Zoo, free admission to the zoo is offered for those bringing a pumpkin larger than their head size-a fun way to contribute to the special project and enjoy the zoo in the often-beautiful October weather.

A $40 zoo membership is a great value that provides free admission for one year for parents and children and the opportunity to visit about one hundred zoos nationwide free. Call the Info Line for complete updates on the zoo and its activities. You can also find out about baby animals through the Info Line or find the information posted on a kiosk in the main plaza area. It is rare to find animal babies in the zoo nursery because they are being well cared for by their mothers. Baby animals are usually born in the spring or summer.

The Sky Tram is fun and allows for a birds-eye view of the animals. The cost is $1 one way per person (children under three are free). The tram is seasonal and weather-dependent. It takes you from the front entrance to Aquaticus. You can

bring your own picnic or buy your lunch from the many concession stands. Whether you buy or bring your food, there are many shaded areas with tables to enjoy your lunch. Strollers are available for $2, and wheelchairs are available for a small deposit. From October-March, the weekday dolphin show at 11 a.m. is a free training show. People "in the know" say that their children can get

*The Butterfly Garden.*

close to the animals and ask questions of the trainers during this special time.

The zoo is busier during nice weather and on weekends. Peak hours are from 11 a.m. to 3 p.m. The animals are most active during early morning and late afternoon.

Consider giving a gift of animal adoption through the "Parents of the Wild" program. Visit the Information Kiosk (located in the main plaza area near the front) for a brochure.

## Oklahoma Firefighters Museum

*2716 Northeast 50th Street, (405) 424-3440. Located near the southwest corner of I-35 and Northeast 50th Street, just east of the Oklahoma City Zoo. Adults $3, children from six to twelve $1.50, children under six-years-old are free when accompanied by a parent. Price for scheduled tours is half the normal admission. Open daily, 10-4:30; closed on holidays. Tours last seventy-five minutes and are given by reservation to any group of twelve (children and adults). To schedule tours, call two weeks in advance.*

The Firefighters Museum is considered one of the top firefighting museums in the country. It displays a wonderful collection of firefighting equipment which dates from 1736 to the present. Two large antique fire engines are on display outside; they are perfect for climbing on and picnicking nearby. Inside, visitors will find exhibits such as a huge wall mural showing several models of fire engines and restored firefighting equipment such as an alarm box that dates to 1900. Be sure to ask the staff for a demonstration of the alarm box; hold your ears, it really works!

### Helpful Hints

Tours are available anytime during regular weekday hours; drop-in visitors need only to ask the staff for a tour. A selection of thirty-minute videos is available for visitors to view during their tours. The videos stress fire safety and related topics.

The Firefighters Museum is most appropriate for children ages six and older; younger children will have difficulty observing the "no touching" rule. Before you leave, be sure to pick up the museum's colorful brochure; it is full of information regarding the collection.

A visit to this museum will inspire parents to check the batteries in smoke detectors and families to develop an escape route in case of a house fire. These simple tasks can save lives!

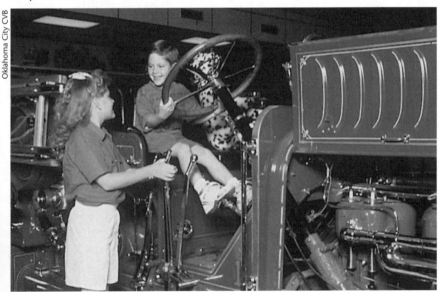

*The Oklahoma Firefighters Museum.*

## Oklahoma State Capitol

*Located at N.E. 23rd Street and Lincoln Boulevard, (405) 521-3356. From I-44, exit at Lincoln Boulevard and proceed south to N.E. 23rd Street. Monday-Friday 8-4:30. Tours last forty-five minutes and begin at the Visitors Information Center on the first floor every hour on the half-hour from 9-3 or by appointment. To make tour reservations, call in advance. There is also a self-guided tour brochure available. Admis-*

*sion is free. The Capitol is handicapped accessible.*

Take a trip to the Oklahoma State Capitol to let your children see their government at work. The Oklahoma Legislature (both the House of Representatives and the Senate) convenes the first Tuesday in February and adjourns the last Friday in May. During these months, visitors may observe House sessions Monday through Thursday from the fifth floor viewing gallery. The Senate Chamber viewing gallery is open during business hours Monday through Friday.

The Oklahoma State Capitol has many interesting features. It is one of only twelve state capitols without a dome, and it's the only one with working oil wells on the property. There are 650 rooms with eleven acres of floor space. The exterior is made of Indiana limestone, and Oklahoma pink and black granite is used for the base. Alabama marble covers the floors, and Vermont marble is used for the stairs and wall bases. The ceilings are hand-carved and hand-painted. During the last few years, many of the areas have been returned to their authentic interior decor and furniture, including the original paint colors; the effect is stunning.

Beautiful murals and portraits fill the capitol. Located on the curved walls of the rotunda are four portraits of famous Oklahomans. Charles Banks Wilson, a native Oklahoman, was commissioned in 1963 to paint these large portraits at a cost of $5,000 each. The first shows Robert S. Kerr, the twelfth governor of Oklahoma and a former U.S. Senator. The second is a portrait of Sequoyah, the inventor of the Cherokee alphabet. The third portrait is Will Rogers, a famous cowboy, entertainer and goodwill ambassador. The fourth portrait is Jim Thorpe, declared to be the greatest athlete in the world due to his achievements at the Olympics of 1912. A recent portrait of baseball great Mickey Mantle was dedicated in May, 1997. In 1976, the historical murals above the portraits were added at a cost of $65,000. These murals represent Oklahoma's early stages of development. Help your children pick out the interesting highlights of the state's history as they study the paintings.

On the north wall of the fifth floor is a captivating mural by Mike Larsen, a Chickasaw Indian artist. Entitled "Flight of Spirit," the mural memorializes five world-famous Oklahoma ballerinas of Native American heritage. Note how the mural seems to "glow" with beautiful color.

Elaine Warner

*As Long As The Waters Flow*

Other highlights of the capitol include the "hidden staircase," the beautiful Supreme Court room, the Governor's Blue Room, and much more. Walk the halls of the Oklahoma State Capitol, where history is made every day!

**Helpful Hints**

The Visitor Information Center on the first floor near the rotunda has much Oklahoma tourism information. Try to plan your tour during nice weather; the rotunda areas are not heated or air-conditioned. A tunnel featuring painted scenes of Oklahoma history is located on the east side of the Capitol; it conveniently exits near the State Museum of History.

## Omniplex

*2100 N.E. 52nd Street, (405) 424-5545. Located in the Kirkpatrick Center. Take I-44 to Martin Luther King Avenue, and go south. The museum will be on your left past Remington Park. Adults ages thirteen to sixty-four $6.50, seniors ages 65 and up $4.50, children ages three to twelve $4. Children ages three and under are admitted free. Group rates for fifteen people or more are available by calling 427-5461 for reservations. This museum is handicapped accessible.* 🏛 ★

With its myriad of activities and educational venues, Omniplex is the ultimate "edutainment" center. You and your children, regardless of age, will relish this learning experience together! Among the main museums and galleries in Omniplex are the Kirkpatrick Science and Air Space Museum, the International Photography Hall of Fame, Red Earth Indian Center, Kirkpatrick Planetarium, and the Gardens and Greenhouse.

The **Kirkpatrick Science and Air Space Museum** includes two major areas, the Hands-On Science Museum and the Air Space Museum. In 1996, *Parents* magazine named the **Hands-On Science Museum** as one of the nation's best museums for children. Over three hundred hands-on exhibits and educational programs enlighten, entertain, and educate the entire family. Visit a weather station monitoring the climate outside, capture your shadow, pet a python, climb through a giant molecule, spin around in the "Aerotrim," journey to the center of the earth by virtual reality, learn about gravity and friction, and much more. The recently-renovated Energy Quest area includes twenty-two hands-on exhibits about Oklahoma's energy resources such as electricity, oil, natural gas, minerals, and more.

Each summer, the museum hosts blockbuster traveling exhibits such as: "Invasion of the Giant Insects!" and "Whodunit?: The Science of Solving Crime." In 1997, the featured exhibit especially appeals to the younger set; Richard Scarry's "Busytown" is full of interactive learning. In Busytown, children (and adults) become actively involved in running the town, including the Grocery Store, Factory, Shipyard, Power Plant, Construction Area, and more.

For more hands-on instruction, science sessions for children ages three and up are held on weekends; week-long sessions are held in the summer. All classes are taught by professional educators who promote interactive learning. Classes should be reserved in advance by calling the education department at 424-5545.

**Kidspace** captivates younger children (ages two to five only) with a variety of activities designed to engage children as they see, touch, manipulate, and modify objects. For example, "Electronic Fingerpainting" introduces children to computer technology, and "Waterworks" explores buoyancy, volume, and kinetic energy. There are also several areas that promote "pretend" play; especially popular are the phones that promote imaginative discussions between parent and child.

Oklahoma's premier public-access planetarium, the **Kirkpatrick Planetarium,** presents shows to over 100,000 visitors each year. Planetarium shows are free but, on busy days, tickets are handed out early to reduce the time people spend in line. Inquire about tickets at the front desk when you arrive. A new aluminum dome, state-of-the-art sound system, plush carpeting, comfortable seating, and informative shows make the visit a sensational one. Planetarium staff members suggest that children should be about eight years old to fully understand and absorb the information shared through the programs. Shows last about forty minutes. Show times vary by season; call in advance for precise times. The Planetarium is closed the first Monday of each month for maintenance.

Learn about Oklahoma's many contributions to the air and space industry and experience "lift-off" at the Air Space Museum, known as having one of the nation's premier collections of aviation and space artifacts, aircraft, and exhibits. Many Oklahomans have become famous pilots and astronauts. Learn about these aviation pioneers and their lives and accomplishments through the exhibits at the Air Space Museum. From early flight pioneers such as Wiley Post to recent world-record holder, astronaut Shannon Lucid, learn and be inspired by these daring and brilliant scientists and aviators.

Blast off into space via a Mercury capsule simulator that recreates the first space mission by a U.S. astronaut. Young astronauts wear a silver jumpsuit and helmet while receiving orders from "mission control" inside the space capsule. Older children slip into an F-16 Combat Flight Simulator and experience aerial warfare or fly a real World War II link trainer. The AWAC's control center allows airplane enthusiasts to fly an actual mission as they are buckled into the seat and push control buttons.

On weekends, the museum offers free tickets for the Cimarron flight simulation room. Register at the front desk of the Air Space Museum for the simulator rides on the day of your visit. The F-16 flight simulator lasts thirty minutes and costs $3 for ages ten and up. Children can experience lift-off into space in the Mercury space capsule simulator for $5. For $10, your child can take the simulator ride and obtain a video of his or her flight.

Popular astronaut and pilot training programs are offered for children ages four through sixteen during the summer. Costs range from $50 to $120 (register early and receive a discount). Call 427-5461 for more information on the program and registration deadlines.

A diverse selection of art, artifacts, and rare collections are displayed in the eighteen **Kirkpatrick Galleries** located throughout Omniplex. View a section of the Berlin Wall, peep inside a real passenger railroad car from the 1920s, watch the toy train collection move through the tunnels and miniature villages, and gaze at the unique collection of hats from around the world. Children and parents will enjoy art work by Oklahoma school children displayed in the Young Artists Gallery. For military enthusiasts, the Navy Gallery is located near the Air Space Museum entrance. African and Asian Galleries explore cultures from around the world, and the Oklahoma State Collection of Art promotes local talents. When you are admiring the popular exhibit of Oklahoma First Lady's inaugural gowns, ask your children to pick their favorite and visit with them about fashion history. Young children will especially like the large Victorian doll house located near the inaugural gowns exhibit.

Tropical gardens, fountains, lush flower beds, and a Japanese Garden are among the pleasures you will find at the **Gardens and Greenhouse**. Enjoy lunch at one of the picnic tables, surrounded by beautiful plant life. In the warmer months, children should be on the lookout for turtles and lizards hiding in the foliage. Playground equipment keeps children entertained while adults sit back and enjoy the peaceful surroundings.

**Red Earth Indian Center** (405-427-5228) is located within Omniplex on the east side of the second floor. This museum presents the heritage of Native Americans through art, artifacts, hands-on exhibits, and more. Imagine the children that rode in the cradleboards of the Deupree collection and visit the exhibit featuring scale models of early-Native American homes. These exhibits will help your children better understand the culture of the Indians.

See a stuffed buffalo in one room and a tepee in another. The tepee is the right size for children to go inside and imagine they are living on the Oklahoma plains. All visitors will appreciate the works of nationally-known Oklahoma Indian artists.

Classes are available Monday through Friday at 10 a.m., 11 a.m., noon, and 1 p.m. for children, preschool age through twelfth grade. Classes offered explore Oklahoma Indians, powwows, and more. The cost is $2.75 per person, with a minimum of ten participants required (twenty-five maximum). The group price includes admission to the museum complex. Call (405) 424-0066 or (800) 532-7652 at least a week in advance.

**Winter Expo** is a festival featuring Native American singers and dancers in traditional dress, as well as crafts for children. The Expo is held the first weekend in February. In June, the Red Earth Indian center hosts the internationally-acclaimed **Red Earth Festival** (see page 231 of this book for more about this "must do" festival).

Your children may want to experiment with the family camera after visiting the **International Photography Hall of Fame** (405-424-4055), located at the west end of the second floor. Here, visitors see permanent exhibits featuring contributions of photography pioneers such as Louis Daguerre and George Eastman and traveling exhibitions of works by outstanding photographic artists such as Tim Ernst, Mark Webber, Jan Watten, and Christina Patoski. Take a trip to the Grand Canyon when you view the world's largest photomural, a 360-degree laserscape.

### Helpful Hints

Several events are held at Omniplex and its many museums. Make a special trip to Omniplex for **Omnisports**, an event for families held each March. Professional and college coaches and athletes give hands-on instruction to children as they are introduced to approximately twenty different sports, including rock climbing, football, fencing, baseball, gymnastics, basketball, wrestling, tennis, and much more! For more information, call 424-5545.

Children of all ages will enjoy the magic of **Treefest**, beginning the day after Thanksgiving and continuing through New Year's Day. Trees representing countries and cultures from around the world are displayed throughout Omniplex. During the opening day for Treefest, dancers and singers in native costume entertain visitors. Visit Omniplex during the holidays and see why thousands of Oklahoma families have made Treefest a family tradition!

Strollers are available at the entrances to Omniplex. You can purchase a variety of hot and cold lunch and breakfast items from the Garden Cafe or bring a picnic lunch; either way, dine indoors or outside in the gardens. The Museum Shop contains an outstanding inventory of science-oriented games, as well as a large selection of T-shirts, stationary, jewelry, toys, inexpensive souvenirs, and more.

## Pumpkin Patch

*2624 N.W. 178th Street, (405) 348-3074. Located between May and Pennsylvania Avenues on 178th Street (in Edmond this is known as Edmond Road or 2nd Street). Prices for pumpkins range from fifty cents to approximately $30. Group tours are $2 per child. Barn parties, which include a hay ride and bonfire, are $3 per person, minimum $100. Other parties for children are held for $2 per person (minimum of ten), plus a setup fee of $25-35. Open daily from the next-to-last weekend of September to October 31, Tuesday-Saturday 9 a.m. to dark; Sunday 1 p.m. to dark; Monday 9 a.m. to 2 p.m. Some parties are scheduled into November.*

Nearby residents flock to the Olsen family farm to enjoy hay rides, acres of pumpkins, and the hands-on "treasure hunt" for their special pumpkin. Since many school tours are conducted during the day, the best times for families to visit are after school and on weekends. Families pay only for the pumpkins they pick.

To book a group visit to the Pumpkin Patch, call at least two weeks in advance; it gets busier every year! Tours include lessons about the farm and, after each tour, children are allowed to pick their own pumpkins. Barn parties are available during the evenings, and two-hour parties, complete with decorations, are available for children.

## Remington Park

*One Remington Place, (405) 424-9000 or (800) 456-9000. Located near the intersection of I-44 and I-35. Exit I-44 at Martin Luther (M.L.) King Boulevard. Travel south to Remington Park, which is located on the east side of the road. From I-35, exit at N.E. 50th Street (Remington Place) and follow it west to Martin Luther King. Turn north to the Remington Park entrance. Valet parking is available at Gate 1 on*

*N.E. 50th Street. General admission: $2.50, senior citizens, $1.50; Clubhouse re-served seats, $5 (includes admission). Parking: general $1, preferred $3, and valet $5. With few exceptions, the first race begins at 1:15 p.m. The gates are open two hours prior to the first race on weekends and holidays and ninety minutes prior to the first race on weekdays. The facility is handicapped accessible.*

Let your heart race at Remington Park, a place where thoroughbreds and quarter horses race year-round! Children of all ages are welcome on all track levels. In addition to watching the races, children will be interested in the Remington Paddock. This area offers a wonderful opportunity to see the horses and jockeys up-close as they prepare to race.

A large family recreation area with a playground, picnic tables, pavilions, concession centers, pari-mutual windows, TV monitors, and more is located at the Infield Park. The Infield Park is open weekends and holidays from mid-March to early November. You may bring a lunch for a picnic at Infield Park or eat at the restaurants at Remington Park; the restaurants serve everything from pizza to prime rib.

## Sensational Garden

*400 North Portland, (405) 945-3358. Located on the Oklahoma State University/Oklahoma City campus. Take I-44 to N.W. 10th Street. On N.W. 10th, go west to Portland and turn south. The gardens are located on the east side of the road. The gardens are accessible at all times but, during business hours, there will be someone available to answer questions. Admission is free; donations are appreciated. The gardens are handicapped accessible. Restrooms are available Monday-Friday 8-5 in a nearby building.*

Pack a picnic lunch and enjoy the refreshing Sensational Garden, a place designed to appeal to many senses. Visit the Children's Garden to view the floral "dinosaur hill," the topiary dinosaur, and the butterflies. Listen to the trickling waterfall, touch the different plant textures, smell the sweet fragrances, and see the colorful plants. Some signs are in Braille. Ask your children if they can think of other ways to enjoy the gardens by using their senses. The peak time for floral display is June.

## State Museum of History

*2100 North Lincoln Boulevard, (405) 521-2491. Located just southeast of the State Capitol. From I-44 exit onto Lincoln and proceed south to N.E. 20th Street. Watch for signs. Monday-Saturday 8-5. Closed Sundays and state holidays. Admission is free, but donations are appreciated. The museum is handicapped accessible. The tours are self-guided and take an hour or more.*

The State Museum of History provides information from prehistoric Oklahoma to the present day. For understanding and appreciating the unique history of Oklahoma, a visit to this museum is essential. Displays include a bison-hide tepee, a wagon used during an Oklahoma Land Run, oil field wildcatter exhibits, original art, and more. Exhibits of interest to children include Native American children's items such as clothing and dolls, and pioneer children's items such as miniature spinning wheels, marbles and clothes.

A diorama of the Battle of Honey Springs is located in the Union Room, and artifacts from early forts are found in the Confederate Room. Before you leave, stop by the Oklahoma Sports Hall of Fame to see portraits of Oklahoma sports heroes. Children will enjoy these displays.

### Helpful Hints

Parking is available behind the museum. A gift shop sells historic Oklahoma coloring books and history books. Due to school field trips, the museum is unusually crowded in the spring.

## Stockyards City

*Located just south of I-40 on Agnew, near downtown Oklahoma City. West on Exchange Avenue leads to Oklahoma National Stockyards. (405) 235-7267. Other than special events, the best days to visit are on Mondays and Tuesdays which are livestock sale days; sales begin at 8 a.m. and continue all day. (If a holiday falls on Monday, the days change to Tuesday and Wednesday.) Admission is free, except for some activities during special events. The Oklahoma National Stockyards is partially handicapped accessible.*

Visit Stockyards City and experience Oklahoma's western heritage just as it was more than eighty-five years ago! People travel from around the world to view the livestock operations and to purchase Western goods from the specialty shops located here. In fact, several famous people have visited Stockyards City, including President Ronald Reagan, Pope John Paul, and President George Bush who enjoyed a steak at the historic Cattlemen's Steakhouse, founded in 1910. Children, ages three and up, and adults will learn a great

*Stockyards City Main Street Project*

*Mutton Bustin' at Stockyards City.*

*Cowboy Christmas at Stockyards City.*

deal about cowboys and ranchers by experiencing the sights, sounds, smells, and fun activities at Stockyards City.

When you are touring the area, your first stop should be the Oklahoma National Stockyards. View the cattle from the steel catwalks and then visit the auction, located near the far northwest corner of the catwalks. See if you can identify the many breeds of cattle or recognize their different brands. Close to the auction building you will see how the cattle are prepared for sale. Once inside the building, notice how quickly the cattle sell. Thousands of cattle are sold each week from Stockyards City, and this process sets the standard for cattle prices around the country. Pigs and sheep are also auctioned here on a limited basis.

After the auction, plan to visit some of the many local businesses such as art galleries, saddle and tack-making shops, retail Western stores such as Langston's, and other shops featuring craftspeople whose work is unsurpassed. One shop, located at 1206 South Agnew, features a western clothier, a hat maker, a boot maker, and a tack maker. These professionals will gladly demonstrate their craftsmanship and answer any questions you may have.

### Helpful Hints

For groups of ten or more, call the Oklahoma National Stockyard's main office at 235-8675 a week in advance for a tour. The IFR Parade is held in January in conjunction with the International Finals Rodeo (held at the State Fairgrounds). The parade features horses, wagons, riding clubs, entertainment, and more. In the style of an old-fashioned street party, the **Stockyards**

**Stampede Festival** is usually held the first weekend in June. This cultural and music festival features bull riding and rodeo clown bullfighting competitions. There is live entertainment from multiple stages, arts and crafts displays, a fine arts show, a barbecue and chili cook-off, and many children's activities. The festival admission is free, but there may be fees charged at some venues. A **Cowboy Christmas** takes place on Saturdays between Thanksgiving and Christmas. Celebrate Christmas the "Western way" with a real cowboy Santa and western entertainment.

## White Water Bay

*3908 West Reno, (405) 943-9687. Exit on Meridian from I-40, traveling north to Reno. Turn east on Reno and watch for the sign on the south side of the street. The park is open from mid-May until the week after Labor Day, sometimes only on the weekends. The park opens at 10 a.m. each day, with rides starting at 10:30. Closing times vary between 6 p.m. and 9 p.m. depending on the day; call for more information. Adults $16.99, children (forty-eight inches and shorter) $13.99. Admission is half price during "Night Water," available after 4 p.m. Group rates are available for groups of fifteen or more. For more information, call (405) 478-2140, extension 214. Double Park Season Passes are available; passes are a good value if you and your family plan to enjoy White Water Bay and Frontier City frequently. The pass entitles guests to unlimited visits to both White Water Bay and its sister park, Frontier City. In addition, both parks include double-park perks such as in-park discounts at select food and retail locations, "buddy day" discounts, and more.* ⑨ ★

When the hot Oklahoma sun is beating down, White Water Bay is a great place to take the family. There are many fun rides and activities to keep you cool. Featuring wading pools, small slides, fountains, and water squirters, the Kids Cove area is reserved for those under forty-eight inches tall. The wave pool is another fun area; it produces four-foot waves every fourteen minutes, and it includes a shallow end for younger children. Castaway Creek is a nice break from other exhilarating rides and slides. This area provides a pleasant current for swimming, floating or just relaxing.

Even though height limits are not specified, the child's swimming skills and ability to adapt to new experiences should be taken into consideration by parents before allowing the child to ride certain rides. The Big Kahuna and Keelhaul Falls are considered the mildest rides. The Big Kahuna is an especially good family ride because four people can ride together.

The Bermuda Triangle and Pirates Plunge are fast slides in the dark, while the Swashbuckler Flumes allow you and a partner to race down two tracks. The swinging rope and cable walk in the Shipwreck Island are challenging and popular with older children. Thrill-seekers will "meet their match" with the Acapulco Cliff Dive Speed Slide.

### Helpful Hints

The park is equally busy during the week and on the weekend, with the weather being the determining factor for crowd size. Peak hours are from noon to 4 p.m. It is a good idea to have at least two adults in your group, especially if there are young children (three and under), because of the varying levels of rides.

White Water Bay has numerous restaurants and snack areas, with prices ranging from $2 to $5 for an adult's meal and about $3 for a child's meal. If you would like to pack your own picnic, you can drop it off at the cooler storage located in the southwest corner of the parking lot before you enter the park. Once inside the park, you'll find the cooler station near the Swashbuckler Flumes ride in the northwest corner. Picnic areas are available, but please note that glass containers are not allowed!

You may rent a locker for $3 with an additional $2 deposit. You may also rent rafts, both single and double. Because the rides requiring rafts provide them, your own raft or a rental raft is useful only for the wave pool and Castaway Creek. Be sure to keep a watchful eye on your raft. If it is taken, you will lose your deposit. Raft rental is $3-5 with a $1 deposit.

The lifeguards at White Water Bay are highly qualified, and they strictly enforce the rules. Available free of charge, lifejackets can be found throughout the park. East of the Big Kahuna ride is the first aid station; it is staffed at all times by trained EMT/paramedics.

Visits usually last from three to four hours; sunscreen is a must for all and should be applied frequently. (Be aware that the rafts rub off the lotion.) Bathhouses are located near the front of the park. Always wear sandals or thongs; the pavement gets hot! Lounge chairs are available, but they are not easy to find during peak hours. Be prepared to carry rafts (especially heavy for the Big Kahuna) up many flights of stairs.

## Events

### Prairie Dance Theater

*Performances are held at the theater at Omniplex, (405) 478-4132. Exit I-44 at Martin Luther King Boulevard. Go south past Remington Park. The Omniplex will be on your left. Use the west entrance. The group includes special programs for children each year. Call for a schedule of events. The February and March performances are free; others cost $5 for adults and $3 for children.*

Prairie Dance Theater was the first professional modern dance company organized in Oklahoma. Since 1978, the company has toured extensively through the Southwest, the Midwest, and the East Coast. Incorporating lighthearted humor to touching drama through dance and multimedia effects, the dance group explores American Indian heritage and encourages harmony and balance among all beings. Each performance utilizes Native American themes and a unique musical accompaniment, including drums and sounds from nature.

Of special interest to families are the four annual performances held in February, March, May, and November and based on Native American stories such as *Rabbit Trickster* and *Night Hawk's Dream*. The February dance is especially geared for children preschool-aged to 5th grade, but all four are appropriate for families. The narrated dances are forty-five minutes in length, and they often involve audience participation. Enjoy modern dance and interesting stories at a Prairie Dance Theater performance!

The Prairie Dance Theater performers are also available to perform shows in your school or community. Call for more information.

## Scottish Games

*Usually held the first Saturday after St. Patrick's Day at Joe B. Barnes, Regional Park. For date and brochure, call (405) 737-3330. From I-40, exit at Douglas and go approximately 3.5 miles to Reno. At Reno, go west. The park will be on the south side of Reno. The games take place from 9-5 on Saturday. Adults $4 in advance, $6 at the gate. Children twelve and under are free when accompanied by a parent or adult.*

The Scottish Games are an exciting celebration of Scottish heritage. Join in the fun as Bag Pipe bands compete and adults take a shot at the Caber Toss. Learn about clydesdales and miniature horses, sheep dogs, and Celtic music.

In the Children's Tent, children watch a puppet show presented in Gaelic language or participate in arts and crafts related to Celtic history. Children also take part in athletic events where they will receive medals.

Don't miss the Scottish food! Your appetite will have a celebration of its own when you try the

*Scottish Games, fun for all ages.*

meat pies, apple dumplings, sausage rolls, and a Scottish pie known as Brady. This is one "not-to-be-missed" cultural event!

NOTE: A similar event is held in Tulsa's Chandler Park in mid-September. For information about the **Tulsa Scottish Games,** call (918) 241-6399 or (405) 525-6070.

## Spring Fair and Livestock Exposition

*Held in mid- to late-March at the State Fairgrounds. (405) 948-6700. From I-40 west, exit May and go north. From I-40 east, exit Portland and go north. At Reno, go east. Adults $1, children twelve and under are free.*

Each year the Spring Fair is held concurrently with the world's largest junior livestock show. Children will enjoy seeing—and petting—the nearly 8,000 farm animals. After touring the barn area, be sure to visit the indoor fun fair. Ride the rollercoasters, merry-go-rounds, and other fun amusement rides. A special "kiddie land" is available for the younger children. For your convenience, there is an indoor food court.

## Red Bud Classic

*Usually held on a mid-April weekend in Nichols Hills, Oklahoma City and Jones. For date and brochure call (405) 842-8295. Races start at N.W. 63rd Street and Pennsylvania Avenue at the Waterford Complex. Entry fees: 10km and Two Mile Events $15, Bicycle Tour $15 and both Bicycle and Run/Walk Events $25.*

Celebrate physical fitness and the advent of spring during the popular Red Bud Classic. The first day of festivities includes a free one-mile run/walk/stroll for children ages one to twelve. Prior to the start, release forms must be signed by a parent or guardian. Afterwards, enjoy refreshments and entertainment provided by the Balloon man, clowns and costumed characters.

On Saturday evening, a healthy pasta buffet is served to help boost your energy. Bring a blanket and stay for the live entertainment and the special activities provided for children.

Test your stamina in the 10-K, Two Mile Run or Two Mile Walk through the lovely setting of Nichols Hills. School teams are encouraged to participate, and strollers are allowed on the two-mile walk. You may win a cash prize if you run the two mile or 10-K event in costume! For the bicycle enthusiasts (ages twelve and older), try the ten-mile, thirty-mile, or fifty-mile bike tours. Child seats and trailers are not permitted, and all riders must wear a bicycle helmet. There is also a wheelchair event.

## Festival of the Arts

*Held at the Myriad Gardens and Festival Plaza for six days near the end of April. From I-40 west, exit Walker and go north. From I-40 east, exit Robinson and go north. Parking is located between Reno and Sheridan. For date and brochure, call (405) 270-4848. Admission is free, but plan to pay for parking, the children's area, etc.*

Founded in 1967, the Festival of the Arts has become one of the top ten outdoor festivals in the country. It is attended by more than 750,000 visitors annually. Art available for purchase includes everything from paintings to three-dimensional pieces such as sculpture and pottery. Continuous entertainment is provided by street performers and stage performers.

Food is one of the main reasons to attend this event. Over twenty International food booths and special family eating areas are available. Try a Singapore Rice Noodle or a Greek pastry. How about a hot dog or Strawberries Newport? There are even peanut butter and jelly sandwiches for children!

The Children's Art Field is a popular place during the festival. For $1.50, children can make their own art for forty-five minutes in a supervised area while parents check out the festival by themselves. At the Youth Emporium, children can purchase original art created especially for them by festival

Arts Council of Oklahoma City

*Art is fun at the Festival of the Arts.*

artists. Prices range from fifty cents to $5.

At the Creation Station, the whole family creates art together. One year, participants placed colorful strips of fabric over nearly life-sized, wire-framed dinosaurs to make prehistoric masterpieces. The Festival of the Arts is a special Oklahoma Ctiy tradition. As one observant eight-year-old said, "There's just something about the Festival that makes me happy!"

### Helpful Hints

Pay attention to the weather when you are planning a trip to the Festival of the Arts; April can be gorgeous, cold, windy, and/or wet! Crowds are thick on weekends and during the lunch hour, when downtown Oklahoma City workers enjoy the festival and the food booths.

A diaper-changing area, information/lost people booth, and first aid station are available. Some events have signing for the hearing impaired. Festival programs are available for twenty-five cents. To avoid stairs, strollers are best used along Sheridan Avenue.

## OKLA-HOE-DOWN

*Held the second Saturday in May in Regional Park, Midwest City. From I-40, exit at Douglas and go approximately 3.5 miles to Reno. At Reno, go west. The park will be on the south side of Reno. For date and brochure, call (405) 739-1293. The festival is free until 6 p.m. After 6, anyone over the age of eighteen must have an arm band to remain for the evening entertainment. The arm bands cost $2, and they can be purchased at the General Store in the park.*

At the Okla-Hoe-Down, visitors can have their picture taken with a 2,000 pound longhorn steer, cheer on the cowboys in the professional bull riding competitions, and watch the beautiful "dance steps" of the precision horse drill team. Attractions include arts and crafts, concessions, children's entertainment, a chili cook-off, Native American dancing, a petting zoo, pony rides, and a car show. At the end of the day, attend a fantastic evening concert.

## Israeli Festival

*Held the third or fourth Sunday in May at Emanuel Synagogue, 900 Northwest 47th Street. For more information, call (405) 528-2113. Admission is free.*

A fascinating presentation of Israeli culture is featured at this festival. Among the activities are a mock wedding and a mock barmitzvah. A special area for children includes games and a moonwalk. You can also purchase gifts from Israel and arts and crafts from local artists. This festival comes complete with traditional foods and dances, magicians and mimes, making it a memorable family event.

## Red Earth Festival

*Held the second weekend in June at the Myriad Convention Center. For dates, brochure and tickets, call (405) 427-5228. From I-40, exit at Walker and go north to Sheridan. Turn east on Sheridan to the Myriad. Although many activities are ongoing throughout the day, the grand entry of dancers in full regalia starts at noon on Friday, Saturday and Sunday. Day events: Adults $6 per day, children under twelve free. All-day passes (which include the night show) for Friday and Saturday: adults $10, children under age twelve $5. Three-day passes are $25; group rates are available in advance.* ▯ ★

A unique, highly-acclaimed celebration, Red Earth Festival encourages visitors to become acquainted with Native American cultures. Over 1,500 Native Americans from the United States and Canada are represented in the art show and dance competitions. Children especially enjoy the excitement of the regalia (each garment tells a story), the dances (described well in the guide available at the festival), the hands-on art, face-painting, and dramatic storytelling available at the festival. Through the art, dances, colors, and sounds, children learn to appreciate and understand Native American traditions. This is a "must do" event for every family!

## Lyric Theatre

*(405) 524-7111. Performances are held during the summer months at the Kirkpatrick Auditorium on the Oklahoma City University campus. From I-235 (Centennial Expressway), exit onto 23rd Street and go west. At Blackwelder, turn north. The Kirkpatrick Fine Arts Building is on the left (west). Family night*

*The excitement of Broadway at Lyric Theatre.*

tickets are $12/person, all other times are $20/adult or child. Season tickets are $92.50 and $110. Call a week in advance for tickets.

For over thirty-five years, Lyric Theatre and its talented actors and singers have thrilled audiences with outstanding musical productions. Only held during the summer months, each season includes a special family-oriented musical. Favorites such as *Peter Pan* and *Annie* have previously been performed. A family night discount is offered the first Wednesday of each production. The best view for children is from the balcony.

## Aerospace America

*Usually held on Father's Day weekend at Will Rogers World Airport. For date and brochure, call (405) 685-9546. From I-40, exit MacArthur and go south. Watch for policemen guiding traffic to the free parking area. Advance tickets are adults $8, children ages six to twelve $3. Tickets at the gate are adults $10, children ages six to twelve $6. Children under six are free.*

You and yours will be dazzled at this one-of-a-kind air show. A wide variety of aircraft—antique, military and speciality—can be seen on the ground and in the air. You can climb aboard the military airplanes and see their fascinating instruments, visit the display of antique and specialty aircraft, or browse through the trade show. Look to the skies  and be amazed as top flying teams such as the United States Navy Blue Angels, the United States Air Force Thunderbirds, and the Royal Air Force Red Arrows captivate the crowd with daring maneuvers and intricate formations. Children of all ages will love the aerobatic performances, wing walkers, sky writers, and parachute teams. Since 1988, Aerospace America has treated crowds with a special nighttime performance. The Friday evening performance is always a big hit with children because it ends with a spectacular fireworks display. If the weather permits, this performance also includes a hot air balloon glow.

### Helpful Hints

For your own comfort, bring blankets, lawn chairs, hats, sunglasses, and sunscreen. Water fountains are located throughout the grounds. No coolers or ice chests are allowed. Be sure to wear comfortable clothing and walking shoes. Small children may become frightened by the loud noises; consider bringing ear plugs. Although the night performance is long, it is an excellent choice for children; the temperature is cooler, the lines are shorter, and the performance is exciting.

Souvenir and concession stands are plentiful. Advance discount tickets can be purchased at Homeland stores statewide, Blockbuster Video and Music stores, Oklahoma Air National Guard, FAA Mike Monroney Aeronautical Center, Tinker Air Force Base, and the OKC All Sports Association.

## Arts Festival Oklahoma

*Held Labor Day weekend at Oklahoma City Community College, 7777 South May Avenue. From I-44, exit 74th Street and go east. The festival will be on the south side of 74th Street. For dates and brochure, call (405) 682-7536. A $2 donation is* requested for the conveniently-located parking. The children's area costs $1 per child.

Arts Festival Oklahoma is a fun celebration of the arts—for adults and children alike. For the adults, more than 160 arts and crafts booths offer pottery, paintings, jewelry, clothing, folk art, and other items for sale. A wide variety of food will satisfy your hunger pangs, and music and dance performances will entertain you.

For the children, a well-supervised play

*Children love art festivals.*

area encourages young ones to make newspaper hats and necklaces or dabble in fingerpainting and face-painting. A large sand pile provides the perfect opportunity to build sand castles. Dress appropriately for a "messy" day of fun outside; you'll all appreciate the convenient outdoor cleanup area.

Outstanding local and regional talent provides continuous entertainment; on Saturday evening, the Oklahoma City Philharmonic Orchestra performs an outdoor concert, followed by a fireworks display. Plan to bring a blanket or lawn chairs; seating is limited.

## State Fair of Oklahoma

*Usually held the last two weeks of September at the State Fairgrounds. For date and brochure, call (405) 948-6700. From I-40 West: exit at May and go north. From I-40 East: exit at Portland and go north. At Reno, go east. Adults $4, children twelve and under are free. Free admission with a grandstand or arena show ticket purchased prior to the opening day of the fair.*

With over one million people passing through the gates each year, the State Fair of Oklahoma is one of the best-attended fairs in the country. From the Ferris wheel to rollercoasters, candy apples to corndogs, and livestock exhibits to baking contests, the fair offers attractions for everyone. Special exhibits include the Victorian Good-Holm Mansion; product and service displays with items from Oklahoma and foreign countries; and the Oklahoma Department of Wildlife Conservation's educational exhibit about Oklahoma wildlife.

The Good-Holm Mansion is an educational stop for the family. This turn-of-the-century Victorian home was donated, cut into three pieces, and transported to the fairgrounds. Each year, local antique stores decorate the home, and thousands of fair-goers visit to imagine what life was like in the early 1900s.

Take the children through the International Trade Building where they can gain an understanding of world cultures through informational exhibits; several of these exhibits are geared toward children. Visit the Oklahoma Wildlife exhibit and learn about the many animals in our state. The Hobby, Arts and Crafts Building, FFA Building, and the 4-H Building are other excellent stops for children, since many of the exhibits are created by their peers.

Try your luck at winning a stuffed animal along the midway, let the little ones experience the "kiddie" rides located in a special area, and watch older children experience the thrills of the faster rides. The whole family will enjoy visiting the barns and looking at farm animals.

Special attractions at the fair include **Walt Disney World on Ice** performances, the **PRCA Championship Rodeo,** and the **Ringling Brothers and Barnum & Bailey Circus**. These fantastic shows will delight the whole family.

Thrilling rides, educational exhibits and dazzling shows make the Oklahoma State Fair an adventure your family will want to experience year after year.

### Helpful Hints

Try to attend the fair on a weekday near the opening, when it is less crowded and the grounds are cleaner. Food booths selling the same products are required to charge the same prices. Watch for discount ticket information in local newspapers and on local television and radio.

## Judd Theater, OCUSA

*From I-35, take the Memorial Road exit and go west past Bryant to the OCUSA campus entrance on the north. (405) 425-5540. The university produces a children's play usually in late September or early October. Admission for the children's program is $5/person. A special rate of $4/person is offered school groups or youth groups of ten or more.*

Fred Marvel/Oklahoma Tourism

Oklahoma Christian features at least one show each year for children ages four and older. Children's favorites such as *The Lion, the Witch and the Wardrobe* and *Winnie the Pooh* are presented in late September or early October. After the show, the cast is available to meet children and answer their questions.

## Czech Festival

*Held the first Saturday in October on Main Street (Route 66) in Yukon. (405) 354-*

*Yukon's Czech Festival.*

*3567. Admission is free; however, there are charges for certain activities.*

Colorful, ethnic costumes and the sweet taste of Kolaches await visitors at the Czech Festival, a tradition in Yukon for over thirty years. The Czech Festival Parade starts at 10 a.m., and by 11 a.m., the authentic Czech meal is being served. You may enjoy the carnival rides or dance in the street to the rousing Polka music. Czechoslovakian souvenirs may be purchased at the Czech Building. Sand art and craft making are available for children.

## Global Oklahoma

*Held the second Saturday in October at Rose State College in Midwest City. From I-40 in Midwest City (east of downtown Oklahoma City) take Hudiburg Drive exit, go north a short distance to the campus. For more information, call (405) 736-0313. Admission is free.*

Oklahoma's diverse heritage is highlighted in this multicultural festival. This educational festival features four stages of live entertainment, art, games, and sports from cultures all over the world. A food court with twenty vendors is also available. Children's activities may include educational videos, coloring or painting, but these activities change every year.

## Opening Night

*Held in downtown Oklahoma City and nearby Bricktown on New Year's Eve. For more information, call (405) 270-4848. Admission: $5 per person, children under age five are admitted free. Buttons can be purchased at Opening Night or ahead of time at advertised stores. Check your newspaper, television or radio for additional information. Downtown parking is $4.*

Celebrate New Year's Eve and the beginning of the new year with your family

Arts Council of Oklahoma City

*Opening Night, celebrating the new year with style!*

in downtown Oklahoma City! Enjoy the live music, dance performances, art, and food. There are many indoor venues such as the First National Center Lobby, City Bank, the Myriad Convention Center, and Bricktown; most are located within walking distance of each other. Children will dance to music and laugh at clowns, mimes and jugglers. They will also be able to listen to storytellers and participate in hands-on arts and crafts projects. These projects cost an additional $1-2 for each activity. The highlight of the evening is the ringing in of the New Year while watching the fantastic firework display.

### Helpful Hints

Opening Night is a safe and fun way to spend New Year's Eve with your family. Parking is available at all downtown parking garages on the perimeter of the event. The Central Oklahoma Transportation and Parking Authority offers parking lots for people with disabilities. Trolleys will run regularly from major parking areas to the central downtown area and to Bricktown.

# Seminole

Named for the Seminole Indians, this town had a population of about 800 until July, 1926, when a well blew just east of the present town and the Greater Seminole Oil Field was discovered. By the next year, the town's population had grown to 35,000! Although the early boom years were marked with violence and less-than-reputable businesses and businessmen, the town was eventually able to restore law and order. This remarkable "boom" event is celebrated through the town's annual **Gusher Days** festival. In more recent years, Seminole has been known for its outstanding hands-on children's museum, the Jasmine Moran Children's Museum.

*Seminole is located approximately fifty-six miles east of Oklahoma City, and about ninety miles south and west of Tulsa. From Oklahoma City, take I-40 east to the Highway 99 exit, then turn south. From Tulsa, go southwest on I-44 then take the U.S. 377/99 exit at Stroud and proceed to Seminole. Seminole Chamber of Commerce (405) 382-3640.*

## Attractions

### Jasmine Moran Children's Museum

*1714 Highway 9 West, (405) 382-0950. From Highway 99, take Highway 9 west one mile. The museum is located on the north side of Highway 9. Tuesday-Saturday 10-5, Sunday 1-5. Closed Monday, major holidays and the first two weeks of January (call to verify). Children ages three to sixty, $5, children under three (with adult) are free, over age sixty $4. Discounts are given for organized groups by reservation; call at least one week in advance to make arrangements. If you attend often, ask about memberships.* 🚻 ♿ ★

The Jasmine Moran Children's Museum offers a host of hands-on activities for children young and old. Children can play the roles of firefighters, grocery store owners and shoppers, television newscasters, teachers, emergency medical technicians, or even jet pilots. They can marvel over a gigantic doll house, experience the inside of a soap bubble, make a music video, or pretend to drive an antique car. Several new exhibits are in the planning stages, including a climbing maze, a law enforcement exhibit, a train, and a Dinosaur Dig where children can become junior archaeologists. Children twelve and under call this museum "Awesome!"

Jasmin Moran Children's Museum is rated as the #1 attraction for childrne in Oklahoma. Don't miss it!

Blowing bubbles at Jasmine Moran Children's Museum.

### Helpful Hints

The museum is designed for children ages two to twelve, and it is equipped with a playroom for toddlers. If you are concerned about crowds, phone a day in advance to ask whether any large groups are scheduled to attend on the day of your visit. Volunteers on duty at the museum are more than happy to answer any questions. An average stay is three hours. There is a lunch room; eat inside or out. A small gift shop sells a selection of learning toys and games for all ages and price ranges. The facility is handicapped accessible.

Located across the street from the Jasmine Moran is the **Seminole Historical Society Museum**. Learn about the early days of Seminole through the exhibits of this expanding museum. Hours for this museum are Monday-Friday 10-4 and the first and third Saturdays of each month from 10-2.

## Shawnee

In 1872, a settlement began here as a trading post near the West Shawnee Cattle Trail. From 1876 to 1892, a post office operated using the name, Shawneetown. Present-day Shawnee was laid out in 1892 when the Shawnee Indian lands were open to non-Indian settlement. Soon after, three railroads arrived in Shawnee; in the 1920s, the town "boomed" upon discovery of the Seminole oil field. Today, Shawnee offers several museums and events for visitors.

*From Oklahoma City, travel approximately forty miles east on I-40. From Tulsa, travel approximately sixty-six miles west on I-44 to Highway 18 (Chandler exit). Continue twenty-eight miles south to Shawnee. Greater Shawnee Area Convention & Visitors Bureau, (405) 273-6092.*

## Attractions

### Beard Cabin

*Broadway and Highland, (405) 275-8412. From Oklahoma City, take the Kickapoo exit south. Travel until you come to Highland Street, turn east. From Tulsa, take Highway 18 (Harrison Street) to Highland Street then turn west. Open Tuesday-Friday 10-4, and Saturday-Sunday 2-4. Admission is free. The cabin is not disabled accessible. The tour is less than fifteen minutes long, but may vary according to size of group.*

Beard Cabin was built in 1891 on newly-opened land; it is now nestled comfortably in the middle of Woodland Park. Shawnee's first postmistress, Etta Ray, built the home before she married Henry Beard, Shawnee's first mayor. The bottom floor of the small cabin is the kitchen area, and it includes a pie safe, stove, rocking chair, cast iron cooking pot, and a spinning wheel. Other authentic pieces found upstairs include an antique bed, trunk, and table.

To arrange for a tour, call the Pottawatomie County Historical Society at least one week in advance.

### Mabee-Gerrer Art Museum

*St. Gregory's College Campus, 1900 West MacArthur, (405) 878-5300. From I-40 east, take the first Shawnee exit onto Highway I-77. Travel south until you come to the MacArthur exit, turn left and continue approximately one mile. You will notice St. Gregory's College on the north side of the road, its entry lined with pine trees. From Tulsa, travel south on Highway 18 to MacArthur Street, turn right*

*Mummies at Mabee-Gerrer Art Museum.*

*and continue west until you see the entry drive. The museum sits on the southwest end of the campus. Open Tuesday-Sunday 1-4. Closed Monday and holidays. Admission is free; donations are accepted. This museum is handicapped accessible.*

Father Gregory Gerrer, a Benedictine Monk of St. Gregory's Abbey, founded this museum in 1915. Exhibits include Egyptian mummies, Renaissance paintings, Native American art, American landscapes, and ivory and bronze artworks. Special past exhibits have included the works of Raphael, Chase and Jerome.

"Is she really in there?" is one of the most frequently-asked questions about the mummy of Princess Menne, one of two mummies at the museum. Before modern technology, unwrapping the mummy was the only way to answer that question. Currently, mummies are X-rayed instead of being taken apart. To prove the answer to this question, the X-rays of Princess Menne hang on the wall next to her linen-wrapped body. Although she is believed to be from the

Ptolemaic Dynasty (400-300 B.C.), the museum continues to research her origins and provides up-to-date information about her. Other displays include a mummified cat, pottery, and jewelry.

### Helpful Hints

Children ages five and up will be amazed at the collection. Ask the tour guide for a copy of an activity sheet listing several works of art in the building that children can identify.

Some exhibits rotate every three months. Call one to two weeks in advance to make group tour reservations. Tours are one hour long and are conducted by docents.

## Santa Fe Depot Museum

*614 East Main Street, (405) 275-8412. From I-40, take the Shawnee/Meeker exit onto Harrison. Travel south about four miles to Main Street then turn west and continue for about four blocks. Look for a castle-like building on the north side of the road. Tuesday-Friday 10-4, Saturday-Sunday 2-4. Admission is free. The museum is handicapped accessible.*

The Santa Fe Depot Museum is full of memorabilia. Exhibits are located in every nook and cranny, from eye-level displays to knee-level displays. Children ages six and older will especially want to notice items such as a life-sized model horse, antique dolls, toys, a foot X-ray machine, and a pump organ that survived the Shawnee tornado of 1924. Other items that particularly interest children include turn-of-the-century equipment from a doctor's office, a Model-T Ford car, and a hands-on model of a farm. Native American artifacts include arrowheads, spearheads, a ceremonial pipe, and a prehistoric stone spear head believed to be used for hunting mammoth. The Baggage Room contains many railroad items from the Santa Fe and Rock Island Lines such as uniforms, a conductor's wooden case, lanterns, timetables, and a miniature train set.

## Bob Townsend Antique and Classic Cars

*North of Shawnee, (405) 273-0330. Located three miles north of I-40 on Highway 18 (exit 186). Open Friday, Saturday and Monday 11-6. Adults $3.50; children ages twelve and under are free if accompanied by an adult. School groups are $2 per child; senior citizens and car club groups are $2 per person.*

Three buildings full of antique and unique automobiles are found at this museum! Mr. Townsend began collecting cars in 1958 and has collected and sold interesting automobiles ever since. The current collection includes cars from the United States and Canada, and cars that were previously owned by Sammy Davis, Jr., Elvis Presley and Mae West. The oldest car is a 1901 Oldsmobile. New to the collection are two Duesenbergs.

This display is open on a limited basis so call ahead to verify times. Be sure your children understand that this is a "hands-off" museum!

## Events

### International Finals Youth Rodeo

*Held for seven days in July at The Heart of Oklahoma Exposition Center. For more information, call (405) 275-7020. Morning performances: adults $6, children ages twelve and under $3. Evening and Sunday performances: adults $8, children ages twelve and under $4.*

Over 700 youth from more than thirty states compete in rodeo events such as barrel racing, bull riding, roping, and other events. It is difficult to believe that these youth are not professionals! You can purchase jewelry, clothing, tack, and rodeo supplies at the IFYR Western Shopping Mall on the Expo grounds.

### Jazz Festival

*Held on Main Street the first weekend of October. For more information, call (405) 878-5300. Free.*

For more than five years, the Jazz Festival has spotlighted superb local and out-of-town musical talent. Recently, a children's corner was added to the festival. For only $1, children (accompanied by a parent) can enjoy their own hands-on craft-making. Various civic organizations have food booths that serve Indian tacos, strawberry crepes, hot dogs, and baked potatoes. In the evening (for about $6), you can indulge in some of the most delicious desserts made by talented local chefs.

# Stillwater

Originally part of Indian Territory, the central part of Oklahoma was taken from different Indian tribes to be used for future Indian resettlements. The two-million-acre area was still unsettled after the Civil War and became known as the Unassigned Lands; it was viewed by all as a mecca of potential wealth. By 1879, a class of professional promoters emerged with the sole purpose of opening this area to white settlers. David L. Payne was prominent among these promoters and he established several "Boomer" camps along the borders of the territory. Boomers would regularly invade the Unassigned Lands and establish small towns. They would stay (illegally) until caught and escorted out by the U.S. Army.

One such group camped on the banks of Stillwater Creek and used the creek's name for their town. The Boomers were later escorted out of the territory but not before their ten-year campaign drew national attention. By 1889, Congress agreed to open the Unassigned Lands to white settlers by way of a land run. The Unassigned Lands were opened on April 22, 1889, and numerous towns, including Stillwater, were suddenly populated. The progressive-minded town leaders worked hard to become the site for the new territory's land grant college. Oklahoma Agriculture and Mechanical College (now known as Oklahoma State University) built its first building—Old Central—in 1894.

Although much of the activity in Stillwater centers around OSU, the community has also preserved its history through museums and has supported several businesses that fall under the category "American Dream." This entrepreneurial spirit is evidenced through several thriving businesses such as Eskimo Joe's, the NY Bagel Shop, and Hideaway Pizza.

*Stillwater is located approximately 65 miles north of Oklahoma City, and about 64 miles west of Tulsa. From Oklahoma City, take I-35 north and Highway 51 east. From Tulsa, travel west on the Cimarron Turnpike, then take either the Perkins Road exit (Highway 177) or the OSU exit south about ten miles. Stillwater Convention and Visitors Bureau, (405) 743-3697.*

## Attractions

### Couch Park and Municipal Pool

*1000 East 12th Street, (405) 747-8070. Located along 12th Street just east of Perkins Road (Highway 177). The park is open daily. The swimming pool is open from the end of May through August, Monday-Friday 1-5 and 7:30-9; Saturday and Sunday 1-6. Admission is $2 for anyone age four and older; ages three and under are free. Family swim is $5 per family during the 7:30-9 session.*

Tennis courts, swings, a large, sand-filled playground, and the outdoor city pool provide families with plenty of recreational choices at this city park. The municipal pool has a diving area, two slides, and a separate wading pool. A snack bar located in the pool area sells pop and snacks.

### Eskimo Joe's Clothes World Headquarters

*501 West Elm, (405) 624-3249. Located one block east of Oklahoma State University campus on Elm Street. Monday-Saturday 10-9 and Sunday 11-8. Handicapped accessible.*

*World-famous Eskimo Joe and his faithful companion Buffy.*

What began as a sideline business to a fun Stillwater bar and eating establishment has developed into an apparel business featuring the world's second most popular T-shirt. The famous Eskimo Joe's logo with the smiling "Joe" and his dog Buffy was designed by an OSU student in the mid-1970s; in addition to the popular T-shirt, the logo is now found on numerous other items such as sweatshirts, jackets, pajamas, golf bags, and computer mouse pads!

The Eskimo Joe's shirt has appeared in movies, national newspapers, and even on the television news program "20/20." Recently, Oklahoma's Shawntel Smith, Miss America 1996, created a flurry of excitement as she distributed a limited-edition, special-design Joe's T-shirt to the fifty 1997 Miss America contestants, the stage crew, and the show's host, Regis Philbin.

As the first official retail outlet for the popular "Joe's" T-shirt and other products, this shop is always busy! Don't miss your opportunity to experience firsthand the entrepreneurial spirit of Eskimo Joe's.

### Helpful Hints

The Eskimo Joe's Clothes World Headquarters adjoins the original (albeit updated and expanded) Eskimo Joe's restaurant. You can also find Eskimo Joe's clothes and products at Joes' Clothes outlets at Penn Square Mall in Oklahoma City and Woodland Hills Mall in Tulsa.

## Hideaway Pizza

*230 South Knoblock. From 6th Street (Highway 51), turn left at Knoblock. The Hideaway is on the left near the OSU campus. Open Sunday-Thursday 11-10; Friday-Saturday 11-11.*

Established in 1957 by OSU college student Richard Dermer, Hideaway Pizza has evolved from a small, popular campus hangout to a family restaurant with a loyal following. Appetizers, salads, hot and cold sandwiches, and pasta are offered, but the main attraction of this restaurant is the pizza. The Hideaway uses olive oil, garlic and sun-dried tomatoes to make these delicious taste sensations. Your family's trip to Stillwater is not complete without trying Hideaway Pizza!

### Helpful Hints

Even if you don't live near Stillwater, you can have frozen Hideaway pizzas shipped anywhere in the United States, including Hawaii and Alaska. Hideaway Pizza has two locations in Tulsa and one in Oklahoma City.

The restaurant is located near an old-fashioned fire station at 600 West University. Children and parents are welcome to stop and visit with the firemen.

## National Wrestling Hall of Fame

*405 West Hall of Fame Avenue on the OSU campus, (405) 377-5243. From Highway 51 (6th Street) and Duck Street, travel north to Hall of Fame Avenue. The museum is located on the southwest corner of this intersection. Open weekdays 9-4, and weekends by appointment. Admission is free. Free parking is available on the west side of the building (no parking stickers are required). This museum is handicapped accessible.*

Wrestling was introduced at the Olympic Games in 708 B.C., and it has been called the oldest sport. At the National Wrestling Hall of Fame, numerous exhibits relating to the history of the sport and its greatest achievers are displayed. Exhibits include photographs, uniforms, awards, and memorabilia. The Hall of Fame recognizes wrestling legends, applauds current competitors, and inspires future participants. This museum will appeal most to sports-minded children and wrestling fans.

## Old Central Museum of Higher Education

*Located on the southeast corner of the Oklahoma State University campus, (405) 624-3220. Take Highway 51 (6th Street) north to Knoblock. Turn west at the end of Knoblock onto University Avenue. Parking is available on Knoblock Street or in the Student Union parking garage. Open Tuesday-Friday 9-5 and Saturday 10-4. Closed Sunday, Monday and holidays; the museum is also closed during the university's Christmas break. Suggested donation: adults $1, children fifty cents.*

Tour this historic site and experience what life was like for OSU students at the turn of the century. Old Central accommodated 144 students its first year and was the only permanent structure on the campus for six years. The building was constructed at a cost of less than $25,000 and included carbide gaslights, a modern central heat system, and complete furnishings. Old Central recently celebrated its hundredth birthday and is listed on the National Register of Historic Places.

Visitors will especially enjoy the restored President's Office and Student Night Watchman's Room, both furnished with period furniture and accessories.

### Helpful Hints

This museum is most appropriate for older children and adults. The museum curator will explain the exhibits and give a background on the building. A tour through Old Central can be short or long, depending on one's interest.

## OSU Sports

*For tickets and schedules of the various sports games, call (405) 744-5745. The ticket office is located on Hall of Fame Avenue, just east of Lewis Field football stadium. Admission ranges from "free" to $30.*

OSU's athletic department offers a variety of sporting events including football, basketball, baseball, golf, wrestling, tennis, and women's soccer. Football is played from September to December on Lewis Field. Of particular interest to families is the annual **Homecoming weekend** at OSU, usually held in early November. Children will enjoy a morning parade and viewing the various decorations in front of fraternity and sorority houses and other locations. From October to March, basketball is played in the small but action-packed Gallagher-Iba Arena. OSU is noted for its outstanding baseball and wrestling teams. Baseball is played at Allie P. Reynolds Baseball Stadium from February to June; wrestling is held at Gallagher-Iba Arena from November to March. Soccer games are played west of the track field from August to December. Other sports and their seasons are tennis, September to May; track, March to

June; softball, September to May; and golf, September to June.

## Pleasant Valley School

*1901 South Sangre, (405) 743-6300. The schoolhouse is located at its original site at the corner of Sangre and 19th Streets. From the intersection of Highway 51 (6th Street) and Sangre, go south to 19th Street. Open by appointment only. Phone the Stillwater Board of Education at (405) 743-6300 for names and numbers of local Pleasant Valley alumni who are willing to give tours. To schedule a tour, call two weeks in advance. The busiest times are from March through May when school groups from around the state visit. Admission for families is free, but there is a $3 per student charge for school tours. The school is not handicapped accessible.*

Listed on the National Register of Historic Places, this one-room schoolhouse brings to life a different time when a single classroom was filled with students of all ages. Pleasant Valley School was built in 1899 on a 2.5 acre lot that cost $5. The school operated until 1943, when students joined the nearby Stillwater school district.

School alumni volunteer as teachers and tour guides. They love to share stories from their school days. One such story is that on cold winter days, each student brought an ingredient to add to the stew simmering on the potbelly stove.

Although families and small groups are welcome to tour the school, fourth graders from across the state can experience a typical day at the school, complete with one-room-school instruction. The students are encouraged to bring their own lunch pails and wear period clothing.

## Sheerar Museum

*7th Street and Duncan. Travel one block south of 6th Street (Highway 51) on Duncan Street in downtown Stillwater. Open Tuesday-Friday 11-4, Saturday and Sunday 1-4. Closed Mondays. Admission is free; donations are appreciated.*

A series of permanent exhibits featuring items from the Land Run of 1889 to the present illustrates Stillwater's history. Among the most noted exhibits at the museum is the Sheerar Button Collection. It contains 3,450 buttons dating from the 1740s to the 1930s. Traveling historical exhibits are also displayed at the museum.

### Helpful Hints

A walking tour brochure of downtown Stillwater is available at the museum; you and your children will enjoy the interesting and often amusing stories associated with the historic buildings in Stillwater.

Ask about a hands-on program for fourth graders. During the program, museum guides pass around items such as school supplies, farm instruments, and household goods, then the guides explain how the items were used. This hands-on process helps children realize the technological and lifestyle changes that have occurred since the beginning of the twentieth century.

## Events

### Allied Arts

*The Seretean Concert Hall is located at the corner of Knoblock and Morill on the OSU campus. Tickets range from $11-14. Children's group tickets are $7 each for groups of ten or more. OSU students are $7.*

Nationally-known musicians and artists are brought to OSU by Allied Arts. Performances vary each year, but previous shows include the Moscow Boys Choir and the Chamber Music Society of Lincoln Center.

### Run for the Arts

*Usually held the third Saturday in April from 9-4 on the west lawn and parking lots of the Payne County Courthouse. The courthouse is located at the corner of Highway 51 (6th Street) and Husband, near downtown. For more information, call (405) 747-8084. Admission is free.*

Honoring the Land Run of April 22, 1889, this juried art show and sale features artists from a five-state area. Art mediums include jewelry, woodworking, blown glass, pottery, sculpture, and paintings. A supervised area is available for children who like to create their own art such as decorating T-shirts, making buttons, and drawing with chalk. Tickets must be purchased for each activity ($5 worth should keep a child busy for about one hour). Jazz bands play throughout the day, and different types of food vendors are available.

### Stillwater Community Band Concerts

*Held every other Thursday evening in June and July on the south lawn of the Payne County Courthouse. The courthouse is located at 606 South Husband Street at the corner of Highway 51 (6th Street) and Husband Street. For concert dates and times, call (405) 747-8003. During inclement weather, concerts move indoors to the Stillwater Community Center auditorium, at Eighth and Duck Streets. Admission is free.*

Bring your family for some summer fun held "under the stars." The Stillwater Community Band Concerts are made possible by volunteer adult musicians who bring back the tradition of outdoor summer evening concerts. Ranging in variety from patriotic tunes to Broadway selections, the music is sure to please the entire family. Parents can relax as children dance to the rhythm of the music. Audience  members should bring lawn chairs, blankets and picnic baskets. Lemonade and cookies are offered for sale.

### Jumpin' in July!

*Held during the month of July. Because many activities take place throughout Stillwater during this event, it is advised to call the Stillwater Chamber of Commerce at (405) 743-3697 for a calendar of events. Hours and admission vary by event.*

A number of different events are held during Stillwater's month-long celebration. To start things off with a "bang," join residents as they celebrate the Fourth of July at the **Boomer Blast**! Visitors to this evening-long event at Boomer Lake are treated to a Classic Car Show, a Boat Show, and a Bungee Jumping. A Sand Castle Contest is held on the banks of the lake. Children ride ponies nearby.

Bands, special entertainment, and food booths contribute to the day's success. Evening brings one of the state's largest and most impressive fireworks displays, reflected in the waters of Boomer Lake.

Also held at Boomer Lake in mid-July is **"Oklahoma's Largest Family Picnic"** and the "Not so Still-water" **Great American Duck Race**. Later in the month, OSU hosts its **Celebrity Alumni Basketball Classic**. OSU alumni, honorary coaches, and television personalities all participate in this classic basketball event. The Stillwater Water Garden Society hosts its summer **Water Garden Tour** in July. The gardens, which add color, sound, beauty, and movement to residents' yards, are the features of this tour. **Krazy Daze** is a city-wide retail promotion featuring sidewalk sales, food vendors, children's activities, arts, and entertainment. This two-day event brings shoppers some of the best retail deals of the year, and it includes special activities such as the Children's Day Parade and a Baby Bikini Contest.

## Constien Pumpkin Patch

*Open during October on a farm west of Perkins. From the intersection of Main Street and 9th Street in Perkins, go west 1.5 miles. Watch for signs. Admission is $1.50 per child (includes their own pumpkin).*

During the week, school groups visit the farm and children enjoy picking their own pumpkins, listening to storytelling, and watching pumpkins and squash being carved by experts. On weekends, families are welcome to come to the farm to buy pumpkins. The pumpkins are sold by the pound.

## Taylorsville Country Fair

*Held the first full weekend (Saturday and Sunday) in October at Perkins. From Stillwater, take Highway 177 south to Mehan Road. Travel four miles east on Mehan Road, then 1.5 miles south on a dirt road. A large gate and signs guide visitors to the fair. (405) 547-2732. Adults and children ages twelve and older $3, younger children are free. This event is handicapped accessible; ask the mounted police in the parking area if you need assistance.*

Come to this country fair and enjoy entertainment such as cloggers and gospel and country bands. Be sure to watch the hands-on demonstrations of skills such as basket weaving, glass blowing, soap making, and bread baking. Arts and crafts booths, food booths, children's game booths, a petting zoo, and gunfight reenactors add to the fun of this old-time event.

## OSU Madrigal Dinner Concert

*Held in the Student Union Ballroom at OSU during one week in early December. For dates and ticket information, call (405) 744-5231. Call several months ahead of time to be placed on the mailing list; reservations are taken in early October, and tickets sell out quickly.*

This dinner is a holiday tradition presented by various OSU departments and their students. It runs from Thursday through Wednesday with one dinner performance each night. The student performers will keep your attention with their cheerful music, poetry, amusing antics, and traditional foods of the Middle Ages.

## About the authors and editor:

A native of Woodward, Oklahoma, editor and publisher **Sarah Lowrey Taylor** is a Phi Beta Kappa graduate of the University of Oklahoma. As director of the Plains Indians and Pioneers Museum in Woodward, she developed a great interest in Oklahoma's history, geography and culture. This interest led her to edit and publish her first book, *Exploring Oklahoma with Children, The Essential Parents' Travel Guide!* Her company has also sponsored the "Exploring Oklahoma Contest" for fourth graders statewide and has produced a curriculum guide that is available in all Oklahoma elementary schools. Taylor, along with her husband John R. Taylor, and their children Kathryne, Reed and Zane, live in Edmond, Oklahoma and have enjoyed many hours exploring Oklahoma together.

### *Our sincere appreciation to the following writers who contributed to this book:*

The primary writer and researcher for the second edition of *Exploring Oklahoma with Children* is **Robbie Scott** of Edmond. A native of Ada, Robbie has a Bachelor of Arts degree in English from the University of Central Oklahoma. In addition to exploring Oklahoma with husband Tony and children Christopher and Jessica, Robbie enjoys writing opportunities in her volunteer work.

Other contributing writers include **Susan Hollingsworth** of Tulsa, **Elaine Warner** of Edmond who also provided many beautiful photographs, **Deborah Bouziden** of Edmond, **Sarah Kobos** of Tulsa, and **Taprina Milburn** of Shawnee.

Writers of the first edition of *Exploring Oklahoma with Children* who provided the original research for the book: **Allison Beilue Thompson**, **Susan Hollingsworth**, **Taprina Milburn**, **Patty Lee**, **Debbie Basore**, and **Janet Varnum**.

Writers of the articles in the front of this book include: **Dr. Lisa Marotta**, **Nona Leatherwood Schoenleber**, **Rebecca Tallent**, and **Trena Thomas**.

This book would not have been possible without the help of **Randy Yates** (graphic design), **Melba Prior** (assistance), and **Martha Jacobs** (advertising sales).

**Back:** Martha Jacobs, Nona Leatherwood Schoenleber, Melba Prior, Randy Yates.
**Front:** Robbie Scott, Lisa Marotta with Lindsay and Katelyn, Sarah and John Taylor with Zane, Kathryne and Reed (pictured on back row).

# Calendar of Events

The following calendar serves as a reference guide to the events highlighted in this edition of *Exploring Oklahoma with Children*. Refer to this guidebook, get your "Events Guide" from the Oklahoma Tourism Department, and watch your local paper for events in your area. *Enjoy!*

▲ indicates that the event is seasonal (season runs for more than one month).

## JANUARY

**Eagle Watch**, Tulsa, page 117
**Bald Eagle Tours**, Wichita Mountains, Lawton, page 163
**Eagle Watch**, Arcadia Lake, Edmond, page 169
**IFR Parade**, Stockyards City, Oklahoma City, page 226
**Bullnanza**, Lazy E Arena, Guthrie, page 177

## FEBRUARY

**Tulsa Indian Art Festival**, Tulsa, page 118
**Children's Western Jamboree**, Lazy E Arena, Guthrie, page 177
▲ **Prairie Dance Theater production**, Oklahoma City, page 227
**Winter Expo**, Red Earth Indian Center, Oklahoma City, page 221
**Chocolate Festival**, Norman, page 189

## MARCH

**Kid's World/Children's International Festival** (bi-annual), Tulsa, page 119
**Easter Egg Hunt**, River Parks, Tulsa, page 109
**Easter Egg Hunt**, Lion's Fun Park, Edmond, page 205
**Public Bake Day**, Fort Gibson, page 74
**Oklahoma Scottish Games**, Midwest City, page 228
**Omnisports**, Omniplex, Oklahoma City, page 222
**Spring Fair and Livestock Exposition**, Oklahoma City, page 228
**St. Patrick's Day Parade**, Bricktown, Oklahoma City, page 194
**Timed Event Championship of the World**, Lazy E Arena, Guthrie, page 177

## APRIL

**Spring Arts and Crafts Show**, Turner Falls, Davis, page 146
**Ardmore Shrine Rodeo**, Ardmore, page 141
**Art Under the Oaks**, Muskogee, page 70
**Summer Season Celebration**, OKC Zoological Park, Okla. City, page 215
**Dogwood Days**, Idabel, page 131
**Azalea Festival**, Muskogee, page 72
**Medieval Fair**, Norman, page 189
**Zoofari**, Tulsa Zoo, Tulsa, page 115
▲ **OKC 89ers Baseball**, Oklahoma City, page 211
▲ **Tulsa Drillers Baseball**, Tulsa, page 111
**Run for the Arts**, Stillwater, page 245
**'89er Celebration**, Guthrie, page 181
**89er Celebration**, Norman, page 190
**Keeper of the Plains**, Enid, page 33
**Red Bud Classic**, Oklahoma City, page 229
**Crystal Festival**, Cherokee/Great Salt Plains Area, page 35
**Gilcrease Rendezvous**, Gilcrease Museum, Tulsa, page 22, 97
**Norman Children's Chorus Concert**, Norman, page 186
**Festival of the Arts**, Oklahoma City, page 229

## MAY

**Grovefest**, Grove, page 65

Oklahoma Steam and Gas Engine Show, Pawnee, page 80

Okla-Hoe-Down, Midwest City, page 230

Mayfest, Tulsa, page 119

May Fair Arts Festival, Norman, page 190

Israeli Festival, Oklahoma City, page 231

▲ Oklahoma Shakespeare in the Park, Edmond, page 171

Iris Festival, Ponca City, page 39

Armed Forces Day Parade, Lawton, page 163

Armed Forces Day Military Timeline, Fort Gibson, page 74

Reba McEntire Pro Celebrity Rodeo, Lazy E Arena, page 177

Heritage Fair, Fort Sill, page 160

Blue Grass Festival, Woodward, page 45

Italian Festival, McAlester, page 133

Chuck Wagon Gatherings and National Children's Festival, National Cowboy Hall of Fame, Okla. City, page 209

Jazz Banjo Festival, Guthrie, page 181

Oklahoma Cattlemen's Association Range Roundup, Lazy E Arena, Guthrie, page 177

Memorial Day ceremony, 45th Infantry Division Museum, Oklahoma City page 199

▲ SUMMERFEST!, Ardmore, page 142

## JUNE

Kids Fishing Derby, Lake Arcadia, Edmond, page 169

Gusher Days, Seminole, page 236

▲ Kid's Days, Enterprise Square, Oklahoma City, page 198

▲ Stillwater Community Band Concerts, Stillwater, page 245

Stockyards Stampede, Stockyards City, Oklahoma City, page 225

Ron Alexander's Car Show, Turner Falls, Davis, page 146

Red Earth Festival, Myriad Convention Center, Oklahoma City, page 20, 231

Father/Son Golf Tournament, Lion's Fun Park, Oklahoma City, page 204

▲ River City Players, Tahlequah, page 83

Jenks Country Fair, Jenks, page 102

Juneteenth, Tulsa, page 120

Aerospace America, Oklahoma City, page 232

Tulsa Powwow, Tulsa, page 20, 119

Sunfest, Bartlesville, page 54

Kidsfest, Woolaroc, Bartlesville, page 53

▲ Pawnee Bill's Wild West Show, Pawnee, page 80

Biplane Expo, Bartlesville, page 54

▲ Discoveryland's "OKLAHOMA!" Sand Springs, page 93

▲ Trail of Tears drama, Tahlequah, page 82

OK MOZART Festival (nine days), Bartlesville, page 54

▲ Picture in Scripture, "The Man Who Ran," through Labor Day, Disney, page 66

Owa-Chito Festival, Broken Bow, page 129

Sandplum Festival, Guthrie, page 181

Jazz in June, Norman, page 190

## JULY

▲ Jumpin' in July, Stillwater, page 245

Fourth of July celebration, Shangri-La, Grand Lake, page 69

Old-Fashioned American Celebration, Frontier City, Oklahoma City, page 201

Christmas in July, Ponca City, page 39

LibertyFest, Edmond, page 173

Bricktown Fourth of July, Bricktown, Oklahoma City, page 194

Boom River Celebration, Tulsa, page 120

Summer in the City, Tulsa, page 120

# Index

# Index

# Index

# Index

# Index

# Advertiser's Index

Our sincere apprecition to the following businesses for their support of this book and their interest in helping Oklahoma travelers. We encourage our readers to patronize these businesses. Please let them know that you appreciate their support!

▲ indicates coupon, or discount offered in ad.

## Statewide Interest
▲ Classic Costumes  266
Discover Oklahoma  260
   Frontier Country Marketing
      Association  274
▲ LaPetite Academy  262
   Oklahoma Beef Industry Council  277
▲ Oklahoma Parks and Resorts  267-268
   *Oklahoma Today* Magazine  276
   Oklahoma Tourism and Recreation
      Department  263
   Red Carpet Country  264
   "Arrive Alive" Safety Tape  266

## Ardmore
   Fireside Dining  277

## Bartlesville
   Bartlesville Chamber of Commerce  263

## Clinton
   Pop Hicks Restaurant  277

## Edmond
A Child's Garden 265
Edmond Conventions and Visitors
      Bureau 275
▲ Jason's Deli  267-268
   London House  277
▲ Premier Travel  267-268

## Enid
Leonardo's Discovery Warehouse and
   Adventure Quest  277
The Sage Room  277

## Guthrie
   The Stables Cafe  277

## McAlester
   Trolley's Restaurant  277

## Medicine Park
   The Old Plantation  277

## Norman
   Coaches BBQ, Pizza and Brewery  277
   Legend's  277
   Norman Conventions and Visitors
      Bureau  274

## Oklahoma City
"Arrive Alive" Safety Tape  266
Casady School  266
▲ Classic Costumes  266
▲ Frontier City/White Water Bay  269-270
   Heritage Hall 265
   International Gymnastics Hall of Fame
   273
   Junior's  277
   KISS FM 98.9 278
   KWTV Channel 9  280
▲ National Cowboy Hall of Fame  269-270
   Oklahoma City Conventions and Visitors
      Bureau  269-270
▲ Omniplex  273
   Quail Springs Mall  279
▲ Waterford Marriott Hotel  269-270

## Sapulpa
▲ Discoveryland  271-272

## Seminole
▲ Jasmine Moran Children's Museum  271-
   272; 274

## Tulsa
▲ Big Splash  271-272
▲ Casa Bonita  271-272
▲ Jason's Deli  267-268
   Philbrook Art Museum  261
   Tulsa Conventions and Visitors
      Bureau  279

## Woodward
   Wagg's Bar-B-Q  277
   Woodward Chamber of
      Commerce  264

# *Discover* OKLAHOMA ℠

## Come Discover Oklahoma With Us!

Join Jane Jayroe, Jim Buratti and roving reporter Steve Neumann every week as Discover Oklahoma explores the best flea markets, museum, family entertainment, diners, restaurants, concerts, festivals, theater events, sporting events, bargain shopping, and much, much more! We'll show you where to go and how to get there! Discover Oklahoma, **It's worth the trip!**

(Check your local listings for time period and channel)

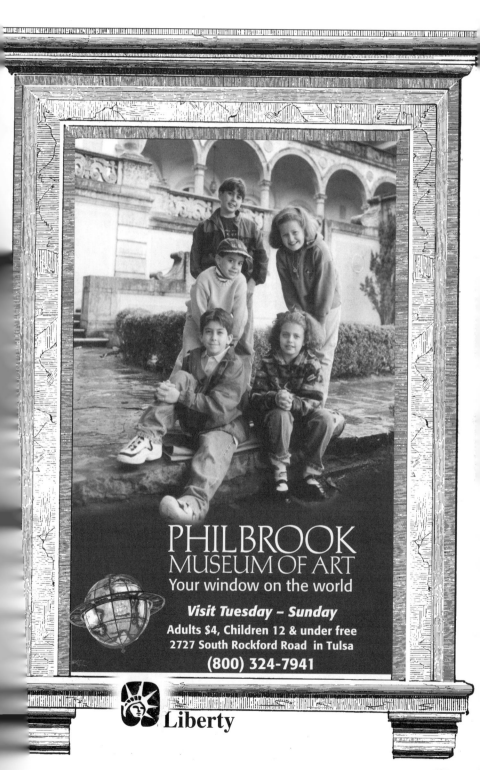

Once upon a time there was a place for child care that was safe and loving, educational and fun, had lots of free sick days and holidays, always let you know what your child was learning and was very, very close to home.

It's not a fairy tale. It's La Petite Academy. Bring in this coupon when you enroll and receive a $50 tuition credit. Ask for details on our Parent's Partner Plan that offers unique benefits like:

- Guaranteed written reports on your child's progress.
- Two weeks' worth of free absence days and six free holidays*, too.
- Extra hours of care during December at no charge.

Call the Academy Director at the La Petite in your neighborhood and reserve a space for your child today.

Benefits may vary according to your child's age and schedule.
*New Year's Day, Memorial Day, July 4th, Labor Day, Thanksgiving and Christmas Day.

# A Child's Garden

### Full Day Developmental Pre-School and Kindergarten

**Degreed Professional Teaching Staff**
**Learning experiences for ages 2 thru 6**
**Quality Theme Based Developmental Curriculum**
**Hands-on Learning Centers and Creative Activities**

*"Planting the Seeds of Knowledge"*

## 340-4300

**729 W. Second**
**Edmond, OK 73003**

*"Our youngest loves A Child's Garden"*–Sarah Taylor, Editor-*Exploring Oklahoma with Children*

---

# Heritage Hall School.

At Heritage Hall, our students, aged 3- 18, are well taught and well prepared — for college and for life. They experience a first rate college preparatory curriculum as well as personal attention in sections of 12- 18 students; and they enjoy endless opportunities to develop their talents and interests in our multi-faceted athletic program and our varied artistic activities.

Heritage Hall is highly respected throughout the southwest and holds a national reputation as a leader in the youth service movement. We teach students responsibility as well as calculus; we teach involvement as well as physics; we teach compassion as well as Shakespeare.

When you think about *your* child,

*Think about her future. Think about his success.*

Think
## Heritage Hall

**1401 NW 115th Street • OKC • 749-3000 • Preschool - Grade 12**
*Heritage Hall admits qualified students without regard to race, religion, gender, physical disability or ethnic origin. Member, National Association of Independent Schools.*

NAIS

The World's only **International Gymnastics Hall of Fame**, has opened its in the heart of downtown Oklahoma City. Located in the East Concourse of the First National Center. Featuring current videos and publications, along with a gift shop and displays from all parts of the globe the emphasis is on current and recent great performers. No admission charge and the Hall of Fame is open from 10:00 to 5:00 Monday thru Friday with group tours available on Saturdays.

*International Gymnastics*
**HALL of FAME**

For more information, call: (405) 235-5600 or Fax: (405) 235-5678.

# EXPERIENCE THE EXCELLENCE
# Edmond

Edmond is rich in history, the proud home of many of Oklahoma's historic sites...First school, First college, and Route 66.

FUN...Arcadia Lake, PGA golf courses, World class tennis facilities, sports abound for all ages.

DINING...Edmond is home to many restaurants ranging from "fast-food-casual" to gourmet.

ACCOMMODATIONS...The Edmond experience allows one to choose from top quality hotel/motels as well as exclusively elegant bed & breakfast for your comfort.

SHOPPING...Browse in Edmond's unique historic downtown for a "one-of-a kind" shopping experience you'll long remember.

ENTERTAINMENT...From Cowboys & Indians to Shakespeare in the park, Edmond has entertainment to be enjoyed by all.

Proud home of 1996 Olympic Gold Medalist Shannon Miller!

Edmond...Experience the Excellence!

**EDMOND CONVENTION & VISITORS BUREAU**
2000 S.E. 15th, Bldg. 300 • Edmond, OK 73013
(405) 341-2808 • edcoc@ionet.net

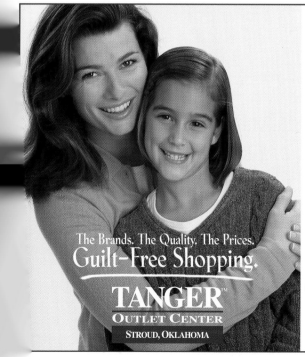

**The Brands. The Quality. The Prices.**
**Guilt-Free Shopping.**

**TANGER**™
**OUTLET CENTER**
**STROUD, OKLAHOMA**

## 1997 Upcoming Events:

**July 4th Centerwide Sidewalk Sale**
July 4th–6th

**Back–To–School Sales**
August 1st–17th

**Labor Day Weekend Centerwide Sidewalk Sale**
Aug. 28–Sept. 1

Buy direct from 53 authentic brand name outlets & save an average of 40% off retail prices every day.

Bugle Boy • Carter's Childrenswear • Levi's Outlet • Liz Claiborne • OshKosh B'Gosh • Toy Liquidators • plus many more...

Halfway Between Tulsa & Oklahoma City On I-44, Exit 179. Phone: 918-968-3566 or 1-800-4-TANGER. Hours: Mon-Sat: 10-9, Sun: Noon-6.

http://www.tangeroutlet.com

275

# Great State. Great Magazine.

## Introducing the Magazine of Oklahoma

Explore the culture, people and places of our state. Subscribe to *Oklahoma Today* and receive six issues of breathtaking photography and award-winning articles. You'll also receive our special Year in Review issue, featuring *Oklahoma Today's* annual choice for Oklahoman of the Year.

Subscribe now for $17.50 and save 42% off *Oklahoma Today's* already low newsstand price. Call (800) 777-1793 or (405) 521-2496 to place your order.

OKLAHOMA
TODAY
THE MAGAZINE OF OKLAHOMA

# BEEF
## 'S WHAT'S FOR DINNER.®

# Discover the Great Taste of Beef in Oklahoma!

### THE OLD PLANTATION
Medicine Park
(405) 529-9641
*Known for world-famous sirloin steaks that hang over the plate.*

### THE STABLES CAFE
223 Division, Guthrie
(405) 282-0893
*Famous worldwide for our BBQ, burgers and steak.*

### TROLLEY'S
21 East Monroe, McAlester
(918) 423-2446
*A family tradition specializing in perfectly-seasoned beef.*

### COACHES BBQ, PIZZA, BREWERY
102 West Main, downtown Norman
(405) 360-5726
*Finest in hickory-smoked barbecue, hand-crafted ales, pizza, and upscale billiards.*

### THE SAGE ROOM
1927 S. Van Buren, Enid
(405) 233-1212
*Specializing in choice aged beef.*

### FIRESIDE DINING
Near Lake Murray, Ardmore
(405) 226-4070
*Our prime rib is truly a mouth-watering experience. 1995 Beef Backer Award.*

### JUNIOR'S
2601 NW Expressway, Oklahoma City
(405) 848-5597
*A fine dining experience.*

### LEGEND'S
1313 W. Lindsey, Norman
(405) 329-8888
*A Norman tradition for 30 years.*

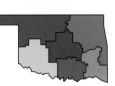

### POP HICKS RESTAURANT
203 Gary Boulevard, Clinton
(405) 323-1897
*A Route 66 landmark for 61 years. Try our delicious chicken fried steak.*

### LONDON HOUSE
1 South Broadway, Edmond
(405) 330-9045
*London Broil steak and more in a casually elegant atmosphere.*

### WAGG'S BAR-B-Q
7th and Oklahoma, Woodward
(405) 256-6721
*Great BBQ in a fun atmosphere.*

# 6:00 - 10:00
## Weekday
## Mornings

# It's more than just the News

## IT'S THE
# SPIRIT
## OF OKLAHOMA

NEWS 9
K W T V
OKLAHOMA CITY